FINDING THE JOB YOU'VE ALWAYS WANTED

Finding the Job You've Always Wanted

BURDETTE E. BOSTWICK

The B. E. Bostwick Company, Inc.
Management Consultants

A WILEY-INTERSCIENCE PUBLICATION

JOHN WILEY & SONS, New York ● London ● Sydney ● Toronto

Library of Congress Cataloging in Publication Data

Bostwick, Burdette E
    Finding the job you've always wanted.

    "A Wiley-Interscience publication."
    Includes index.
    1. Applications for positions.   2. Vocational guidance.   I. Title.

HF5383.B568   650′.14   76-25431
ISBN 0-471-09059-X

Printed in the United States of America

10 9 8 7 6 5 4 3 2 1

To my wife Betty, my son Pete, my daughter Sherry, my son-in-law Peter Bishko, and such others as are consanguineous or affinal; and friends who by reason of acquaintance have been influential in my life.

PREFACE

If you are out of work in times of economic downturn, your most important consideration will be to gain employment—any employment. When times are good, your first objective will be to obtain exactly the kind of job you want. It is the purpose of this book to assist you in both cases.

There is no perfect time to look for work. If you have decided to make a job search, start *now*. Do not put it off because summer or Christmas is approaching, or you wish to take a vacation, or business is poor. Jobs are available in depressions and recessions, in summer and winter, at Christmas and Easter—if you know how and where to look.

Most people are not aware of the special techniques needed to conduct a job search. They equate ability to sell themselves with ability in their jobs. Nothing could be less valid. Persons new to the job market as well as those who have enjoyed longtime employment tend to waste time, and sometimes lose sight of their objectives, by using inadequate job search methods. The correct methods are discussed in this book.

Some of the material included here is new, some is controversial, and some is the standard knowledge of those experienced in the personnel field. All of it has been success-proved in practical experience. Among the many suggestions given choose those that best fit *your* needs. A new element for a book of this kind is the concept of personal career planning—an exploration of your life-style preferences and their relation to your career, and of the corporate mind and its relation to you. Before being interviewed, familiarize yourself, if possible, with the corporate atmosphere: an atmosphere of achievement, figures, charts, goals, profits, relationships, competition. This will help to make your job or career search successful.

I shall be delighted if this book contributes, even in some small way, to your finding just the job you are looking for.

BURDETTE E. BOSTWICK

New York, New York
July 1976

CONTENTS

Chapter 1   **Introduction: How to Find Employment or a New Career**   **1**

Finding a Job—A Sales Function, 2
Preparing for the Job Search, 4

Chapter 2   **Planning Your Career**   **5**

At Ages 18 to 29, 6
At Ages 30 to 39, 12
At Ages 40 to 49, 24
At Ages 50 to 64, 25
At Age 65 and Beyond, 28

Chapter 3   **Analyzing Your Job Personality**   **31**

The Facade Elements of Job Personality, 34
The Operational Elements of Job Personality, 36
The Four Vital Steps in the Job Search, 40

Chapter 4   **Step One: Planning and Preparing the Résumé, the Covering Letter, and the Broadcast Letter**   **41**

The Résumé, 41
The Nature of the Résumé, 41
The Elements of the Résumé, 43
Common Résumé Criticisms, 54
The Ten Résumé Styles, 55
Identifying Your Accomplishments, 129
Effective Short Résumés, Letters, and Advertisements, 131
Writing the Résumé, 132

Answering the Analytical Questionnaire, 135
Typing the Résumé, 140
The Covering Letter, 140
The Broadcast Letter, 147
Rewriting and Resubmitting the Résumé, 152

Chapter 5   Step Two: Using Your Résumé   153

Employment Agencies, 155
Executive Search Firms, 155
Advertising Space Salesmen, 156
Help Wanted Advertisements, 156
Broadcasting Your Résumé, 156
Using Lists, 157
Choosing among Companies, 159
Evaluating Your Job Competiton, 161
Follow-up Telephone Calls, 162
Handling Interview Travel Expenses, 162

Chapter 6   Ploys for Employment   163

The Personal Odyssey, 163
''Advice'' Visits, 164
The ''High-Powered Rifle'' Approach, 164
Relocation, 164
Some Unusual Approaches, 166
Upper Management Job Search, 167
Writing, 167
Advertising, 168

Chapter 7   Step Three: Preparing for Your Interview   170

Personality, 171
Types of Interviewer, 172
''Catch'' Questions, 173
Examples of Interview Questions, 173

Chapter 8   Step Four: Conducting Your Interview   176

The Obvious Factors, 177
Beginning the Interview, 177
Sense of Humor, 178

Examples of Answers to Interview Questions, 178
Questions You Can Ask, 186
After the Interview, 187

Chapter 9   Psychological Tests   188

Types of Psychological Test, 189
Relation of Psychological Testing to Executive
Competence, 192
The Employment Application Form, 193

Chapter 10   Salary Negotiations   195

Salaries, 195
Bonuses, 197
Fringe Benefits, 197

Appendix A   Résumé Language   201

Appendix B   Typical Job Responsibilities   209

Appendix C   Executive Search Firms   220

Appendix D   Business Directories   230

Appendix E   Professional Résumé and Career Services   238

Index   241

INTRODUCTION: HOW TO FIND EMPLOYMENT OR A NEW CAREER

This book is intended for executives, managers, and administrators commanding annual salaries of $12,000 to $100,000 or more, who wish to discover the quickest route to employment, or to better or different employment. It is also appropriate for those who are just beginning careers aimed at management.

A job search can be fun and exciting if you have a position and are under no pressure to make a change. It can be challenging and fascinating if you have never been employed. It can be frustrating and heartbreaking if you are out of work and must become reemployed as quickly as possible. Whatever your situation may be, do it right and you will be rewarded. The techniques of a search are much the same in all situations, varying only in emphasis and details.

Preparation is the best shortcut to success except one: good fortune. Lady Luck can make all the procedures unnecessary but do not build your search on the hope of her intervention.

The success of a job search rests on the proper development and implementation of a rather complex program. There are four most important steps and like the proverbial sticks of wood they are powerful when tied together but weak taken separately.

This book focuses, possibly for the first time, on the critical relationship among these four most important procedures for a successful job search and explains in detail how to prepare for each. It provides the methodology for the most effective job campaign that can be conducted.

It also examines and suggests a wide assortment of supplementary techniques that have worked well for certain people under certain circumstances.

All are placed within the context of the corporate environment to help you tune your approach to a fine pitch, based on what employers are looking for. How does a company assess its employees? How does it evaluate them? How can you evaluate yourself? What factors are important to your goals?

A chapter on personal career planning is included. In today's world of speed, invention, expanding technologies, and greater competition for jobs, no one looking for a career can fail to assign top priority to personal planning.

FINDING A JOB—A SALES FUNCTION

Most people find that selling oneself is the most difficult sale of all. You would not think of trying to sell a product without preliminary indoctrination about what the product can do, its competition, its price, its market, and its presentation. In selling yourself, you, too, must become a sales professional because getting a job is a *sales* function. It is significant that the majority of résumé users, for example, are in some area of marketing (Figure 1)—marketing specialists are aware of the value of selling by method.

In selling yourself you may need to become a "cold canvasser." You may be a salesman following up leads and calling on "retailers" or "wholesalers." You may be a mail order product, or a premium product selling only at list price or higher (with plus "points" as in some mortgage transactions), or a "discount" product. As a job candidate you are very much a "product," subject to factors similar to those involved in the sale of any consumer or industrial product or service. For example:

- **Cold canvasser.** Calling on prospective customers (employers) without previous introduction.
- **Salesman following up leads.** A salesman who makes calls arising from inquiries from advertising or referrals generated by other means.
- **Mail order product.** A product sold by means of a catalog or circular distributed by mail (the job seeker who mails a résumé or broadcast letter to potential employers) relying on a small percentage of responses to a mass mailing.
- **Retailer.** The business that presents products to consumers. As a job seeker you are a "retailer" if you sell yourself directly to the hiring source.
- **Wholesaler.** The middle man between manufacturer and retailer. You "call" on "wholesalers" when you deal with an employment agency or an executive search firm.
- **Premium product.** A product much in demand for which the highest price can be obtained.
- **Discount product.** A product on which the price is temporarily reduced to attract purchase.

You will use most of these, as well as other, selling methods when you conduct an efficient search for a position.

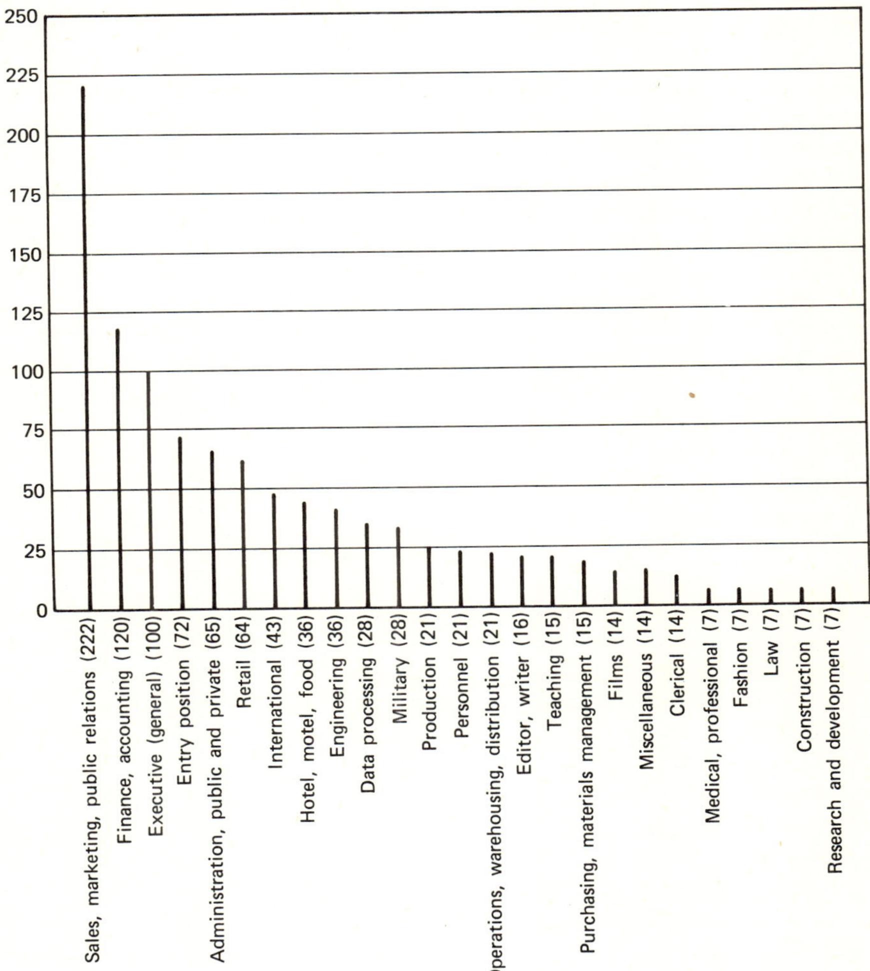

Figure 1   Résumé users by job classification (from a sample of 1000).

PREPARING FOR THE JOB SEARCH

The proper preparation can reduce the time spent on the job search itself by at least 50%, or perhaps by as much as three to six months. Preparation time will consist of the following:

- Reading and understanding this book.
- Analyzing your background and preparing its presentation: a half hour to an hour for each year of experience.
- Writing and polishing your résumé: six to eight hours.
- Preparing a general letter: one hour.
- Researching companies (a minimum of 200) to which you wish to present yourself: eight hours.
- Addressing envelopes, inserting letters, stamping, and mailing: two to three hours.
- Studying and practicing interview techniques: eight hours.
- Traveling, waiting, indecision, and similar items: add a half hour to each hour listed above (as a safety factor).

For example, if you have had 10 years of experience, you will need the following preparation time:

- Five to ten hours of self analysis.
- Six to eight hours for résumé preparation.
- One hour for appropriate covering letters.
- Eight hours for name research (200 companies).
- Two to three hours for mechanics of mailing.
- Eight hours to sharpen interview techniques.
- Eight hours—safety factor.

Thus 45 to 57 hours are required to prepare for a job search. It will be time well spent.

One difficulty many people encounter in searching for a job is that they do not really know what they want to do or where they intend to go as far as their careers are concerned. You will find it helpful to take time to think through your objectives and desires before beginning your job search at any age.

Many mature executives have wished that, early in their careers, they had thought more carefully about the future. Problems with a company or an individual sometimes never go away, or grow slowly over the years, to unstring or ruin what promised to be a fulfilling career. Take time to plan.

The chapter that follows should be of help.

PLANNING YOUR CAREER

Personal career planning is becoming more prevalent as a greater number of qualified and ambitious individuals competes for fewer jobs. Future projections of the jobs-to-people ratio are bound to be imprecise, but it is safe to estimate that in the next 10 years there will be more people than jobs in the area in which you prefer to work. If *you* plan your career, however, you may be among those who *will have* the desired position, one that meets both your life-style objective and your immediate job objective.

Career planning, best done early but better late than never, varies with the following factors:

- **Age.** It becomes more difficult, though not impossible, to obtain a job as the years build up beyond 40.
- **Sex.** Women still face handicaps in certain job classifications. As these handicaps are removed, the job opportunities for women will increase manyfold.
- **Education and personal development.**
- **Job experience.**
- **Objectives.** Two types of objective must be kept in mind: job objective and life-style objective. If your chosen life-style is at odds with your employment, seek new employment.
- **Family responsibilities.** Heavy family responsibilities require that *extra* thought and preparation be given to job changes—unless your job endangers your health or family life, do not surrender it until you have a new position.

Though much of the success or failure of your career depends on fortune—being or not being in the right place at the right time, chancing upon the right or wrong company and boss—planning will reduce the possibility of adverse fortune.

Career planning is a matter of choices. Ask yourself such questions as the following:

- Do I need more education?
- Should I remain with my present employer?
- Should I move to a different company area to gain different experience?
- Am I compatible with my boss?
- Is my company or industry too small or too static?
- Would I rather be my own boss?
- Should I ask for a raise?

Such questions will sprout analysis, decisions, and actions, greatly influencing your future either positively or negatively.

Many executives recognize that their personal planning is as important as planning for their companies. With your personal plans well established and moving in the right direction, you will be of more benefit to your company and happier in your family relationships. Review your progress every four to five years to make sure that you are still going where you want to go at the proper speed.

The working part of your life can be divided into four periods, during each of which you play a different role. The years 18 to 29 are generally those of preparation, and you are the stage manager setting the scene for the action to come. Ages 30 to 40 are the years of development, with you as the understudy. During the polishing years of 41 to 50 you play the supporting actor, reaching the pinnacle—playing the lead—between 51 and 65. Your career planning should vary accordingly.

The age ranges given are, of course, somewhat arbitrary. The job lives of some individuals will develop faster or slower, but most persons should find the age thresholds here coinciding with their own career and life thresholds.

AT AGES 18 TO 29

The direction of your career will probably become established during this period. Your formal education is completed. You are a salesman, an accountant, a copy writer, a production worker. Your success in stage-managing your vocational or professional future depends on your continuing preparation and education beyond the college, secondary school, or elementary school levels.

It has been shown that the earnings of college graduates exceed those without a college education by a wide margin. The influence on earnings of continuing vocational preparation has not yet been documented. We do know that some people with unusual ability earn as much money in a few years as the average manager does in a lifetime. There is also the type of person whom Herbert Hoover called "the uncommon man" who is so talented that he can and does attain high levels of achievement regardless of the degree of formal training or education. Either by rare precocity or perhaps by the circumstances of birth some individuals quickly gain high career objectives. The "average" person, however, would do well to study the statistics on education presented below.

Earnings and Education

The latest U.S. Department of Commerce* data on the earnings of college graduates and those at other levels of education were gathered in 1972 and give the lifetime earnings from age 18 to death, from age 25 to death, between 18 and 64, and between 25 and 64. In all categories persons with four or more years of college are shown to earn 55.5% to 61.7% more in a lifetime than do those without a college degree. The extra income amounts to $229,000 for the ages 18 or 25 to death and $234,000 for the ages 18 or 25 to 64. Viewing the cost of a college education as an investment in an income producing instrument, we know of no other financial venture that produces an equally high and assured return on investment.

The earnings advantage of a college education, calculated on the bases, appears to have eroded slightly since 1961; though the percentage is insignificant, and the 1974–1975 recession may further adversely influence the figures. Nevertheless, the financial edge in possessing an undergraduate degree seems well established. We here make no attempt to evaluate educational advantages other than greater material return, regardless of their importance.

A relevant graduate degree would, over a period of 39 years, return ($2900 x 39) $97,500, bringing the earnings advantage over the high school graduate to about 85%. It would not be unrealistic to say that the possession of such a degree as the Master of Business Administration will double lifetime earnings as compared to those of a high school graduate.

A college or graduate degree also begins to open doors to upper level management, where the financial reward may be four to eight or more times greater than are the earnings of the high school graduate.

The effect on earnings of one to three years of college (without graduation) is relatively minor—they are 13 to 17% above those of the high school graduate.

The value of education, like other traditional values, is now being questioned. Certainly many individuals are not suited for higher education. Many others go through four years of college learning very little. Statistical surveys do not separate those who gain little from their college experience from those who gain much. If the second group could be separately analyzed, its lifetime earnings would tower even more over those of noncollege individuals. Individuals who do poorly scholastically, however, learn in college how to get along

* *Statistical Abstract of the United States,* U.S. Department of Commerce, Bureau of the Census, Washington, D.C., 1974.

with their peers, which is a unique educational value by itself.

A degree is also a door opener—job applicants are often screened during the first round by eliminating persons who do not hold a degree. It is difficult to foresee that this will change. All professional people and most managers have at least an undergraduate degree.

Earnings by education and occupation are shown in Figure 2 and Table 1.

Type of Company, Career, and Life-Style

If you are in a position to choose the company for which you would most like to work, use the following criteria:

- Management excellence.
- Reputation.

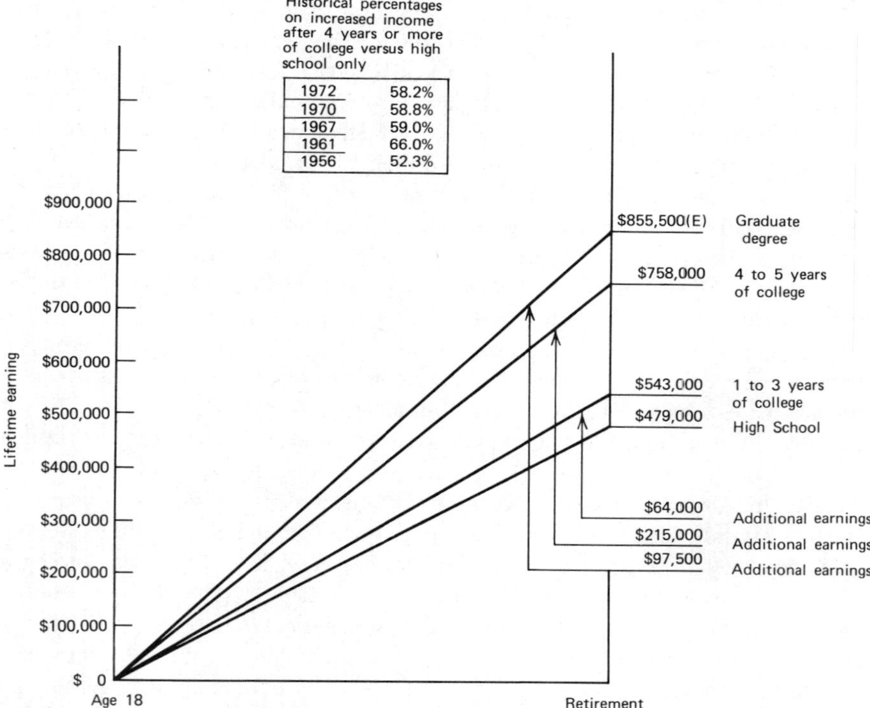

Figure 2   Lifetime earnings by level of education. Data from the *Statistical Abstract of the United States*, Department of Commerce, Bureau of the Census, Washington, D.C., 1974.

Table 1   Earnings by Education and Occupation

Median Lifetime Income by Education

Less than eight years of schooling	$189,000
Eight years of schooling	247,000
One to three years of high school	284,000
Four years of high school	341,000
One to three years of college	394,000
Four years of college	508,000
More than four years of college	542,000
More than five years of college	587,000

Median Annual Income by Education, Ages 18 to 64

High school graduates	$11,269
One to three years of college	12,724
Four years of college	15,530
Five or more years of college	18,159

Lifetime Earnings by Occupation, Ages 18 to 64

Manager	$551,000
Professional	418,000
Farmer	266,000
Clerical	262,000
Sales	387,000
Craftsman	323,000
Operative	229,000
Laborer	189,000

Data from the *Occupational Outlook Quarterly,* Vol. 12, No. 4, U.S. Department of Labor, Bureau of Labor Statistics, Washington, D.C., 1968. (These figures are low by current standards.)

- Financial soundness.
- Growth record.
- New product frequency.
- Location.
- People.

Such an investigation may be time consuming, difficult to conduct, or even irrelevant. Or it may pay off handsomely in the future. Many careers have been short-circuited by lack of sufficient care in job and company selection.

Such concerns as I.B.M., Eastman Kodak, and General Motors are noted for management excellence, and require no further investigation. Most companies, however, do not have formal recognition of this type. You might gain interesting information about them by doing the following:

- Calling on one or two local customers of the company.
- Calling on a banker for information.
- Drawing a Dun and Bradstreet report.
- Looking at a copy of the company's annual report.

It is more difficult to form a judgment about the company's people. Ideally, you should like the person for whom you will be working as well as others who might have influence on your career. Ask to see some of the other executives. Many promising careers have been ruined by personality conflicts. Try to judge whether there is any reason for such a conflict to develop. Though largely a matter of feeling, interpersonal likes and dislikes can be influenced by such factors as age, sex, educational background, jealousy, social background, color, religion, or simply chemical reaction. If you do not like the people you would be working for, look for a different position.

Of course, luck plays a part in success, but you can reduce its adverse influence a little by advance research. Remember, though, that not everyone can be a chief executive officer. Success is knowing yourself and making the best of your talents. Only about 1% of jobholders rise to the top positions of vice-president and president—for the simple reason that only so many top positions are available. Furthermore, some of them are filled by family members or other individuals with an "in" of some kind.

Most people work in lesser positions throughout their working lives. They either find happiness in their work and in their outside activities or hate their work and live in continuous frustration. Here enters the concept of life-style. For most people work is not an end in itself. It is a means to attain the chance to do what they like most: at home, traveling, on vacation, socially, and so on. Essentially, one earns money to have the pleasure of spending it. While career planning can help you on your way to your objectives, it can ruin your happiness if overdone.

If your life-style demands more money than you earn, and expect to earn, you must look around for ways to augment your income: subcareers in investing, buying and selling real estate, or moonlighting.

From a management point of view a "fast-course" employee may be a continuing problem. Not every business grows 20 to 50% a year. Some fine businesses are relatively static. The comfortable employee for many employers is one who is not too demanding. If you can be happy in such a position, your total life enjoyment may be greater than if you continually flagellate yourself about lack of job progress. Though a chief executive is usually paid more than persons of lesser rank, other positions compare well in job importance and possible job satisfaction. The generalist can coordinate the technical experts in production, marketing, and finance and symphonize their efforts to reach the highest levels of their respective capacities. The marketer might contribute more than does a chief executive officer by generating sales. The financial manager might contribute more by his ability to guide the organization through the reefs of money problems. The production executive might contribute more by invention, better methods, and cost savings.

Do not measure your success only against the company's top position or the highest salary range. Measure it against your objectives in relation to your capacities and their use. You are successful, no matter what your job level, if you are making use of your full potential and are happy in your work. Success is lacking if you unhappily perform work that underutilizes your abilities.

Consider, too, how the company's "life-style" fits in with your life-style. In strongly achievement-oriented concerns (such as Xerox) you will be expected to work hard to get ahead—perhaps harder than you would like. Which of the following do you prefer:

- Small town or big city?
- Job pressure or lack of pressure?
- Emphasis on earnings or emphasis on balancing home and office life?
- Leisure time or work emphasis?
- Access to a broad spectrum of cultural opportunities or satisfaction with a nominal amount?
- Highly structured or loose corporation?
- Be boss or work for someone else?
- Career orientation or family orientation?
- Business travel or a 9 to 5 workday?

Most people never stop to think about how they want to live their lives. Though qualified to become a chief executive officer of a large company with all the perquisites of the office, you may prefer life in a small town and away from the pressures inherent in business management positions. You may not want to be in the "rat race."

If your career plans include top management positions, you will wish to think about which area of a company offers the best overall experience toward that end. In my opinion it is marketing, if supplemented with formal or home study training in finance. Marketing is the dynamism of most businesses, and finance is the language of business in its upper levels. Production is important, but in a growing business it only reflects what marketing wants. A good marketer, in turn, reflects what the consumer wants or needs. Marketing provides insights into the marketplace: dealer, wholesalers, consumers, competition, pricing, personnel needs, advertising, public relations, promotion, packaging, delivery, warehousing. It can tell all other areas of business what must be done to *improve* the business. Finance (except on a financial company) is basically a support function that provides the fuel (money) for justifiable growth.

The upcoming executive with the capacity to observe will of course have plenty of opportunity to see the whole picture in any division of the company (see the description of the ideal manager, p. 29).

Whatever the position you hold, do not waste your time on unnecessary minutiae. Look for additional activities from which you can learn and which serve a necessary purpose for your employer. Talk with other executives. Find out what is going on. Have lunch occasionally with people who can inform you. Talk with salesmen. Ask questions.

To sum up, here are some of the decisions that you must make in your teens and twenties:

- College or no college?
- Graduate studies or no graduate studies?
- Work for a small company or for a large company?
- Work for yourself?
- Work in marketing, finance production, or some other area?
- Be guided by the work ethic or follow a more relaxed living style?
- Pursue a career, raise a family, or do both?

AT AGES 30 TO 39

The ages 30 to 39 are the years of development, during which your education and your experience are merged. In this period you will make very important decisions about your job, your company, your satisfactions, and your frustrations.

Once you have gained job experience and have learned about your capacities you will wish to decide whether to stay with your company or look for a more satisfying or better paid position elsewhere. A suggested rule of thumb: stay as long as you are learning and growing. If you cease to learn and fail to move forward (and upward in pay) over a period of months or a few years, tell your company you are unhappy with your job, discuss it with management, and endeavor to be transferred to a more satisfactory position. If this effort is unsuccessful, begin a quiet search for an employer who would put your talents to better use. However, do not give up your job when you run into your first setback. Give it another try, and then another one. If you work for a boss who is not going anywhere, change your job. There is no stigma attached to the job changer today, if the change is made for personal development and not because of employment inadequacy. Many of the most successful executives have changed jobs every four or five years before finding the position best suited to their preferred life-style. Very frequent job changes, however, are looked upon askance, such as one job change every year, or four or five over a period of 10 years.

It will help you in your career planning if you know a company's corporate attitude toward those who work for it.

Analyze Your Income and Position

At this point in your life you can begin to analyze your income with relation to your productivity. There are many ways of measuring your income and job progress, such as by age (see Figure 7) or by comparisons with other executives in the company. For example, if the vice-president is 35 and you, at 38, are only an assistant vice-president, you are being bypassed and must accept it, fight about it, or look for new employment. You may lack popularity at an important corporate political level, or you may not be qualified, or you may not have sufficiently exposed yourself, or you may have let yourself get stuck in a narrow job classification.

Whatever position you hold, find out about the requirements of your boss' job. Get a copy of the job description and begin to prepare yourself to fill that position as quickly as possible. You can apply the same principle to jumping over your boss' head—a frequent occurrence in rapid corporate progress. Appendix B lists the job responsibilities in selected job classifications. You may find it helpful to know what is expected at various corporate levels. You will probably achieve management maturity during your late thirties. By then you will either have established yourself in a satisfactory position or will know that your present work cannot satisfy you. Analyze your income and your position, and take appropriate steps.

At age 35 you should have an earnings goal (inflation and deflation change the values), and your income should continue to increase during what are considered to be the most highly productive years, 35 to 60. Sometimes it is worthwhile to accept nontaxable perquisites in place of additional salary, such as insurance, major medical coverage, an automobile, a club membership, an expense account, stock options, deferred compensation, a superior pension plan, or a termination agreement (but never just a title, a larger office, or a key to the executive washroom!).

Another factor to consider is your place in the company. Every company has an organization chart—perhaps little used in smaller corporations, but usually very important in larger ones. Your own job description relates to the organization chart. Where are you or where will you be? Employers have sometimes made job offers, accepted in good faith, that overstated the nature of the position. Many an employee has thought to be clothed in authority that did not exist. If your job is at a level to be recognized on an organization chart, ask for assurance that your position is as described by the recruiter. A basic reason for job changes is authority promised but not given.

As a job applicant interviewee be aware that the organization chart has many important uses besides identifying reporting relationships. As an employee it would help you understand the different needs of people at different levels. For example, suppose you are a part of the management information systems (M.I.S.) area; the organization chart will help you identify the different kinds of data to be supplied at different organizational levels. Again, it distinguishes between staff and line. It will also show you how you have to prepare yourself for the next step up. Typical simple organization charts are shown in Figures 3 through 6.

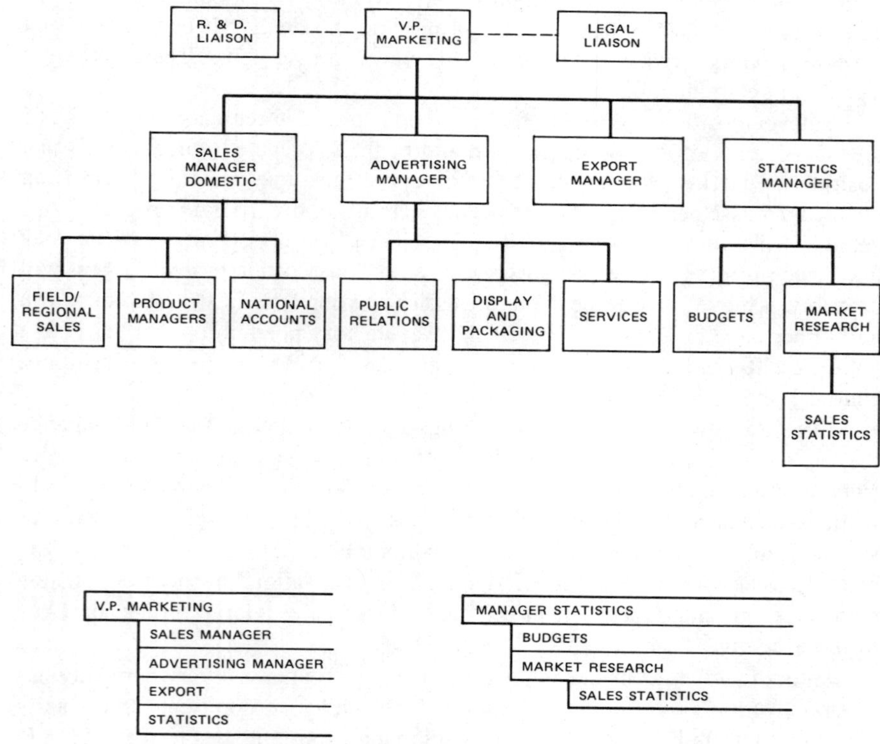

Figure 3   Simple organization chart: marketing.

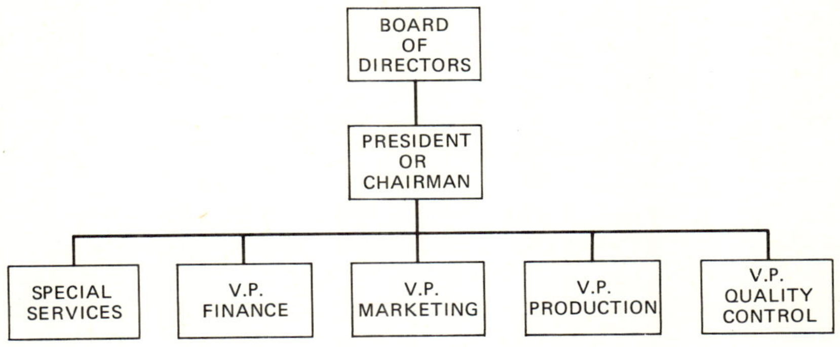

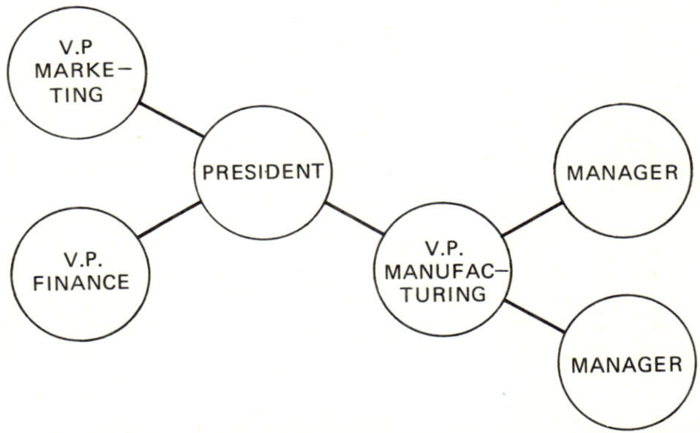

Figure 4   Simple organization chart: top management.

In general, if you are sure of your ability and hold a suitable position, participation in profits is more rewarding than a higher salary, except in times of recession. You contribute to profitability by increased sales or by cost savings. If what you do can be measured, arrange to be compensated by a commission, a bonus, or a percentage. Note, however, that for breakeven productivity for your company you would have to achieve extra business or efficiency at least 20 to 33 times your income based on 3 to 5% earnings after taxes. This is a minimal contribution at the management level. It is very important that you fully understand how a company evaluates the contributions of its employers, and how your salary is controlled by your value to the company.

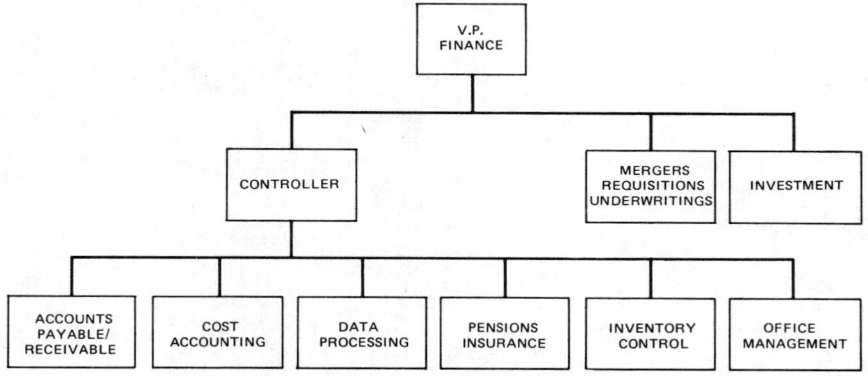

Figure 5   Simple organization chart: finance.

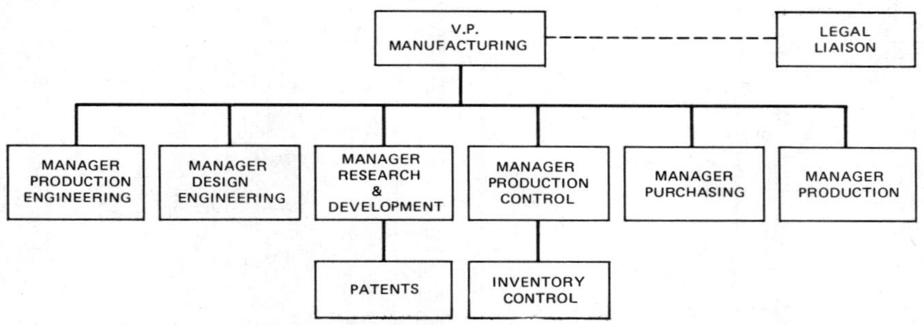

Figure 6   Simple organization chart: manufacturing.

How A Corporation Evaluates You

The basis of business analysis is numbers: simple arithmetic, advanced mathematics, statistics, comparisons. Your value to the company is also ultimately determined by numbers because what you do is translated into numbers: your remuneration compared with what you produce; your influence on profit and loss; your productivity compared with that of other employees.

Most manufacturing companies have a sales volume ranging from $20,000 to $40,000 per employee. Labor-intensive companies have income at the lower part of the scale; high-technology companies at the higher part; banks, at $35,000 to $40,000; some insurance companies, at $60,000; others as high as $90,000.

Age	1950	1953	1956	1962	1965	1968	1971	1974	1977	1980	Annual income in thousands $
65											Over 100
											90
61											80
											70
57											60
53											55
49											50
45											45
41											40
37											35
33											25
29											30
25											20
21											15

Figure 7 Charting your income.

The example that follows shows the relationship of sales to employees and the volume attained per employee by selected classifications (Table 2). Assume a company with a sales volume of $30,000 per employee, a total volume of $30 million, and 1000 employees. Labor constitutes 90% of employment, that is, 900

Table 2   Possible Distribution of Expenses per Each $30,000 Employee Unit in a Manufacturing Company

Volume per individual employee			$30,000
Total number of employees		1000	
Production employees (labor)		900	
Clerical, administrative, executive staff		100	
Costs of goods sold	70%	(of 100%)	$21,000
Gross profit	30%		9,000

Distribution of Manufacturing Expenses

Labor	35%	(of 70%)	7,350
Material	15%	(of 70%)	3,150
Overhead	50%	(of 70%)	10,500
Total	100%	(of 70%)	21,000

Distribution of Sales Expenses

Direct sales cost (salesmen)	3%	(of 100%)	900
Support of salesmen	5%	(of 100%)	1,500
Advertising	4%	(of 100%)	1,200
Total	12%		3,600

Distribution of Administrative Expenses

Salaries	4%	(of 100%)	1,200
Overhead	2%	(of 100%)	600
Total	6%	(of 100%)	1,800
Grand total, all expenses	88%	(of 100%)	$26,400
Profit before taxes	12%	(of 100%)	3,600
Total expenses and profit			$30,000
Profit after taxes (52% of 12%) *	6.24%		1,872
Distribution to stockholders (dividends)		(60%)	1,123
Retained earnings		(40%)	749
Total dividends and retained earnings			$ 1,872

* The bottom line.

employees. The clerical, administrative, and executive staff is 10%, or 100 employees.

> In a manufacturing enterprise labor usually receives the largest amount after overhead. Each salesman in the example requires $50,000 in support activities and $40,000 in advertising. Support factors include displays, catalogs, and other printed material, shows and exhibits, allowances, equipment, warehousing and shipping, and regional managers. Each salesman is thus responsible for $1 million of volume. (Real-life territories are not so uniform, of course.) Percent of overhead is actual overhead divided by the cost of labor. In the example, manufacturing overhead is 130%. Advertising means media advertising, and advertising production. Outside legal, auditing, and consulting fees are administrative costs that are not identified in the example but in real situations affect the distribution of the administrative budget.

The size of the company used in our example is not significant. Large companies treat a million dollars as small companies treat $1000, except that the job marketplace puts a ceiling on individual earnings. An executive salary of $125,000 in a $30 million company would not increase a hundredfold in a $3 billion company, but would have a ceiling of possibly $500,000.

In a profit organization the emphasis is always on the bottom line, that is, on profit after taxes. The continuing effort is to reduce the percentage of all costs by cost reductions, to increase volume, or both. If volume goes up, percentage cost is reduced. If cost is less, cost percentage goes down and the profit percentage rises.

The $30,000 employee unit pays only a portion of the salaries of many types of employees who together make up one employee. For example:

$$
\begin{array}{l}
78.0\% \text{ of 1 worker (labor)} \\
3.0\% \text{ of 1 salesman} \\
10.0\% \text{ of 1 clerical worker} \\
7.3\% \text{ of 1 administrator} \\
\underline{1.7\% \text{ of 1 executive}} \\
100.0\% = 1 \text{ employee}
\end{array}
$$

To earn salary and expenses of $30,000 per year and defray costs of support activities and advertising the salesman must *produce* 33.33 times his cost or $1,000,000.

Clerical, administrative, and executive employees would divide a total of $1,200,000 (4% of $30 million) somewhat as follows. (In static jobs, in which it is difficult to make a profit on job contributions those who show promise are promoted to dynamic jobs where contributions are measurable). These are the static jobs:

| 40 clerical employees | @ $12,000 | $480,000 |
| 14 administrative employees | @ 15,000 | 210,000 |

(In dynamic jobs the incumbent is expected to contribute to increased profitability by savings or volume increases). These are the dynamic jobs:

5 administrative employees	@ $ 20,000	$ 100,000
3 executives	@ 30,000	90,000
2 executives	@ 60,000	120,000
1 executive	@ 75,000	75,000
1 executive	@ 125,000	125,000
		$1,200,000

Neither laborers and clerks nor lower level administrators are synergistic. A job at these levels is worth only a certain amount of money. If you are unwilling to do it at that price (your salary), someone else will. Each position has a salary range, but you need to be promoted to increase your earnings after reaching the top of the range.

The dynamics of business develop at upper level administrative and at executive levels, where a single decision can be worth tens of thousands, hundreds of thousands, or millions of dollars. Many executives have contributed millions of dollars to their companies by invention, by investment, by a new sales method, by a change in product, or by cost savings.

The total profit of this $30 million company is $1,872,000 after taxes. An annual increase in sales of $1000 affects profitability only by $62 in the example. A salary increase, however, is a direct cost, requiring an offsetting sales increase. Thus to justify a salary increase of $1000 you must increase sales by at least $33,000 annually (direct sales costs are 3% of total sales).

To earn a profit of 5%, gross sales of 20 times the profit must be generated (Example A). An increase in sales usually carries with it an increase in all other supporting costs. (Example B). If so there is no improvement in percentage of profit.

	Example A	Example B
Gross sales	10,000,000	11,000,000
Cost of goods sold	7,000,000	7,700,000
Cost of selling	1,200,000	1,320,000
General and administrative expenses	800,000	880,000
Total cost	9,000,000	9,900,000
Gross profit before taxes	1,000,000	1,100,000
Net profit after taxes*	500,000 (5%)	550,000 (5%)

* For simplicity a tax rate of 50% has been used.

When extra sales can be gained without increasing expenses, other than the cost of goods sold, the following happens:

	Example C
Gross sales	11,000,000
Cost of goods sold	7,700,000
Cost of selling	1,200,000
General and administrative expenses	800,000
Total cost	9,700,000
Gross profit before taxes	1,300,000
Net profit after taxes	650,000 (5.9%)

When costs can be reduced the reductions go immediately to the bottom line:

	Example D
Gross sales	$10,000,000
Cost of goods sold	6,300,000
Cost of selling	1,200,000
General and administrative expenses	800,000
	8,300,000
Gross profit before taxes	1,700,000
Net profit after taxes	850,000 (8.5%)

A cost saving of 10% in the cost of goods sold is more valuable than a sales increase of 10%.

Profits are divided as follows (simplified):

Dividends to stockholders	50%
Investment in business	40%
Retained for surplus	10%

Of the net profits after taxes a business retains only 10% or less. This further multiplies the magnitude of contribution necessary to justify an increase in salary. If there are 500,000 shares of stock outstanding, the earnings of the corporation are $1 a share (Example A), rising to $1.10 a share (Example B), justifying perhaps an increase in the value of the stock by 10%. This is the basic reason for stock option plans.

We cannot investigate here all the possible variations of such calculations. The point should be clear, however, that personal earnings carry with them the need to make contributions to profit. The degree to which you make such contributions will determine your earnings. There are many formulas for calculating employee value. Nevertheless, at the executive level your value is measured basically by your contribution to the bottom line. Your value at other levels is determined by the marketplace.

The example given here is in the nature of a profit and loss statement. Some influences of management activity are expressed only in the balance sheet, such as the effect of inventory on the company condition or of investment size on company profits. For example, an excess inventory of $1.2 million could wipe out the possibility of paying a dividend for a company without a strong surplus position, even though profits were good. Or if the profit is only 3 or 4%, the invested capital might be used to better advantage in other ways.

Assume that you are the manager of inventory control at a salary of $20,000. The budgeted company inventory is $7.5 million. Turnover goal is four times. The company has been plagued by inventory excesses that show up as too much raw material, too many finished products in certain classifications, and a parts overstock. The actual inventory is $8.7 million, reducing turnover to 3.4 times and cash flow by $1.2 million. Every reduction of $100,000 that you can make in inventory without affecting availability of product is worth $6240 in profit after taxes. You might think that your value to the company after balancing the inventory would be 12 times $6240 or $74,880 in extra compensation. This would not be true. You have only reduced the inventory to the level at which it should be. If you have thus corrected a chronic problem, you are entitled to a routine salary increase. However, if you reduce the budgeted inventory by $100,000 while retaining all service levels, your contribution is definitely reimbursable to a measurable extent because you have improved upon the acceptable management yardstick.

Suppose that you are a salesman. You increase your territory from $1 million to $1.1 million. This increase makes a change in every figure shown in the preceding example. The cost of support services and advertising may or may not have risen according to the circumstances. Labor and material costs may remain constant in percentage; overhead may be reduced. Your accomplishment was probably aided directly or indirectly by your regional and divisional managers as well as by the executive staff in the home office. Therefore the extra bottom line earnings must be diffused among many levels. It is unlikely that you, *all alone,* are responsible for effecting this strong improvement. An extra $100,000 of sales must not only be sold, but produced, financed, and shipped on time to accomplish the final result. Most corporate growth is the result of team effort, and it is easier to reward employees by a percentage of existing salary level than by individual evaluation. Do point out the extraordinary value of your contribution or participation where appropriate. An individual contribution that can be identified should be compensated proportionately.

In accomplishing a territory sales increase the following chain of events could be established. Salesman Smith's territory produced the increases.

The regional manager says: "I hired Smith."
The divisional manager says: "I trained him."
The sales manager says: "I motivated him."
The advertising manager says: "I increased the consumer response."
The vice-president of marketing says: "He carried out my ideas."
The production manager says: "I provided the extra manpower to make the extra production."
The shipping manager says: "I shipped everything on time so stock was always available."
The R.&D. manager says: "I developed the product that was most important to the sales increase."
The financial manager says: "I provided money by means of a very sophisticated underwriting."
The president says: "I coordinated all the elements that made these sales possible."

This short review should suffice to show the methods of personnel measurement, as well as the interplay of the many forces that influence the result. Consider what *you* can contribute. Every company, no matter how well managed, has areas that can be improved.

Upgrade Your Pension Plan

Most companies have pension plans, although recent government regulations have made them too expensive for some smaller companies. Your pension plan (if you have one) will be extremely important to you at some point in your life. Under existing tax laws you will probably be unable to save enough money from salary and bonuses to ensure the life-style you want. Nor are Social Security payments likely to provide the income you will need. We therefore recommend that you put a study of your penion plan high on your planning agenda.

Analyze your pension plan or a pension proposal with particular reference to the conditions of payment of the primary annual figure. Suppose that your agreement provides for an annual pension of $15,000. This usually means for your lifetime. You might wish to make a part or all of your pension payable to your wife after your death. Such an addition to a pension agreement, however, substantially *reduces* the annual pension payment—possibly to a level that might be unsatisfactory for your standard of living. Study all the permissible options of your pension plan to find out what you will receive under the conditions that are most appropriate to your circumstances before you agree to terms that might turn out to be disappointing. Keep in mind also that federal tax law provisions affect the method of payout.

Consultation with a pension specialist now might save you tens or hundreds of thousands of dollars later.

Maintain Contacts Outside of Your Day-to-Day
Business Relationships

It is important that you and your abilities and talents be known not only within your company, but outside it. Others need to be aware of your value in case you must change jobs, for example. You might do the following:

- Accept committee memberships or chairmanships in a trade association or an educational or charitable institution and perform your duties conscientiously.
- Express your views (if you think you have something important to say) on such occasions as community affairs meetings.
- Accept opportunities to speak before groups on subjects about which you are knowledgeable.
- Accept memberships on the boards of directors of reputable companies or organizations (if you have the time to be a productive member).
- Write for trade and other magazines on subjects in which you have some expertise.
- Help competent individuals to obtain jobs by notifying them of job openings.
- Get acquainted with customers or clients and maintain contacts with them.
- Participate in the activities of industry organizations, whether social or business in character.

Make certain that the reputation you establish this way is a favorable one, however. Beware of being overly aggressive, speaking or writing about subjects that you are not qualified to discuss, talking too much, as well as being an eager beaver. A good reputation, on the other hand, will stand you in good stead throughout your career—and you will have benefited others while procuring it.

AT AGES 40 TO 49

Statistics indicate that while it is the age group between 25 and 30 that makes the most use of résumés, the second largest group of résumé users is between 40 and 49. Many people experience disenchantment, dissatisfaction, boredom, and lack of challenge during this decade in their lives—and realize that any unfulfilled career objectives must be remedied now. These may also be the years of maximum achievement.

Employment or a new career becomes progressively more difficult to obtain with each succeeding year after 40. Corporations put a premium on youth, which legislation cannot prevent. Many prefer to train their own executives rather than bring in outsiders. Pension and other costs increase with age inhibiting the hiring of "older" persons. You should make your move between the ages of 40 and 49. We hold no brief for the corporate attitude that induces this condition, but report it as a fact.

Being in your forties can also be an advantage in job hunting—emphasize such assets as the following:

- Physical endurance.
- Leadership proficiency.
- Experience.
- Supervisory skills.
- Reliability.
- Judgment.

Some corporations have suffered financial and other woes by having management teams composed exclusively of young managers. A business that is moving upward can be managed by a person of average ability and experience. But business is cyclical, and when conditions turn down, seasoned, *experienced* management shows its real value. The experienced manager recognizes the danger signs and knows what to do under adverse conditions—not only when to move forward but when to remain in a neutral position lest the next move be down. A well-managed corporation therefore will have a management team that is balanced not only in departmental expertise but also in age levels. Corporate management has been unsophisticated in believing that a young man with a master's degree in business administration and minimal experience is automatically qualified to assume top level corporate responsibilities.

Experience also shows in performing tasks more quickly, recognizing mistakes, initiating new procedures, being aware of both successful and unsuccessful precedents (thus eliminating the need for expensive experimentation), not requiring consultants in one's own area of specialization, and possessing the accumulated lore based on one's successes as well as failures.

It is an anomaly that your job search becomes more difficult as you near 50 when your real value to a company has actually increased.

AT AGES 50 TO 64

These are the years of peak efficiency by reason of experience, assurance, and knowledge. Most individuals have attained their professional goals by this time. Others may wish or need to seek a new job—a task that is more difficult at this age, but by no means impossible. The assets listed in the preceding section apply also to the 50 to 64 age group, some of the assets even increasing in value with advances in age.

Table 3   Life Expectancy

Age	Those with Adequate Income	Those Not Financially Secure
50	29.6 years	23.63 years
55	25.0 years	19.71 years
60	20.8 years	16.12 years
65	16.8 years	13.90 years
70	13.3 years	10.12 years

From CS0 Table 1958 (Commissioner Standard Ordinary Mortality Table). There is no published updating, although one has been in preparation since 1968.

At age 50 you have probably 20 years of contributory efficacy remaining. Based on insurance actuarial tables, at age 55 you still have 16 years of productive employment potential. At age 60 you have 12 years, and at age 65 you have 8 years. *The older you become, in good health, the farther your proportional productive years extend* (Table 3).

The employment opportunities at 50 or over include the following job classifications:

- Executive.
- Directorship.
- Administration.
- Interim general management.
- Counseling.
- Assistant.
- Research.
- Clerical.
- Retail selling.
- Planning.
- Real estate.
- Consulting.
- Teaching.
- Special projects.
- Sales.
- Communications.
- Correspondence.
- Nursing.
- Insurance.
- Brokerage.

- Retailing.
- Franchising.
- Self-employment.

Consider "assistant" or "assistant to." Topflight managers are often over-worked and could benefit by having at their disposal an experienced advisor who—independent of the official staff and free of routine administrative du-ties—could handle special assignments. An experienced and qualified person aged 50 to 64 or more could be an invaluable assistant. In fact, a top level ex-ecutive with good earnings, much of it paid in taxes, might add greatly to job effectiveness by paying such an assistant out of personal funds for advice in areas in which he or she is less than expert (a fact that may need to be kept from corporate associates) or in areas in which it may be best for the official staff not to participate. Offer yourself in this capacity.

Or consider "interim manager." A family corporation or a small corporation with a thin management staff may not be able immediately to replace a top ad-ministrator who resigns or dies. An experienced, qualified individual could manage the organization or department for a period of years, training the younger executive or executives until they are ready to take over.

Some unemployed older executives or administrators have contributed thou-sands or millions of dollars to the profits of former employers. If it was ac-complished for one or more companies, it can be done for others as well. It costs a company nothing to employ a *qualified* individual, because he or she always produces more than the remuneration paid.

Your planning at this age level should also include planning for retirement. Suppose that you are 50, are employed, do not like your position, see little prospect for advancement, have reached an earning plateau, and are marking time looking forward to retirement. Do what more and more persons are doing today: plan a second career. Perhaps there is something you have always wanted to do: turn an avocation into a vocation, go into business for yourself, make a career change, teach. Many today are retiring early, with plans to con-tinue their businesses or pursue some other useful activity. A second career takes on special importance for those who can retire after a certain number of years of service on full pension or at half pay (such as military personnel). If you start making your plans well ahead of time, the transition will be much eas-ier. Your second career may even bring you greater success and satisfaction than did the first one. "Let me caution persons grown old in active business, not lightly, nor without weighing their own resources, to forego their custom-ary employment at once, for there may be danger in it"—Charles Lamb, *Essays of Elia* (1775–1834).

As one handles a job with greater facility and assurance there is a concomi-tant danger that is always around like a shadow on a sunny day—complacency.

It becomes increasingly important, as self-assurance grows, continuously to re-examine decisions and habits and make new measurements against the changes that take place constantly, sometimes without our noticing, until it is too late. Failures at this age level occur because it is easier to move about on a plateau than on a hill. Companies would increase productivity if they gave employees, particularly at the executive level, some formal, academic reeducation on a rather regular basis and at least every 5 or 10 years.

Use your fifties to consolidate the objectives of your personal career plan—and continue planning.

AT AGE 65 AND BEYOND

Obviously, getting a job is more difficult at 65 or above than at any other age. Nevertheless, many executives have obtained very fine positions even into their seventies. Health is a major factor. People mature and age at different times. Some are old at 50 and some are still young at 80—for reasons that are only partially subject to personal control.

Early retirement or retirement at the mandatory retirement age of 65 is beneficial for the person who has lost vigor and interest, as well as for his employer. For the person who retains vigor forced retirement can be hapless. In fact, retired individuals make excellent workers in almost any position that does not require great physical stamina.

The purpose of this book is not to discuss how to live happily in retirement, but how to find employment or a new career at any age. In your fifties, sixties, and seventies plan as if you were going to live forever. Your plans may work out better than you believed possible.

SUMMARY

At any age, finding the right job takes time. If you are unemployed and for economic reasons need to get back to work as quickly as possible, and have been unsuccessful in finding what you want, take any reasonable position offered even if you are greatly overqualified. You can continue your search for a better position while employed, using your résumé, newspaper advertisements, and other sources to turn up leads. You are in a better position to find new employment while employed. This is contrary to some advice but my experience indicates that it is a sound recommendation.

If you need a job quickly, consider sales; it is often easier to get a sales position than other types of position. Some companies will hire salesmen on a commission basis. Make certain that the company is reputable and that its products are salable, however.

You may also wish to consider a career change. Insurance companies, stock-brokers, and some other industries train qualified individuals while paying them a salary.

Each age period has its advantages and disadvantages in the job market. You are a better employee if you sometimes think not only about your job, but about yourself as well. Many people become so deeply involved in their day-to-day business problems that little or no time remains for recreation, family, investments, and planning. As you go through your life stages *take* time to think about *your* future.

You might find it interesting to measure yourself against the following description of the ideal manager:

What is the ideal manager? The ideal manager sees what needs to be done and does it, or delegates its accomplishment to others. Seeing is an art. It can apply to something as subtle as a relationship between two people or to something that has the impact of a drophammer. The accomplishments of people are infinite: increasing cash flow, improving R.O.I., expediting the handling of cash, finding new markets, improving a product, developing a better system of management information, finding a better way to diagnose an illness, discovering a different word for an advertisement, creating a new surgical technique, finding an antitoxin for disease, leading a fashion trend.

The ideal manager can look at the details of a business and formulate a plan for its improvement or growth which is then to be tested in its various parts. The specialist, such as an engineer, tends, by training, to look at the parts first. The generalist looks at the whole first, creates a hypothesis, and then tests its parts. In this respect the good generalist has an advantage over the specialist.

The ideal manager uses the figures of a business to determine the relationships among cost, market, competition, turnover, sales (geographical, customer, territory, salesman, demography, etc.), price, profitability, and production to arrive at an assessment—improvable, neutral, unfavorable—from which an affirmative plan emerges. An affirmative plan can be such diverse things as the expansion of a plant, a new method of marketing, the closing of a plant or the discontinuance of a product, and the firing of an executive.

The ideal manager recognizes the talents and deficiencies of office staff, balances them, corrects the deficiencies where possible, provides training and example, assures the continuity of management by having a successor or successors available, places the good of the business ahead of all except family, country and personal well-being. If the job is in conflict with more important loyalties, the manager resigns (first finding another job).

The ideal manager is a leader who can motivate others to accomplish goals that he or she may have failed to attain.

The ideal manager is educated, though not necessarily formally, to know all that is required to perform the job responsibilities.

The ideal manager is understanding, thoughtful of others, fair, disciplined, innovative, far-seeing, right more often than wrong, able to play as well as work, perceptive, decisive, profit oriented, and with a sense of humor and proportion.

The ideal manager sets an objective, and makes decisions based on their effect on the objective.

The ideal manager's work is superior to that of all others operating in similar capacities in other companies.

The ideal manager is right about two thirds of the time, using the skills and advice of others to be correct in important decisions nearly 100% of the time.

The ideal manager is concerned about self and family, and recognizes the need for others to do the same.

Is there such a person? No. But the ideal is always a measurement to use in evaluation. Measure yourself.

ANALYZING YOUR JOB PERSONALITY

Now that you have thought about yourself and have begun to learn how to make the most of yourself, how to evaluate your contribution, and how and why to plan, you may find it intensely interesting to measure your job personality. The method we present here for analyzing the personality you bring to the job market will also help you to understand who and what you are. You will discover how you compare with others. You may be superior, in which case you must continue to increase your superiority. An average score indicates need for improvement. If you score poorly, you need help. Do not be afraid to ask for help. A little boost over an obstacle may help you to surmount a problem that would otherwise remain a permanent block. Since your *job personality* (which is not the same as social personality) can greatly help or hinder you in your job search, you should *prepare* it for the task ahead.

Our job personality test is different in that it is based on pragmatic rather than psychological considerations. If you score well the chances are that you have been or will be successful. The values established for the various elements of job personality might be disputed. Remember, however, that they apply only to those seeking a position. Different values would be assigned for a person happily established in a job. By whose standards are the scores validated? The scoring is based on my own experience as to the importance of certain factors in job success. They may lack acceptance by some readers.

To achieve meaningful test results, you must score yourself honestly or ask a friend or associate to score you.

Interviewers use their own formal or informal methods of assessment to gain the same kind of information.

Some employers require that job applicants at certain levels take psychological tests. Most mature people, we believe, know their aptitudes and expected levels of accomplishment without undergoing psychological testing, which can even be harmful. The few individuals who would benefit from it can make use of industrial clinical testing by qualified practitioners at a cost of about $300 to $500.

Table 4 Job Personality Evaluation

Based on the value assigned to each category in columns 1 to 5, enter *your* score in column 6. Use the number that best fits you. If you judge the degree of your articulateness to be midway between superior and good, for example, enter a score of 70. At the end of your evaluation, enter your grade in column 7.

Job Personality Trait	Base Score					Your Rating	
	Superior (1)	Good (2)	Average (3)	Unsatisfactory (4)	Poor (5)	Your Score (6)	Your Grade (7)
The Facade Elements of Job Personality							
1. Articulateness	80	60	40	20	0	________	
2. Dress	30	22.5	15	7.5	0	________	
3. Enthusiasm	30	22.5	15	7.5	0	________	
4. Extrovert/introvert	20	15	10	5	0	________	
5. Facial appearance	40	30	20	10	0	________	
6. Figure	40	30	20	10	0	________	
7. Grooming	50	37.5	25	12.5	0	________	
8. Posture	40	30	20	10	0	________	
9. Sense of humor	30	22.5	15	7.5	0	________	
10. Voice	40	30	20	10	0	________	
Subtotal						________	
Divide subtotal score by 4 to obtain your grade						________	

The Operational Elements of Job Personality

11.	Age	110	82.5	55	27.5	0	__________
12.	Breadth	40	30	20	10	0	__________
13.	Common sense/ impracticality	50	37.5	25	12.5	0	__________
14.	Creativity	70	52.5	35	17.5	0	__________
15.	Education	60	45	30	15	0	__________
16.	Experience, qualifications, accomplishments	270	202.5	135	67.5	0	__________
17.	Fairness to others	50	37.5	25	12.5	0	__________
18.	Health	80	60	40	20	0	__________
19.	Integrity, honesty	80	60	40	20	0	__________
20.	Job effectiveness	50	37.5	25	12.5	0	__________
21.	Leadership capacity	80	60	40	20	0	__________
22.	Past success	60	45	30	15	0	__________

Subtotal
Divide subtotal by 10 to obtain
your grade   __________

TOTAL SCORE   __________

Divide TOTAL SCORE by 14 to obtain your TOTAL JOB PERSONALITY GRADE   __________

A grade of 100 = superior; 75 = good; 50 = average; 25 = unsatisfactory; 0 = poor. The grades of 100 and 0 should be impossible.

Analyzing yourself is a very difficult assignment. "Make it thy business to know thyself, which is the most difficult lesson in the world"—Cervantes, *Don Quixote,* Part II. "There are two sentences inscribed upon the Delphic oracle, hugely accommodated to the usages of man's life: 'Know thyself,' and 'Nothing too much'; and upon these all other precepts depend"—Plutarch, *Consolation to Apollonius.* The phrase "know thyself" is ascribed also to Plato, Pythagoras, Philo, Thales, and others.

Many books and articles suggest self-analysis, telling the reader to determine capabilities, rate of career progress, and the like, as if all these injunctions were readily accomplishable. They are not. If you need further assistance, do not hesitate to pay a qualified professional advisor $50 to $75 a hour (for less than a day probably) to help you in your self-evaluation.

Our job personality evaluation (Table 4) will give you a start on self-analysis.

THE FACADE ELEMENTS OF JOB PERSONALITY

1. Articulateness

Many well-educated and intelligent persons have difficulty in expressing themselves—for such reasons as lack of clear thinking or lack of assurance. Try to learn to talk about yourself fluently and unhesitatingly when looking for a job. Groping for words will make a bad impression. Preparing a résumé will help you to know and to express yourself.

Articulateness also includes English language proficiency, which is *essential* to career success in the United States. Attend classes to increase your language proficiency; almost every community has adult education courses in English. A hard-to-understand foreign accent or a speech disability will hinder you in finding a position, though other qualities and qualifications may compensate for such deficiencies.

2. Dress

Dress is an expression of your taste. Employers vary in the importance they attach to it and in their views on the type of dress. Dress conservatively for your interview. "To succeed in this world, we do everything we can to appear successful"—Rochefoucauld (1643–1680).

3. Enthusiasm

Enthusiam is a quality that carries others along. Being contagious and generating confidence, enthusiasm is essential in salesmanship, which in turn is essential in every job at some time. Employers are favorably disposed toward enthusiastic people.

To be enthusiastic, you must be sincere and must wholeheartedly believe in what you are saying. Enthusiasm does not mean fast-talking attempts to overwhelm a listener. It means saying what you believe in sincerely, factually, with expression and verve, and always under complete control.

4. Extrovert/Introvert

Both extreme extroversion and extreme introversion are undesirable. You are an excessive extrovert if you are overly friendly, tend to show off, talk compulsively, talk at length to strangers, and call attention to yourself by any means, whether appropriate or not. You are overly introverted if you seldom express yourself, tend to remain on the fringes of a group never saying anything or saying little, avoid people, and are embarrassed by interpersonal relationships.

Normality lies between these extremes. Give yourself a score of 15 if you think you are normal, and between 15 or 20 if you consider yourself to be an "interesting" conversationalist. If unable to decide, ask others what they think of you in this regard.

5. Facial Appearance

Your face is usually the first impression that others have of you, and on a job interview it is first impressions that carry the most weight. Facial appearance in this context does not refer to beauty or handsomeness, but only the juxtaposition of features that gives the impression of good looks, strength, charm, or average appearance. Such qualities as intelligence, goodness, enthusiasm, humor, liveliness, evil, and dourness can sometimes seem to emerge from one's facial expression.

If you have a facial defect that makes you self-conscious, consider correcting it by cosmetic surgery, rather than letting it inhibit your entire career. One of my salesmen—a well-educated, handsome man of 50—had a walleye (an eye directed outward), which was very disconcerting in daily business and social relations. Upon my urging, he investigated, found that the eye was readily correctable, and had it corrected. He became a better salesman, increased his friendships, remarried, corrected his drinking problem, and became a much happier and more successful person.

Choose your eyeglasses with the same care as you select a suit or a dress. They can greatly affect your appearance.

"A fair exterior is a silent recommendation"—Publilius Syrus (42 B.C.).

6. Figure

General trimness and reasonable figure proportions will affect your job search. Recent studies indicate that overweight people have more difficulty in getting jobs then do normal-weight people.

7. Grooming

Good grooming enhances your natural attributes and camouflages liabilities. Grooming includes cleanliness, complexion, hair, makeup, clean fingernails, unwrinkled clothes, and shined and clean shoes.

8. Posture

Good posture provides a strong aura of personal pride, health, vigor, value, and importance. Slouching makes a person appear older, discouraged, unhappy, or even unhealthy, while an erect carriage projects a better personality and compensates for any less than perfect aspects of appearance.

If your posture is affected by a physical handicap, score your posture as 0, but add 40 to some other classification in which you are superior.

9. Sense of Humor

A sense of humor, including the ability to laugh at yourself, is an asset in rating your job personality, but not one to be indiscriminately demonstrated in a job interview.

10. Voice

The tone, timbre, and inflection of your voice tell your listener a lot about you, your level of education, your exposure to culture. Is your voice monotonic, nasal, guttural, loud, angry, shrill, flat, froggy, foreign, musical, intonational, harmonious, flexible, expressive, melodious, mellifluous? Your own ear should be able to indicate the nature of your voice compared with voices you admire. If you think your voice makes a bad impression, take professional training to improve it.

THE OPERATIONAL ELEMENTS OF JOB PERSONALITY

11. Age

Age is a major factor in the decision to hire or not hire an applicant, and is even more subject to illegal discrimination than race or creed. Score yourself arbitrarily as follows: ages 28 to 32, score 110; 33 to 39, score 83; 40 to 47, score 55; 48 to 55, score 28; age 56 or over, score 0.

12. Breadth

The variety and extent of your reading, hobbies, community activities, and awareness of major national and international events in economics, politics, sports, religion, social events, fashion, entertainment, the arts, trends, and sociology are all a measurement of your total stature as an individual. In general the man who must always work overtime is a poor manager; he will also have no time left over in which to achieve the quality of breadth.

You can expand your horizons by reading (newspapers, newsmagazines, books about current affairs or historical events, novels), meeting new people, introducing interesting topics when conversing with friends and acquaintances, attending meetings, seminars, conventions—and by leaving your work at the office. Do you do these things? Measure yourself according to your answer.

13. Common Sense/Impracticality

Common sense is that indefinable quality which permits some individuals to get to the heart of a question and arrive at a solution or method of approach that a seemingly more qualified person may overlook. It is practical judgment.

14. Creativity

Though a manager *can* manage effectively without being innovative, there is no *great* manager who does not have this quality. Some poor administrators are great innovators. The ability to create is an invaluable asset. Tangible creativity with respect to things is inventiveness. Intangible creativity can be genius. At its highest level (genius) creativity has a grade value equal to the total maximum grade value of all other attributes. Such a measurement is impossible on a normal scale, because it would apply only to about one out of every 100,000 persons.

15. Education

Education is your preparation to meet the world. Education here is used to mean formal education (experience is informal education). If you are at a stage in your career where education outweighs experience, give yourself a triple score for education and zero for experience. Score as follows:

A graduate degree, three or fewer years of experience	180
A graduate degree, more than three years of experience	60

An undergraduate degree, three or fewer years of experience   135
An undergraduate degree, more than three years of experience   45
An associate degree (or two years of college), three or fewer
   years of experience   90
An associate degree (or two years of college), more than three
   years of experience   30
High school graduate, three or fewer years of experience   45
High school graduate, more than three years of experience   15
Less than complete high school   0

The greater your experience, the more it outweighs your education. For maximum job effectiveness, you must continue to learn by both formal and informal means.

16. Experience, Qualifications, and Accomplishments

Your job experience, combined with education and job effectiveness, are the highest-scoring elements among the operational aspects of your job personality. Education and experience, in turn, determine your qualifications. After 10 or 15 years on the job, experience becomes decisive in measuring your contributions to a company or institution. Your past accomplishments are the strongest possible assets in an affirmative employment decision.

17. Fairness to Others

How fair are you toward those who work for you or are directly or indirectly affected by your decisions. You cannot be a good manager if you are biased or inequitable. You show fairness by leading unproductive employees to become productive rather than firing them, for example. This quality will be evidenced by your reputation, your record in training others to assume greater responsibility, and the stature of your leadership in present or past positions.

18. Health

The state of your health determines the degree of effective effort that you can give to your work. You demonstrate good health by the firmness of your handclasp, your movements, your posture, your voice, your enthusiasm, and your appearance. Let these factors be in evidence during a job interview.

19. Integrity

Integrity is an essential ingredient in an affirmative job personality. You can demonstrate your integrity only through character references or by your record.

Some individuals do exude trustworthiness, while others of equal honesty can seem shifty in their mannerisms.

You should be aware of the importance of honesty to your career, as well as of the difficulty of cultivating this quality. Many people who think of themselves as completely honest are not so in the strict sense of the word intended here.

20. Job Effectiveness

Though experienced and qualified, you may not be bringing full effectiveness to your job for such reasons as lack of leadership or lack of breadth. Are you giving your job the full power of your experience and qualifications?

Measurements of job effectiveness include judgment, decisiveness, aggressiveness, the ability to analyze, plan, and implement, and perhaps technical knowledge, industry knowledge, manual skills, and profit orientation.

You can demonstrate job effectiveness in both your résumé and your interview by showing that your brought more to your position than was required by the job description. For example, you were a more effective salesman if you studied your customers' reasons for buying your product, analyzed their success with your product, notified your management about needed product changes or competitive advantages, helped your lesser customers to improve by telling them how others had succeeded and provided extra service during emergencies.

Did you go beyond the strict perimeters of your job to be extra productive? You may have failed to do so merely because you did not like your job—an awareness of the factors that held you back should help you to be more productive in your next position.

21. Leadership Capacity

All effective managers are leaders. They know how to lead others, to train them to do what they want, and to develop and maintain their loyalty. It requires initiative; implicitly encompasses fairness toward others. It is based on a recognizable superiority in interpersonal relationships.

22. Past Success

Past success is a measure of ability. It could have been brought about by luck or accident. If you have not been successful, the score assigned will not affect your total grade unduly. It will affect your score as a part of qualifications, however. Accomplishments in present or past jobs have a strong influence on employment. "Most people judge men only by their success or their good fortune"—Rochefoucauld (1613–1680).

If you scored well in your job personality test, you already have invaluable assets to assist you in your job search. If you scored less well, consider now what steps you should take to decrease deficiencies. Remember that serious deficiencies in your job personality will have a continuing detrimental effect on the success of your career plan. If necessary, enlist outside help to rectify your deficiencies.

Appendix B lists the elements of selected job classifications. Brush up on what you are expected to know within certain job categories as a part of *preparing* yourself for your job search.

THE FOUR VITAL STEPS IN THE JOB SEARCH

Now that you have organized your thinking about what you wish to do, what you can do, and what you will do, take the following four vital major steps before presenting yourself on the job marketplace:

1. Write a résumé and a covering letter (or a *broadcast letter* if you are at an upper management level).
2. Plan and implement your exposure to prospective employers in person and by mail.
3. Prepare for an interview.
4. Learn how to handle the interview.

STEP ONE: PLANNING AND PREPARING THE RÉSUMÉ, THE COVERING LETTER, AND THE BROADCAST LETTER

THE RÉSUMÉ

The purpose of a résumé is to gain an interview. Almost 90% of the *display* advertisements offering employment ask for a résumé (see Figure 8). There is almost no substitute for a résumé in a successful job search. It is the most accepted form of initial communication between a candidate and a prospective employer. The reason is that a résumé is an executive recruiter's time-saver. It takes three hours to conduct an in-depth interview, but only a few minutes to read a résumé and decide whether or not to interview the applicant. The résumé will screen out 90% of the applicants. If you are to be one of those chosen for an interview, your résumé must be superior. We shall teach you to write a superior résumé. This requires research—your research of your mind. "Style is the dress of thoughts"—Philip Dormer Stanhope, Earl of Chesterfield (November 24, 1749).

The physical appearance of your résumé has a strong affect on its effectiveness. You cannot give too much attention to the details of spacing, paragraphing, headlines, underlining, uppercasing and lowercasing, margins, hyphenations, and centering. "Whatever is worth doing at all, is worth doing well"—Earl of Chesterfield (March 6, 1742).

THE NATURE OF THE RÉSUMÉ

Your résumé is your evaluation. Your prospective employer wants to know not only what your responsibilities are or were but what you are doing or did to meet them. List both your responsibilities and your accomplishments.

A survey of 1000 "help-wanted," "positions available" advertisements in *The New York Times* (Sunday) and *The Wall Street Journal* was conducted over a period of 5 to 6 weeks. The results were as follows:

1.	Ask for résumé specifically	757
2.	Ask for reply with full details (probably requiring résumé)	118
3.	Ask for reply only	74
4.	Ask for reply by telephone	51

Total   1000

Items 1 and 2, involving résumés, came to 87.5%. Adding item 3, for which a résumé would be the most appropriate reply, we find 94.5% of the advertisements to be résumé related.

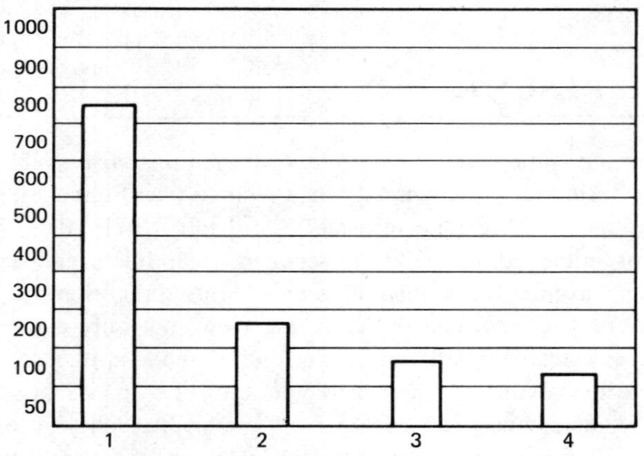

Figure 8   Help wanted display advertising.

Responsibilities (example):

- Mailing and administering audits to about 400 accounts monthly.
- Test and final runs, on computer, of monthly statistics report.

Accomplishments (example):

- Improved collections from creditors.
- Reduced monthly unresolved exceptions from 15 to 5.
- Increased cash collections from 60% to 80% of outstanding totals.
- Introduced new invoice analysis methods and increased departmental efficiency by 25%.

Describe your accomplishments as specifically as possible; give amount, percentage, size, volume, degree of efficiency or accuracy, and so on.

THE ELEMENTS OF THE RÉSUMÉ

What to Omit

The following information is usually best omitted from your résumé:

1. **Omit date.**   Your résumé should remain current for an extended period of time. Place the date in your covering letter.
2. **Omit race, religion, political affiliation, and the like, unless part of the main thrust of your résumé.**   Since the law forbids discrimination for such reasons, you should not offer them as a basis for selection, which you do if you include them in the résumé. Disregard this advice if you know your prospective employer to be partial to certain kinds of people. Thus a Catholic parish would not only employ a Catholic priest rather than a Baptist minister, but might also tend to hire Catholic clerical workers—a tendency that holds equally for any religious institution.
3. **Omit matters that are negative, detrimental, or awkward to write about.**   ''Without some dissimulation no business can be carried on at all''—Earl of Chesterfield (March 6, 1742).
4. **Omit salary requirements.**

   - A leading reason for seeking new employment is to improve compensation. Avoid being restricted by your past salary level.
   - You are entitled to the income level of the position being offered. The company should indicate what it is prepared to pay.
   - Salary is negotiable—based on the nature of the position and your expected contribution to it.
   - Compensation includes many things besides salary: working conditions, responsibilities, opportunity, fringe benefits.
   - It is unwise to commit yourself to a salary level before the interview because you might underrate your potential.
   - In the same way a salary that the employer finds unacceptable from a mere reading of your résumé (causing the résumé to be discarded) might become acceptable after the interview.

Some qualifications are in order, however. If an advertisement asks for salary information, you might supply it. Write it in by hand at the end of the résumé, together with bonuses and fringe benefits, if substantial, or combine all in an inclusive lump sum. I am ambivalent about this. In a very strong résumé, salary disclosure can probably be avoided even when specifically requested.

Furthermore, very significant salary growth—from $12,000 to $40,000 within a short time—shows that your employer has recognized your merits in the most important possible way, and this in turn indicates strong functional progress. In such a case, making salary data known, showing your salary growth by percentages or graphically, is another way of buttressing your accomplishments.

Finally, if your earnings are or have been at a certain level that you are confident you can match in your new position, you might safely include your income expectancy in your covering letter.

5. **Omit references.**

- An employer should have no interest in your references until after he has become interested in you—after the interview.
- A prospective employer might consult the persons given as references before interviewing you. This is undesirable because you wish to be the first one to describe yourself.
- Persons named as references can become irritated by too many calls.
- You will not wish to have your present employer called as a reference before employment interest in you has been indicated.

However, any extraordinary references that you might have can be included. Extraordinary references would include famous people, individuals of stature in your area of competence, important political figures, and the like.

What to Include

The elements to be included in résumés are discussed below. The starred items are those essential to any résumé.

*1. **Your personal directory.** Name, address (with zip code), and telephone number (with area code) are obvious essentials that must appear in your résumé. The only exception is the case in which the employer is dealt with by way of an intermediary for reasons of confidentiality. The third party approach is of course less effective than the direct approach and should not be used without good cause. Make sure that the intermediary disclaims any right to compensation for services rendered.

Note that many avenues in the job search are closed to you if your search must be confidential. If confidentiality is a "must," there are very few people with whom you can discuss your plans and you will have to place even greater reliance on a mail campaign.

If you are employed, list your business telephone number, provided that privacy of conversation is possible. Repeated unanswered calls to an applicant's home may negatively affect the prospective employer's interest. Immediate availability can be crucial in the decision to hire.

*2. **Objective.** Your résumé should be geared to your job objective. State the objective clearly at the outset. If you know the experience and qualifications needed for a job, direct your résumé to describing, as specifically as possible, your ability to meet the criteria. Most applicants lack such information, which sometimes can be obtained from friends, acquaintances, bankers, competitors, annual company reports, and similar sources. Usually, however, a résumé is intended to meet the qualifications of more than one specific job and must be written more broadly. Among the objectives toward which a résumé can be directed are the following:

- An entry position in marketing, finance, or production.
- A management position in marketing, finance, or production, or in any subdivision of these functions.
- A career change—from a profession to business, from military service to business, and the like.
- An office administrative position.

These are general categories. For your résumé, choose as specific a job classification as possible from the thousands of categories in existence. A prospective employer should not have to guess what kind of a job you want.

3. **Qualifications: A brief summary, a paragraph long summary, or an expanded full page summary.** Having stated your job objective, you must present your qualifications for it. Qualifications include courses of study, past work experience, and even character traits that can be supported:

- *Ambition* can be indicated by having worked one's way through college.
- *Motivation* can be manifested by having achieved good grades.
- *Commitment* can be shown by a long term ambition to pursue one's objective and enrollment in training toward that end.
- *Intelligence* might be indicated by a high class standing and receipt of awards.

If you have substantial work experience, a summary page is in order. The method of preparing such a page is explained later.

You can describe your qualifications either objectively or subjectively. Allowing your personality to come through will add warmth to an otherwise sterile document, especially if the résumé is short. Objective evaluations can come from official reports on personnel, such as those used by the armed forces and increasingly by many private companies that review their personnel annually, making the results available to the employee.

*4. **Experience.** In describing your experience give the dates on which you began and terminated the job. Use the phrase "to present" to indicate current employment. State the name and location of the company, except when present employment must be kept confidential.

The methodology described should be followed for each different position in a company and for each different company. The information may be used in a *Chronological Résumé* or revised to accord with another form.

The most important information you can give to a prospective employer is a record of real accomplishment for another company. The expression of such achievement is the same as showing a rare object of exquisite beauty to a connoisseur. Your résumé, properly written, could make you wanted sufficiently that price is no object.

*5. **Education.** As a rule education appears near the beginning of a résumé if one has no work experience, and after work experience when experience begins to outweigh education after a year or so in a job. One exception is the *Professional Résumé* for reasons explained later.

An academic degree or attendance at a college makes any mention of graduation from high school superfluous, though you might wish to list a "name" preparatory school. The high school graduate who did not go to college must mention the fact of graduation. The noncollege graduate should deemphasize education as early as possible in the résumé. Any continuation of education should be noted and described, regardless of the level.

Show your class standing if it is high; otherwise omit it. Mention the honors, awards, and scholarships you have earned.

If your education or individual courses you have attended are particularly relevant to your objective, say so in your résumé (this will be self-evident in the *Professional Résumé*). Advanced degrees should be stated. At this writing a master's degree in business administration (M.B.A.) is the most valuable business degree and commands a compensation advantage of $2000 or more annually. For the nonprofessional a doctoral degree is an advantage if related to the job objective. It is an asset for a researcher, teacher, scientist, writer, and public administrator.

6. **Extracurricular activities.** Listing extensive extracurricular activities can add flavor to a résumé. Omit them if they are few, however, and after you have gained substantial work experience—their significance tends to erode with time. Do list teaching assistantships, tutoring, waiting on ta-

bles, elective student organization offices, sports participation, school newspaper experience, and special distinctions of any kind. They enable the employer to know you better and may strike a responsive chord that might provide an edge in selection for employment.

7. **Summer work while attending school or college.** Employers look with favor on those who have used their school or college holidays for constructive activities. Therefore, summer employment is a worthwhile addition to a résumé, and so is having partially or wholly worked one's way through college. This entry in the résumé is a character building block.

8. **Military service.** Your service in the armed forces, with an honorable discharge, has a place in your résumé. Usually its mention should be brief. Extended description is in order, however, if military service forms a major part of your background—the young man who has been in the armed forces for two to five or more years and has no other employment experience or the career military man who seeks a new career after retirement from the service. Your service record supplies a wealth of information from which interesting, persuasive, and relevant material can be drawn as the basis for a highly effective résumé presentation. Take care to avoid an overlong discussion of your military career, no matter how extensive—stress the factors that are most relevant to your civilian job objective.

9. **Professional membership.** Membership in professional and trade associations denotes an ongoing interest in expanding one's vocational experience. Some memberships are almost mandatory for certain job classifications. Any industrially, commercially, or professionally recognized membership should be listed in your résumé.

10. **Community activities.** Some companies, highly conscious of their local image, favor employee participation in fund drives, charitable board memberships, and community assistance activities. Participation in community activities may characterize you in the eyes of a potential employer as an individual with broad interests and the potential for greater managerial responsibilities. There are, of course, individuals who participate in such activities for personal aggrandizement only; the preceding comment will not apply to them.

11. **Accreditations and licenses.** Include all accreditations and licenses related to your vocation in your résumé. Examples are C.P.A., C.L.U., Licensed Engineer, Licensed Real Estate Broker, and R.N. Honorary degrees should also be listed.

12. **Patents and publications.** Patents, particularly important to the research scientist, the R.&D. manager or employee, and the engineer, as indicators of original thinking should always be included in a résumé.

Publication carries special weight in teaching, business consulting, law, and other professions. They serve as tools in evaluating you, and as a basis for a constructive and interesting interview.

*13. **Personal data.**   Personal data are date of birth, marital status, sex (if name is ambiguous), state of health (if excellent), citizenship (if potentially unclear), number of children, home ownership, willingness to relocate, geographical employment preference (if any), availability for employment (if not immediate), extensive travel experience, height, and weight.

The laws relating to equal opportunity employment make it illegal* for an employer to discriminate by reasons of age, color, creed, race, religion, and sex. You must judge for yourself whether to include all these data in your résumé. Give age if you are young; omit it if you are over 50. On the other hand, if no age is given, the employer may infer more years than the actual number. Approximate age can be guessed quite accurately from dates of graduation and from the length of your career. You might also consider excluding all dates from your résumé. Age is one of the greatest deterrents to employment for many reasons, such as pensions and other benefits, which become costly to employers for new employees of advanced age, and the partiality of many large companies to training their own executives.

Other personal data, we think, need not be excluded from your résumé. The employment opportunities for qualified blacks and other ethnic groups are expanding; an equal opportunity employer may be able to utilize information about your race to your advantage. Employment opportunities for qualified women are growing apace. Your height and weight will be of value only in the entertainment field. We prefer that separation or divorce be stated in a résumé, but this is a matter of personal preference.

14. **Hobbies.**   Mention interesting hobbies; omit commonplace ones, except golf and tennis, which accomplish wide rapport. Outstanding excellence in any sport or hobby should be mentioned.

15. **Languages.**   A knowledge of languages other than English may be mandatory in an international business and important or helpful in many other activities. Include any language proficiency.

16. **Reason for leaving last job.**   Personnel executives consider this information to be an important part of a résumé. We prefer its *omission* because the explanation can be cumbersome and disadvantageous. Furthermore, it can normally have no positive influence on gaining an interview. *The reason for leaving your last job is a matter to be discussed at a personal interview when you can explain it at length.* However, almost

---

* In some states organizations employing five or fewer persons are exempt from E.E.O. rules.

everyone has had one disastrous job experience. It may even be an advantage—one story, possibly apocryphal, has it that a large employer receiving hundreds of applications for a position decided to exclude all résumés that did not show one job failure!

Several jobs held in a short period of time need to be explained if the period is important to the chronology of the résumé. The period can be omitted entirely if it occurs early in your career, for example.

Employment gaps should be explained or closed as fully as possible. Gaps occurring during a recession will be understood by your prospective employer. For those gaps very difficult to justify you might consult your friends or former employers. Such terms as "consultant" and "freelance worker" are poorly received except in areas where freelancing is common (artists and writers, for example).

17. **Security clearance.**   If your past or present employment is security sensitive, specify the level of your security clearance.

18. **Aptitude and psychological tests.**   Employers tend to think that most tests other than their own have little validity. In fact, such tests frequently are too generalized or diffused to be of significance. Omit test results from your résumé, unless excerpts of singular appropriateness can be used to show qualifications objectively.

19. **Photographs.**   Most of the executives recruiting for business do not consider photographs important. Nevertheless, a résumé impact can be increased by including a small (2½ by 2½ inches) clearly defined candid snapshot in color (passport-type photographs are usually of poor quality). Remember that photographs with the subject posed for artistic effect are inappropriate in business résumés. Paste the photograph in the upper left or right hand corner of the first résumé page. Photographs are essential in the résumé of an entertainer or model and should be 8 by 10 inches or larger.

20. **Art decoration.**   Simple decoration can improve a résumé. However, because "one man's meat is another man's poison" use art devices with great care.

21. **Graphs and charts.**   Graphs and charts usually add little to a résumé unless of professional quality. A simple curve showing sales increases is not impressive. On the other hand, a 10 year bar chart of sales and profit increases or a curve of dramatic increases in your income can make valid points. Figures 9 through 12 contain graphs that are suitable for inclusion in a résumé.

22. **Testimonials.**   Testimonials can serve effectively as objective evaluations, provided that you can present them without appearing to be boastful. Testimonials can be placed in any appropriate part of your résumé, particularly on a summary page or in a summary paragraph, or when discussing your handling of important responsibilities.

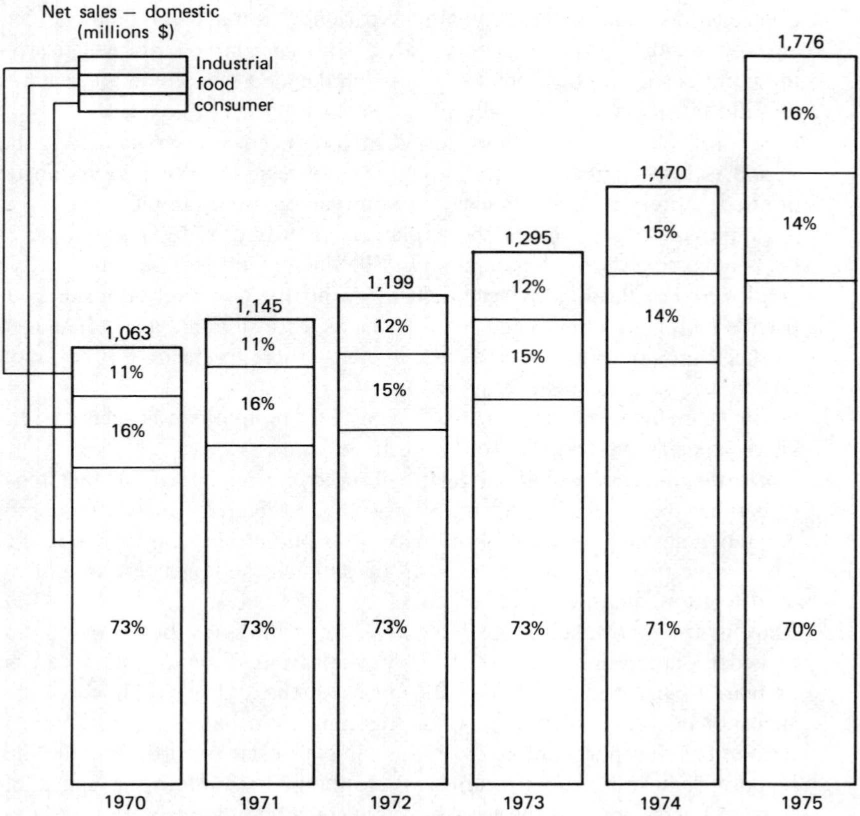

Figure 9   A bar chart.

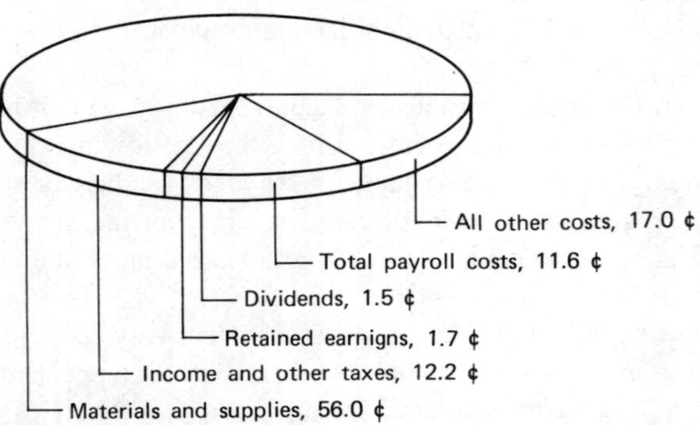

Figure 11   An interesting chart, using a coin to show the distribution of a dollar.

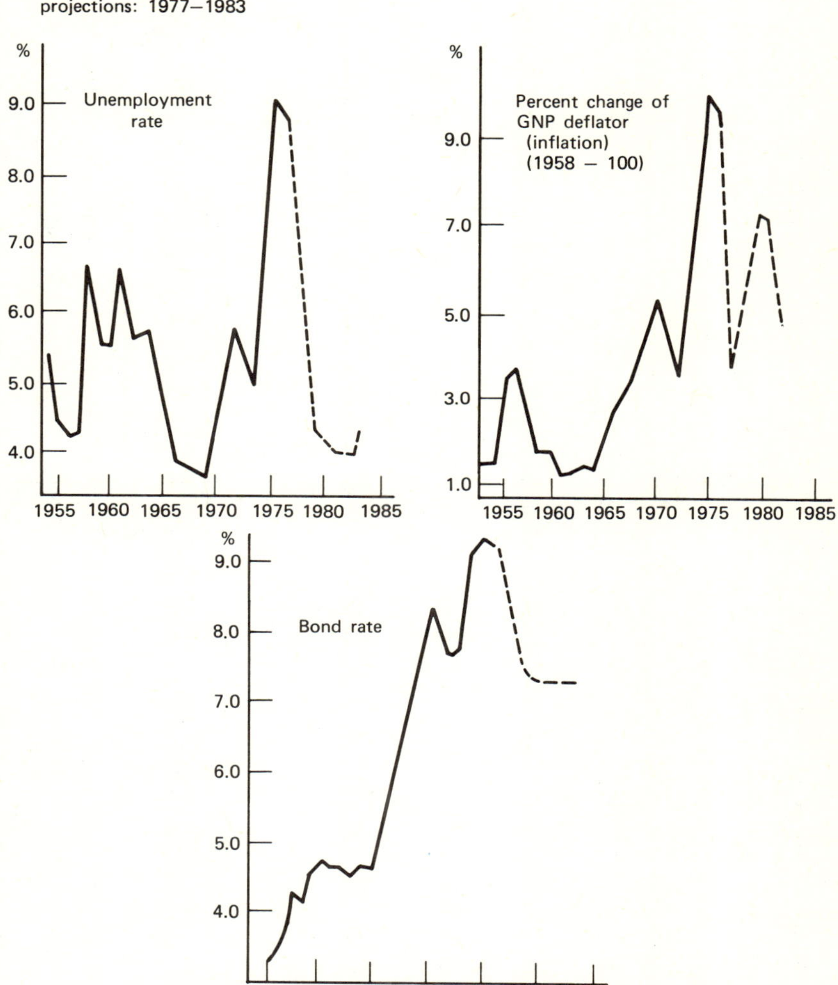

Figure 10   Examples of graphs. *Source:* Ross R. Proston, Director, Wharton Long-Term Forecasting Model.

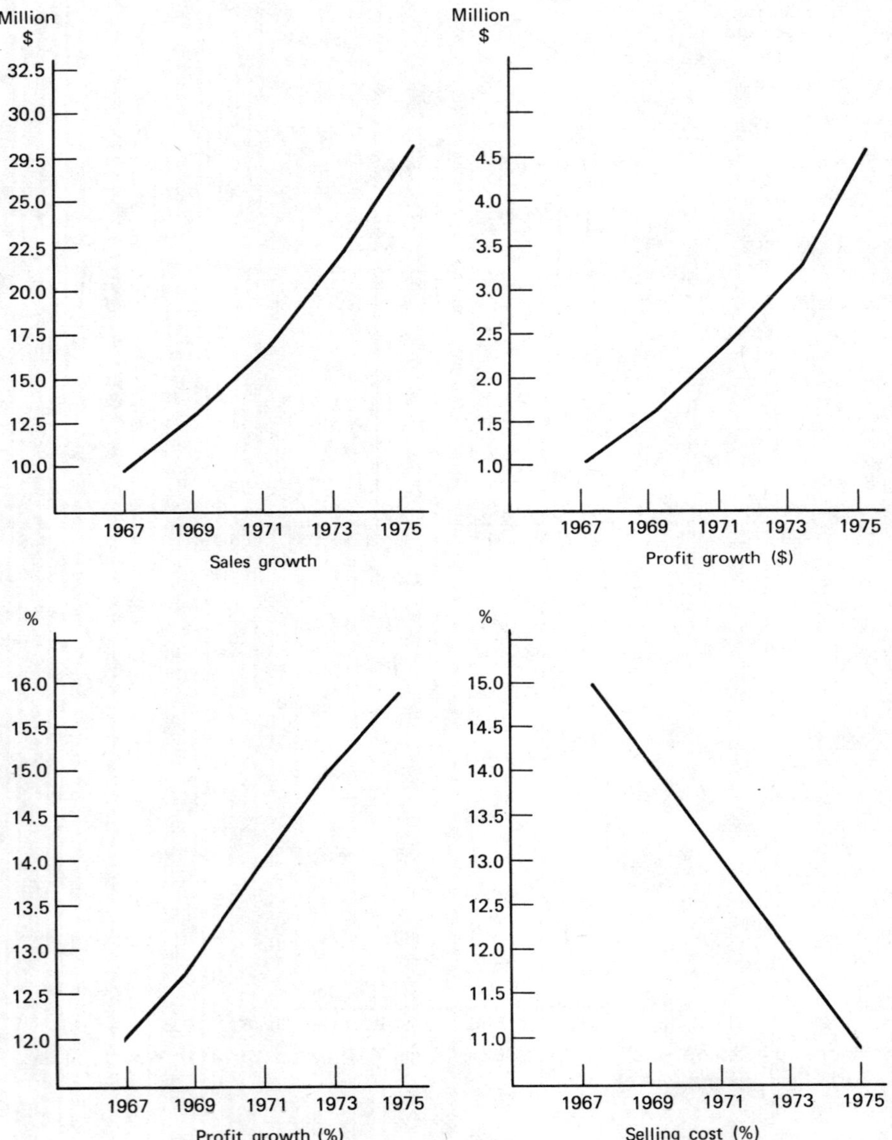

Figure 12   Examples of graphs suitable for inclusion in a résumé.

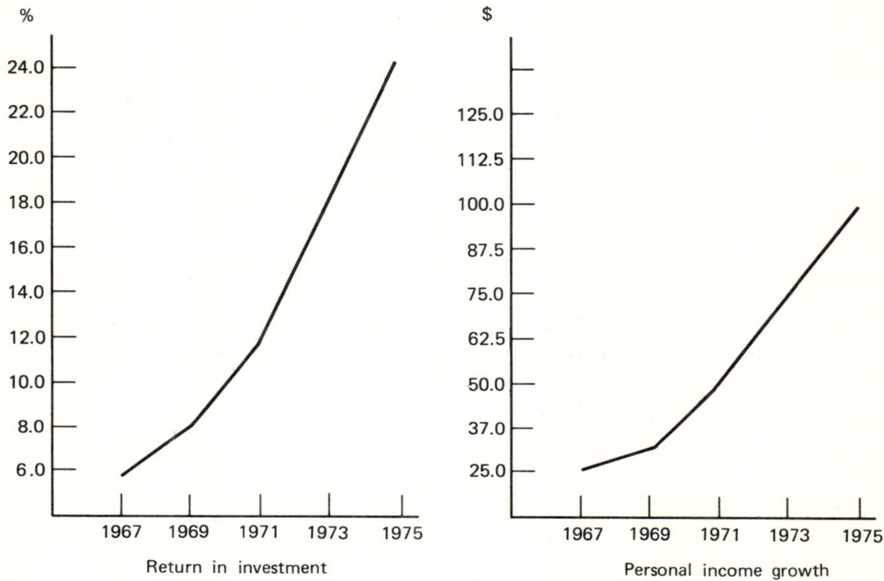

Graphs in Figure 12 are based on the
following data (000 omitted):

	1967	1969	1971	1973	1975
Sales growth	$10,000	$13,000	$16,900	$21,970	$28,561
Profit growth	1,200	1,690	2,366	3,295	4,569.76
Sales cost (%)	15	14	13	12	11
Return on investment (%)	6	8	12	18	24
Income growth	$25	$32.5	$50	$75	$100

23. **Civil service grades.**   In seeking a job with the government or in in-
    dicating the governmental level of your responsibilities to a private em-
    ployer, mention of the civil service grade is useful.
24. **Date of availability for employment.**   Specify the time of your avail-
    ability only if it is more than 30 days in the future.
25. **Willingness to relocate.**   A willingness to relocate expands your job op-
    portunities and should be noted. A position that is ideal for you might
    turn up far away from the location where you thought you would like to
    work.

COMMON RÉSUMÉ CRITICISMS

The criticisms listed below are those most commonly expressed by résumé readers. You will observe that many of them are in exact opposition. There is no way to write a résumé that will appeal to every reader. Fit your résumé to the type of individual whom you expect to be reading it.

1. **Too long.**   The résumé is not concise, interesting, and relevant. A person required to read hundreds or thousands of résumés, however, may find any résumé that exceeds one page to be too long. Keep a résumé short if it is aimed at a lower echelon personnel executive or an employment agency.
2. **Too short.**   The résumé does not give the reader an opportunity to make a proper evaluation.
3. **Too condensed.**   Paragraphs and sentences are too closely written for easy reading. It is preferable to expand spatially sentences, paragraphs, and white space rather than to try to get two pages of easy-to-read writing on one page.
4. **Too wordy.**   The description is verbose, with several words used for what could have been expressed in one or two.
5. **Too slick.**   The résumé is so well prepared as to be inappropriate for the individual presenting it and must therefore have been written by someone else. This evaluation leads the reader to suspect that the subject's qualifications are exaggerated.
6. **Too amateurish.**   The applicant cannot express himself, which would be a liability on the job.
7. **Poorly reproduced.**   The résumé is carelessly reproduced, especially when duplicated by photocopying.
8. **Misspellings and bad grammar abound.**   Spelling and grammatical errors in a résumé show lack of the primary skills necessary for accomplishment. Poor spellers need not be low achievers, but a poor speller who does not compensate for this deficiency by having another person proofread the résumé shows bad judgment. Bad grammar is inexcusable at the executive and professional levels.
9. **Reason for leaving last job omitted.**   This has been discussed elsewhere in this book.
10. **Date of availability omitted.**   If you apply for a position months ahead of the time when you can start work, include the date of your availability.
11. **Geographical preference omitted.**   Any geographical preferences or limitations regarding location of employment should be specified in a résumé.
12. **Objective omitted.**   This has been discussed elsewhere.

13. **Poorly expressed.**   If you are unable to prepare your own résumé, have someone else write it for you.
14. **Résumé is boastful.**   Boastfulness is an unattractive quality. Be realistic about yourself, but do not bluster, overestimate, or exaggerate.
15. **Résumé is dishonest.**   You have claimed to have expertise that you do not possess.
16. **Salary information lacking.**   This has been discussed elsewhere.
17. **Résumé is "gimmicky."**   It contains words, structure, decoration, or material that depart so much from the norm that the résumé is unacceptable.
18. **Sufficient data lacking.**   The material is insufficient for a proper evaluation. You may have tried to condense to one page experience that requires several pages for explanation.

THE TEN RÉSUMÉ STYLES

The 10 basic styles of résumé are discussed below. The word *chronological* is used in this book to mean the arrangement of data in a résumé in the *reverse* order of their occurrence. That is, a résumé, unlike a biography or a history, describes one's most recent experience first and one's oldest experience last. The body of the *Chronological Résumé with Summary Page* (starting with p. 2) is chronological in form. The *Summary Page* is a brief interpretation of the *succeeding* pages.

The word *functional* refers to a style of résumé that describes activities in each area of experience separately without reference to the companies for which the function was performed or to the time of performance. For example:

EXPERIENCE

GENERAL MANAGER	Held P. & L. responsibility for $10 million division. Reorganized production and cost accounting departments. Reduced costs. Set up new marketing strategies. Increased sales. Also consolidated two manufacturing plants for improved efficiency.
MARKETING MANAGEMENT	Surveyed market for power tools. Established share of market goals for each territory; assigned quotas; installed new salesmen's compensation plan. Redirected advertising. Increased sales 37% within 2 years for one company and 23% for another company.

EMPLOYMENT HISTORY

J. D. Blair Company, Chicago, Ill.
Anderson and Sloan Company, Portland, Me.
Smith and Steele Company, Newark, N.J.

These experiences (described in summary form here) might apply to one, two, or all three of the companies named.

Brief descriptions of the various résumé styles, together with our recommendations, are given below. Detailed analyses appear later.

1. **Basic Résumé.**   The best form for one entering the job market or having very limited experience.
2. **Chronological Résumé.**   The second best form (sometimes the best) for a middle or upper management executive, since it permits the sharpest delineation of accomplishments.
3. **Chronological Résumé with Summary Page.**   The best form for a middle or upper management executive—in addition to permitting a clear listing of accomplishments, it also contains a *Summary Page*.
4. **Functional Résumé.**   An excellent form, especially for one with experience in several job functions, such as marketing, finance, and general management. A preferred form for educators at the administrative level. Some personnel executives profess a liking for this form.
5. **Functional-by-Company (or Institution) Résumé.*** Advantageously associates function with the company for which it was performed, but loses the impact of the pure *Functional Résumé*.
6. **Harvard Résumé.**   Has an excellent appearance, but less effective, from both the job seeker's and the employer's point of view, than the styles discussed so far.
7. **Creative Résumé.**   For special uses only. Has no definite structure.
8. **Narrative Résumé.**   A specialized form that may serve well in situations deviating from the norm.
9. **Professional Résumé.**   For lawyers, doctors, teachers, and other professionals whose education and accreditation are of primary importance to the rader.
10. **Accomplishment Résumé.**   Not generally recommended because its raison d'être is to obscure.

---

* Company: an incorporated or unicorporated business; institution: an organization with a social, educational, or religious purpose, such as schools, churches, hospitals, prisons, foundations, and libraries.

These evaluations are based on personal opinions and on experience.

The selection of a résumé form may also change with your career. You might start with the *Basic Résumé,* graduate after a few years to the *Chronological Résumé,* and finally proceed to the *Chronological Résumé with Summary Page* or to the *Functional Résumé.*

A *covering* letter is an essential short introduction to a résumé. Of the samples included in this book there will be one more "right" for you than any of the others, which you can then amend to fit your circumstances. A *broadcast* letter—different from a résumé and a covering letter—is also fully explained.

The word *résumé* (from the Latin resūmere, "to take up again," and the French résumer, "to resume, summarize"), pronounced ráy zū māy, is defined by *Webster's Third International Dictionary* as "a short account of one's career and qualifications prepared typically by an applicant for a position."

Résumé Length

There is no standard résumé length. A résumé should be as long as it needs to be to present important information concisely and interestingly. Successful résumés have been as short as one page and as long as six pages. It is conciseness, relevance, and interest that matter. A six page résumé can be concise; a three page résumé, verbose.

Résumé Language

The language of a résumé must be succinct, crisp, trenchant, expressive, interesting, and personal. Words, phrases, sentences, and paragraphs illustrating this type of writing appear in this book (Appendix A). Use the specialized vocabulary of your job area. Scientists, data processors, lawyers, financial people, economists, engineers, social workers—each specialization has its own nomenclature. However, a résumé must never be so technical that those outside your discipline fail to understand it. If you have experience in a vocation, your language will naturally reflect it. If you have little or no experience, ignore this aspect.

Avoid the personal pronoun "I" in a résumé (it is acceptable in a covering or broadcast letter, however) because its repetition is tiresome and creates an atmosphere of boastfulness or egotism.

While conforming to the conventions of modern résumé writing and language, make your résumé reflect your personality where possible. Of the effective words, phrases, sentences, and paragraphs suggested in Appendix A select those that not only are appropriate but seem natural *to you,* or use a synonym that does correspond to your natural way of expression. Make your résumé a portrait in words. Remember that a skilled portraitist brings more to his subject than is disclosed in a photograph. A photograph, no matter how great, reflects a moment in time; a portrait is an enduring record.

The Basic Résumé

The *Basic Résumé,* best suited for those entering the job market, should contain the following items (their order may vary).

1. Name, address with zip code, and telephone number with area code.
2. Personal data (age, martial status, health, willingness to travel or relocate, date of availability).
3. Objectives.
4. Education (honors, awards, high class standing).
5. Extracurricular activities.
6. Languages other than English.
7. Summer jobs.
8. Military service.
9. Hobbies (if interesting).

This is a standard form. We reccomend that job qualifications be added, if they can be properly expressed, immediately after objectives. Keep this résumé to one page. Use the *Basic Résumé* whenever work experience is very limited. Any important job experience that does exist should be described before education.

Examples of *Basic Résumé* follow.

EXAMPLE OF BASIC RÉSUMÉ

23 Redondo Drive   (123) 456-7890
La Jolla, California 12345   R E S U M E
                                         of
                                    RICHARD SMITH

<u>PERSONAL DATA</u>: Born 3/10/51, single, excellent health.

<u>OBJECTIVE</u>:

Association with a communications or other company in an entry position with
opportunity for general management consistent with ability to contribute.

<u>QUALIFICATIONS</u>:

Good education, consistently high academic grades, willingness to work hard
to establish capability; concerned with and interested in major U. S. and
world problems; active in causes; experienced in working with general public
during summer jobs and in retail selling since graduating from college.
Volunteer work 1974 to date. Harmonious, articulate, diligent. Senior year
of high school in Thailand. Rudimentary knowledge of French and German.

<u>EDUCATION</u>:

<u>B. A.</u>, Government, University of Pennsylvania, Philadelphia, Pa., 1973.
Courses in Government: U. S., South Africa, Latin America, France.
Courses in: Principles of Management, Economics I and II, International
             Business, Business Ethics, Fundamentals of Public Speaking,
             Oral Interpretation. Dean's List, 2 years.

<u>EXTRA-CURRICULAR ACTIVITIES</u>:

Football, lacrosse, handball; librarian assistant; mail room messenger,
R. O. T. C.

<u>BUSINESS EXPERIENCE</u>:

<u>Nov. 22-Dec. 24, 1973</u>   THE MAY COMPANY, Long Beach, California

TOY SALESMAN for branch of leading department store.

<u>SUMMER JOBS</u>:

<u>1969-1973</u>   DEPT. OF PARKS AND RECREATION, La Jolla.

June to Nov. 1973, GATE ATTENDANT, beach area; June to Sept. 1972, POOL
GATEMAN; June to Sept. 1971, LOCKER ROOM ATTENDANT; June to Sept. 1970,
LOCKER ROOM ATTENDANT; June to Sept. 1969, PARK ATTENDANT. Collected
revenues, checked residency, painted, cleaned beach.

<u>HOBBIES</u>: Numismatics, philately, chess.

<u>REFERENCES AND FURTHER DATA ON REQUEST</u>

DISCUSSION

Basic Résumé.   The Richard Smith résumé arouses interest at once. The advantages of youth and good health are stated immediately. Here is a young man who knows the genral area in which he would like to work and without boastfulness expresses the qualifications he knows he possesses. The qualifications have a good relationship to the objective. Probably only a few students could be selected for study in Thailand. He attained academic honors in college. He worked during summer vacations at a job that he can show to have increased his ability to develop and maintain harmonious human relationships. Some employers give preference to applicants who have worked their ways through college, partially or wholly.

Mr. Smith's extracurricular activities are broad. His hobbies are intellectual, original, and interesting. He chose his studies with a business career in mind. He has some language proficiency.

The résumé is easily readable and logical in sequence, with education taking precedence over business experience because of its greater significance at this career stage. If previous employment had included important learning experience relevant to job objective, however, it might have preceded education. The important elements of the résumé are all headlined. The language is personal.

EXAMPLE OF BASIC RÉSUMÉ

10 Learning Avenue   Home (201 345-0987
Essex, N. J. 07007   Office (201) 888-9779

Curriculum Vitae
of
PAMILA W. PIZER

TEACHER

Personal Data: Age 23 (b. 4/2/52), married, excellent health.
                    S. S. No. 123-45-6789

Objective: Teacher, common grades 1-3.

Qualifications: College training in teaching; intense interest in children; summer
                    and part-time jobs throughout college; recipient of scholastic hon-
                    ors; valuable experience in student teaching with commendations.
                    Characterized as a talented first grade teacher. Hold New Jersey
                    State accreditation for teaching in private schools. Expect accred-
                    itation for public school teaching as soon as examinations are
                    given. Plan to enter graduate school to earn Masters Degree in
                    Education, reading specialty.

Education: B. A., Montclair State College, Upper Montclair, N. J. Dean's
                    List: 1973, 1974, 1975. Graduated Magna Cum Laude. Cumula-
                    tive Index 3.6. Interpersonal Communication Index 3.9 (major).
                    Elementary Education Index 3.8 (minor).

Extra-curricular   1973-Present, Administrative Assistant, Montclair State College,
Activities   Doctoral Students' Council, typing, receptionist, student liaison,
Part-time and   office management.
Summer Jobs: Feb.-May 1974, Avon Avenue Elementary School, Newark, N. J.,
                    Student Aide, 2nd grade. Feb.-May 1974 (concurrently, same
                    school), tutored reading, 3rd grade.
                    1970-1973 (concurrently), Montclair State College, Student Teach-
                    ing Office, Student Aide to Coordinator of Student Teaching. Or-
                    ganized day school for children and taught reading, math, language
                    arts, dramatics; conducted field trips.

Teaching   Sept.-May 1974, Bergen Street School, Newark, N. J. Student
Experience: Teacher. Taught 1st and 3rd grades in own reading, math and
                    language arts groups, daily and unsupervised. Received "A"
                    grade. Commended by cooperating Teacher, Supervisor and Princi-
                    pal. Taught Dramatics at summer classes in Stratford, Conn.

Hobbies: Tennis, dance, acting, creative dramatics.

Availability: At once.

REFERENCES AND FURTHER DATA ON REQUEST

DISCUSSION

Basic Résumé. In the Pizer résumé it is the *qualifications* paragraph that helps to give personality to this young teacher who has just graduated from college. She is more than merely another job applicant. She says she has an intense interest in children. This is supported by her activities listed under part-time and summer jobs.

She was commended while a student teacher. Her scholastic grades were excellent, giving great promise of excellence in her chosen field. Motivation is indicated by extracurricular activities and summer and part-time jobs. The whole résumé is laid out for logical sequence and readability.

When you have accomplished great victories, small details become insignificant and can be omitted. When you are on the threshold of achievement, small pieces of activity shine out of proportion to their importance.

The Chronological Résumé

The *Chronological Résumé* is the one most frequently used by applicants who have job experience. The form offers the writer the best opportunity to "highlight" achievements and the reader the best opportunity to gauge the applicant's qualifications. The work experience is shown in reverse chronological order, the last or present job being given first. The various positions held at one company should also be described in reverse chronological order. This order shows the applicant's growth and development—characteristics of great interest to employers. The elements of the *Chronological Résumé* are as follows:

1. Name, address, and telephone number.
2. Objective.
3. Name of the company of most recent or present employment.

   - Brief description of the company.
   - Responsibilities.
   - Accomplishments (treat each level of assignment as if it were a different employer).

4. Name of the company of next most recent employment.

   - Brief description of the company.
   - Responsibilities.
   - Accomplishments.

   Continue as above for each relevant employment, going back to your first job. If earlier employment is unrelated to your present objective, summarize it briefly in a catchall sentence or paragraph. Omit mention of inappropriate or undignified jobs—jobs that are unrelated to the one being sought, or jobs that poorly reflect your qualities.
5. Military service (delete this heading if inappropriate).
6. Education.
7. Extracurricular activities (including summer jobs).
8. Accreditations (C.P.A., C.L.U., Real Estate Broker, Licensed Engineer, and so forth).
9. Professional memberships.
10. Community activities.
11. Hobbies.
12. Personal data.

The *Chronological Résumé* may be two or more pages in length. Remember the rules: conciseness, relevance, and interest.

   Examples of *Chronological Résumé* follow.

EXAMPLE OF CHRONOLOGICAL RÉSUMÉ

605 Dock Avenue   (123) 456-7890
Boston, Mass. 02108

R E S U M E

of

<u>MERILLE LYNCH</u>

Employment Objectives in the Following Areas:

INVESTMENT BANKING   Municipal financial consulting; new issues; new
                              business; private placements; financial services;
                              institutional sales; research.

COMMERCIAL BANKING   Urban affairs; money market; municipal lending;
                              financial services.

Education Includes:

M. B. A., B. S., superior grades, 3.7 on 4.0 scale. Finance major.

Personal Data:

Age 34, divorced, excellent health; interested in financial analysis, riding, sports, travel, writing.

Record of Experience:

<u>1968-1973</u>   KUHN MARX & CO., Hancock Street, Boston, Mass.

ANALYST, Institutional Department for investment banking company and full-service retail and institutional brokerage. This department over the past $5\frac{1}{2}$ years handled approximately 35 new capital projects per year for Connecticut municipalities involving general obligation or revenue bonds of about $200 million.

Responsible for:

- preparation and dissemination of information to facilitate new issue financings by serving as intermediary between municipality and investor.

- assistance to debt issuer to obtain best credit rating possible together with lowest interest cost.

- creating environment to provide maximum marketability of bonds.

- preparation and finalization of all Official Statements including organization of all pertinent economic and financial data needed for evaluation.

over please

MERILLE LYNCH   PAGE 2

The above responsibilities entailed:

- participation in all preliminary financial discussions with architects, bond
  counsels, house counsel, municipalities solicitors, trustee banks and/or
  paying agents, syndicate members, issuers, investors and major banks and
  insurance companies, financial firms and salesmen.

- risk analysis, financing concepts and closing sales. Personally responsible
  for many salesmen's orders up to $2.6 million.

- examination of feasibility of capital proposals, reviewing feasibility reports
  prepared by consultants and major accounting firms, suggesting modifica-
  tions as necessary to assure successful underwriting, inclusion of security
  provisions, rate covenants, earnings tests, reserve capitalization, analysis
  of financial statements including balance sheets, break-even points and re-
  checking to assure validity of risk/equity relationship.

- contacts with regulatory agencies at state and federal levels.

The carrying out of these various responsibilities resulted in:

- saving issuers thousands of dollars in basis points by achieving higher ratings from rating services through personal presentations, i. e.: upgrading
  ratings, holding marginal ratings, reversing lower ratings, sometimes getting
  a higher rating from one service than another and thereby mitigating the lower rating.

- ability of firm to underwrite issues in difficult markets.

- specifically, for example, causing both Moody and Standard and Poor's to
  upgrade one $15.9 million Refunding School Authority Issue in 1973 which
  otherwise might have produced an underwriting loss.

- reduction of underwriting and other market risks.

- protection of firm against civil or criminal suits for non-disclosure with con-
  comitant result of full profit.

- repeat business for the firm.

<u>1964-1968</u>   DUN AND STANDARD CORP., 27 Wall Street, New York, N. Y.

MEMBER OF EDITORIAL STAFF, WRITER, ANALYST of and for "Bond Outlook"
for publisher of financial data on securities with well-known investment advisory service to clients.

- prepared weekly analysis of new bond issues.

- reviewed and evaluated municipal credit.

over please

MERILLE LYNCH   PAGE 3

- analyzed economic, social, political and geographical data.

- reported on city and state general obligation, revenue and construction bonds.

- studied and evaluated annual municipal financial statements, audits, budgets, capital improvement programs.

- evaluated debt structures, histories and trends.

- reviewed and weighed qualitative factors of administration, organization, structure, efficiency and growth factors.

- utilized all types of financial data, Federal Reserve and Census Bureau publications.

Accustomed to personal interview and liaison activities with municipal officials, business managers, financial advisors and consultants and bank executives.

Experience additionally included:

- training analysts.

- analysis of Standard & Poor's ratings on 8,000 issues.

- development of advertising themes.

- providing data and story-lines for financial writers.

- diversified special reports, summaries and analyses.

<u>1961-1964</u>   WACHOVIA TRUST COMPANY, New York, N. Y.

RESEARCH ASSISTANT after starting as Statistical Clerk for one of largest banks in the United States.

- worked directly with Senior Municipal Analyst and Senior Vice-President.

- prepared analystical reports on municipal securities for Officers Investment Committee and Board of Directors.

- provided reports forming a basis for portfolio decisions.

- provided complete supporting statistical data and analyses.

- utilized all sources of financial and economic data as appropriate.

- maintained financial and economic charts.

<u>REFERENCES AND FURTHER DATA ON REQUEST</u>

DISCUSSION

Chronological Résumé.   The Lynch résumé is very comprehensive. It could have been written also as a *Functional Résumé* or a *Chronological with Summary Page Résumé*. The *Chronological* form was chosen because the sequence of experience shows continuous growth.

The summary page was omitted to shorten the résumé; in fact, the obvious high qualifications of the subject require no further explanation or summing up.

The language is that of a professional expressing competence in her vocation with literacy and compactness. Her work is specialized and complex.

The sequence and explanations are logical, indicating the ability to analyze and to write complicated reports with lucidity and expressiveness. Financial expertise was used to assist salesmen in situations where their technical grasp of financial details was wanting. It was also used to upgrade bond ratings and reduce carrying costs for issuers. The subject went beyond her normal duties to provide significant profitability assistance to her employer.

Any reader will know at once that here is a highly capable individual with substantial potential for future growth. Despite the comprehensiveness of the résumé, there is still plenty of room for exploration in a personal interview.

Age, education, and personal data are clearly and briefly expressed at the outset because most are highly favorable and need no extended comment. Experience takes strong precedence over education; just enough is said about education to indicate a high level of intelligence.

EXAMPLE OF CHRONOLOGICAL RÉSUMÉ

75 Executive Drive
Patience, Ga. 00000

Home (100) 123-4567
Office (101) 321-1234

R E S U M E

of

ROBERT EXEMPLAR

OBJECTIVE: HEALTH CARE ADMINISTRATION

QUALIFICATIONS: Experienced in every facet of hospital administration and in
planning and implementing improved hospital expansions and
renovations. Accustomed to supervision of all departments,
Board relationships, nursing, volunteers, public relations,
outpatient development, E.D.P. utilization. Age 35, married,
M.P.H. and B.S. degrees.

1970-Present   AUGUSTA MEMORIAL HOSPITAL, Augusta, Ga., a 400-bed
acute general hospital recently expanded from 200 beds and
renovated in old section.

1973-Present

ACTING ADMINISTRATOR, CHIEF EXECUTIVE OFFICER, in absence of Administrator recuperating from severe illness.

Responsible for:

- completing move from old facility to new $10 million wing; and for renovating
old section.

Accomplishments:

- rearranged departments to achieve more functional and more efficient operations.
- supervised installations of intensive care burn unit, the only one of its kind
within 500 miles.
- held meeting and made agreements with other hospitals to eliminate under-
utilized duplicate services and share facilities; reduced operating costs by
17%.

ROBERT EXEMPLAR   PAGE 2

- reorganized administrative structure to give added authority with responsibility to department heads.
- established capital spending and operating budgets; employed construction consultant and reduced costs in excess of budget to meet budget while maintaining integrity of plans.

1970-1974   ASSISTANT ADMINISTRATOR

- Assigned complete responsibility for EKG, laboratory, emergency services, developing expanded outpatient program, pharmacy, physical therapy, food and dietary, records.
- Developed contract specifications for new hospital wing.
- Purchased $3 million of new equipment.
- Established unit dose and other new systems in pharmacy to attain better control.

1968-1970   ADMINISTRATIVE INTERNE at Medical Center at Ithaca, N. Y.

Responsible for study of operations, reports, recommendations. Made recommendations relating to budgets, operating controls, School of Nursing, new executive suite facility, pressure chamber for improved treatment of acute fractures. All were implemented. Used experience to complete M.P.H. degree thesis requirement.

MILITARY SERVICE:

U. S. NAVAL AIR FORCE, 1965-1968, Lt. Comm. Administrative Officer in aircraft carrier hospital off Vietnam for two years after flight training. Assigned to organize expanded hospital facilities in South Vietnam involving several hundred thousand population area.

EDUCATION:

M.P.H., Hospital Administration, Cornell University, Ithaca, N. Y., 1970.

B.S., Business Administration, University of Chicago, (Ill.), 1962. Dean's List. Graduated Cum Laude.

PROFESSIONAL MEMBERSHIPS:

National Association of Health Care Administrators
Georgia Hospital Administrators Association

HOBBIES: Scuba diving, target shooting, golf.

PERSONAL DATA: Born March 31, 1941, married, two children, excellent health. Willing to relocate.

REFERENCES AND FURTHER DATA ON REQUEST

DISCUSSION

Chronological Résumé.   The résumé shows Mr. Exemplar to be qualified, by experience and education, for the position he seeks. His experience chronologically proceeds forward throughout his career, culminating in the position of acting administrator affording two years of chief executive experience during the illness of the administrator. One can read between the lines that the subject is unwilling to return to an assistancy on the senior officer's recovery from illness.

Few administrators have the learning opportunity afforded by the task of planning a new hospital and renovating old facilities.

Although the résumé is relatively brief, almost every important fact of hospital administration is commented upon. The reader is left in no doubt as to the comprehensive qualifications of the candidate. He is cost conscious, and made use of a construction consultant to save money on construction costs. His use of administrative internship is interesting and contributory.

The facilities available at this hospital are very much like those found at larger urban institutions, thus qualifying the subject for enlarged responsibilities.

The word *SCUBA* in the résumé is an acronym and should have been capitalized.

The Chronological Résumé with Summary Page

The *Chronological Résumé with Summary Page* is the most effective form of résumé for middle to upper business management as well as in some other vocations. The summary page interprets the résumé and quickly provides the gist of the applicant's case. Remember that the summary page is always the *first* page of the résumé. It is written *last,* however, because it is based on the material appearing in the chronological part of the résumé, which must be written *first*.

A summary page establishes rapport and interest and creates the curiosity to learn more about the applicant's background in the subsequent pages. Psychologically it compliments the reader by recognizing that his or her time is valuable and by providing the opportunity to make a quick appraisal.

The summary page can also be used to "beef up" a basically weak résumé.

The summary page, however, is an extra page. If you are concerned about the length of your résumé, eliminate the summary page or reduce its content to a brief paragraph or two to be placed at the beginning of the résumé. You will find examples of résumés with full summary pages and with reduced summaries.

Because *Chronological Résumé with Summary Page* is difficult to prepare, it is explained in detail in the pages that follow. In our annotated example page 2 appears first because the summary page, page 1, is *written last.*

Examples of *Chronological Résumé with Summary Page* are given below.

EXAMPLE OF CHRONOLOGICAL RÉSUMÉ WITH SUMMARY PAGE

375 Broadalban Road
Ephrata, Va.

(177) 377-4777

RESUME

of

<u>DUNCAN SMITH</u>

Qualified As

<u>SENIOR MANAGEMENT EXECUTIVE</u>

This is the
Summary Page

***   Record of consistent profit contributions amounting to millions of dollars in general management, marketing, production in the U.S., Canada and internationally; accustomed for the last ten years to autonomous multi-division P. & L. responsibility and responsible for at least eight turn-around situations involving significant figures.

***   Equipped to use latest management sciences including PERT, CPM and other network techniques to accomplish company goals.

***   Intimately familiar with the metal-working industry and with sophisticated machinery and equipment in a broad area of manufacturing.

***   Characterized by others as an inspiring leader, incisive in identifying problems, imaginative in finding and implementing solutions, strong in comprehensive, accurate planning leading to improved profitability.

(FOR FURTHER DATA, PLEASE SEE FOLLOWING PAGES)

EXAMPLE OF CHRONOLOGICAL RÉSUMÉ WITH SUMMARY PAGE

DUNCAN SMITH

<u>BUSINESS EXPERIENCE</u>:

<u>1970-Present</u>   LEAF MACHINERY DIVISION, BRF, INC.
                                 Winston-Salem, N.C.

VICE PRESIDENT, GENERAL MANAGER of $45 million tobacco machinery manu-
facturing division of $700 million leisure products conglomerate. Reported to
parent corporate Group Vice President. Supervised V.P., R. & D., Controller,
Director of Marketing, European and South American Directors.

Responsibility:

- P. & L. responsibility for U.S. division and plants in France, U.K., Brazil,
  and marketing headquarters in Switzerland.

Achievements:

- U.K. Division lost $250,000 first quarter 1970; by August Division was
  operating profitably with earnings of $80,000.
- Reduced inflated U.S. payroll by $235,000.
- Successfully introduced three new products of complex technology.
- Improved return on assets from 13.8% to 14.6%.
- Prepared, submitted and implemented five-year plan yielding compounded
  annual growth in pre-tax profits of 13.3%.

These accomplishments were engineered by the use of PERT, Critical Path Method
and other net-work techniques to improve production, eliminate bottlenecks; by
repricing; by implementing plans which had been made but not acted upon; and
by creating a new sales program.

<u>1967-1970</u>   THOMAS & SESSIONS, Springfield, Mo.

<u>1969-1970</u>, ASSISTANT to the PRESIDENT of $80 million manufacturer of meters,
electric sub-assemblies, fractional horsepower motors and other products.

<u>1967-1969</u>, PRESIDENT of autonomous Canadian Division with sales of $15 million.
Responsible for:

- Management of complete staff: finance, sales, manufacturing.
- Divisional profit and loss.
- Assisting the President of parent company.
- Presiding at Directors' and Stockholders' meetings.

Accomplishments:

- In 1967 losses were above $$\frac{1}{2}$$ million annually; by end 1969 losses were
  eliminated and profits stood at all-time high of $1.137 million.

EXAMPLE OF CHRONOLOGICAL RÉSUMÉ WITH SUMMARY PAGE

DUNCAN SMITH

This was accomplished by consolidating motor operations, reducing overhead, eliminating ineffective department in production area, re-aligning production facilities, changing sales plans and reassigning sales responsibilities.

1962-1967   W. H. THOMPSON & CO., Harrisburg, Pa.

This company manufactures castings, wire, rod and strip, electrical wire and cable, fractional horsepower motors and other industrial products. Volume $300 million.

1964-1967, VICE PRESIDENT, INTERNATIONAL OPERATIONS. Reported to President. Supervised Director of International Marketing and Managers in Canada, Mexico, Brazil, U.K., Europe, Australia. Responsible for:

- Profit and loss responsibility for 17 international plants and all exports.

Accomplishments:

- Increased pre-tax profits from $1.07 million to $1.69 million, including complete amortization of start-up costs in five new plants.
- Increased volume of manufactured product from $40 million to $45.5 million.
- Restored profitability to Canadian plant operating at a loss of $52,000.
- Achieved turn-around in SARE Division from loss of $350,000 to profit of $120,000; similarly for Netherlands and Brazilian companies.

1962-1964, VICE PRESIDENT, W. H. Thompson & Co. of Canada, Toronto, Ontario. Supervised General Sales Manager, Controller, and three plant managers. Responsible for:

- Profit and loss for three manufacturing locations and six product lines in $12 million division.

Achievements included:

- Improvement in pre-tax profit from $396,000 to $578,000.
- Increased revenue from $13.0 million to $15.1 million.
- reversed severe loss trend at Canadian wire plant to profit over a period of three years rising from $127,000 to $374,000.
- Improved operation at Rubberoid Plant from loss of $50,000 to a profit of $400,000.

1953-1962   VANADIUM METAL WIRE WORKS
                                   ALLOY DIVISION, E. H. HUMBOLT & CO.
                                   Pittsburgh, Pa.

GENERAL MANAGER with supporting staff of Assistant Works Manager, Plant Superintendent, Accountant, Metallurgist, Production and Quality Control Managers and Chief Industrial Engineer.

EXAMPLE OF CHRONOLOGICAL RÉSUMÉ WITH SUMMARY PAGE

DUNCAN SMITH

- started as District Sales Manager and progressed successively to Regional Sales Manager, Assistant General Sales Manager, Sales Manager.

Accomplishments:

- in first year of responsibility as General Manager turned loss of $20/30 per month to profit of $300,000 with subsequent increase to $600,000.

MILITARY SERVICE:

1941-1943   UNITED STATES AIR FORCE

CAPTAIN.

EDUCATION:

B.S., Engineering, 1949, University of Pittsburgh, Pittsburgh, Pa.

Graduate work in Business Management at Northwestern and Michigan State.

COMMUNITY ACTIVITIES:

Chairman, Board of Directors, National Hospital, Winston-Salem, N.C.

Chairman, Community Chest, Winston-Salem, N.C.

Member, National Presidential Committee to Study Government Options.

HONORS:

Winston-Salem Citizen-of-the-Year Award.

HOBBIES:

Tennis, golf, shooting (National 12 Bore Champion).

PERSONAL DATA:

Born 3/31/28, married, two children, excellent health, willing to relocate.

REFERENCES AND FURTHER DATA ON REQUEST

DISCUSSION

Chronological Résumé with Summary Page.   The Duncan Smith résumé is a good example of an executive's résumé. It is longer than most because the subject has a long history of accomplishments. Those who hire executives want a comprehensive picture of the subject before expending, and perhaps wasting, time on an interview of several hours. The form of résumé was selected because there is nothing to hide in his chronology, with achievements increasing in each successive position. Furthermore, the *Chronological* form permits maximum capitalization on accomplishments. A résumé of this kind could be written only by a man who is supremely confident that there is no area of management in which he does not have experience and knowledge to support his claims.

Evidence of continuing formal management study is indicated by the use of network techniques to reach decisions (PERT, CPM). Experience in all the elements of management is shown: marketing, finance, production, general management. Used to being known for qualities of leadership and imagination, he does not hesitate to state them in his résumé, because he knows that the readers of his résumé will not learn about these qualities unless he tells them.

Mr. Smith's résumé creates a favorable attitude. If his interview techniques and his actual experience as brought out in an interview are as good as his writing, he is assured of employment.

The summary page is used in this instance to highlight some areas in his career and some material that contributes to his total image. It should make the reader want to read the body of the résumé.

The résumé provides a strong basis for selection for an interview and for an interesting interview discussion.

EXAMPLE OF CHRONOLOGICAL RÉSUMÉ WITH SUMMARY PAGE

103796 Western Way
Los Angeles, Cal. 99999

(000) 000-0000

R E S U M E

of

<u>EMERSON WORDSWORTH</u>

qualified as

<u>C.E.O., VICE PRESIDENT, GENERAL MANAGER</u>

***   General management competence built upon a strong financial and accounting background. As chief executive
officer currently, effected turn-around recovery in one
year reversing 30% loss to 9% profit; by first researching, validating and then implementing successful move
into new directions.

***   Experienced in bank relations, arranging long- and short-
term financing, production planning and incentive programs, top level marketing, optimum E.D.P. utilization
and accounting systems; effective labor negotiator.

***   Record of consistent promotion by and significant contributions to all employers, starting first employment as
office boy and rising to Treasuryship in six years.

***   Possess ability to communicate effectively, develop
staffs, motivate, innovate and create extra profitability
on sound bases founded upon well-rounded experience
in all facets of general business administration.

(FOR FURTHER DATA PLEASE SEE FOLLOWING PAGES)

EXAMPLE OF CHRONOLOGICAL RÉSUMÉ WITH SUMMARY PAGE

<u>EXPERIENCE</u>:

1969-Present   PARKAY CO., Maspeth, Cal.

PRESIDENT (1972-Present), V. P.-TREASURER (1970-1972), TREASURER/CONTROLLER
(1969-1970) for $5 million manufacturer of threaded products. Report to Chairman.

Responsible for:

- total operation of Company; including P. & L.

Accomplishments:

- redirected Company which was losing business by reason of too heavy concentration in hand tool field to new areas: aircraft, military manufacturing, automotive; recovered $1 million of sales in 1972 vs. 1971.
- arranged bank credits of $500,000 long-term and $300,000 short-term which pre-
  ceeding executive was unable to accomplish; by expressing Company's plans and
  new products; with major California bank.
- instituted new system of recording production on hourly basis by individual, by
  job; set up daily summary vs. predetermined standard; organized complete work
  force into efficient, harmonious group.

<u>1967-1969</u>   CARBORUNDUM CORPORATION, Chatsworth, Cal.

TREASURER/CONTROLLER

<u>1965-1967</u>   EXPERIMENTAL LABORATORIES, INC., Casablanca, Cal.

VICE PRESIDENT OPERATIONS, TREASURER

<u>1964-1965</u>   CRESCENT CO., INC., Los Angeles, Cal.

ASSISTANT CONTROLLER of nationally known manufacturer of wrenches.

Responsible for:

- all accounting and related functions.
- supervision of seven department managers and 60 employees.

Accomplishments (in words of immediate superior):

- "excellent administrator with capacities beyond accounting."
- reorganized general and cost accounting departments resulting in "a more uni-
  form work flow and in a program for training individuals in all phases of accounting."
- "designed improved production and inventory controls to create significant cost
  savings."
- developed budgets of exceptional value in analyzing problems and suggesting
  solutions.
- performed valuable services in converting from punch-card to 370/60 computer.

EXAMPLE OF CHRONOLOGICAL RÉSUMÉ WITH SUMMARY PAGE

EMERSON WORDSWORTH   PAGE 3

<u>1952-1964</u>   INTERNATIONAL TESTING LABORATORIES, Redwood City, Cal.

TREASURER, MEMBER, <u>Policy Making Committee</u>, ASSISTANT CONTROLLER.

Responsible for:

- all accounting functions.
- operating P.&L. statements.
- analysis and recommendation with respect to all financial statements.
- operating budgets for each Division as well as for Company.

Accomplishments:

- originated and developed plan for consolidating billing, accounts receivable,
  inventory control, warehouse shipping release and credit and collections of
  all Divisions through use of computer.
- devised a Company approved Sales Managers & General Sales Managers Compensation and Bonus Plan.
- improved order handling system and mechanized sales payroll and sales recording procedures.
- developed Budget System to evaluate departmental contributions to overall Company profits.
- represented management in arbitrations regarding job standards and classifications.
- reorganized Data Processing Department, developing procedure for Inventory Recording and Control, Production Scheduling and Cost Accounting.

MILITARY SERVICE:

U. S. Army, 1950-1952.

EDUCATION:

<u>B.S</u>., Accounting, U.S.C. at Berkeley, Berkeley, Cal. Dean's List.

MEMBERSHIPS:

National Association of Accountants, Past President.

HOBBIES: Coin collecting.

PERSONAL DATA: Born 3/17/30, married, 4 children, excellent health.

<u>REFERENCES AND FURTHER DATA ON REQUEST</u>

DISCUSSION

Chronological Résumé with Summary.　Written in 1973, the Wordsworth résumé describes an individual whose background in finance led, within a few years, to enlarged responsibilities in general management. His accomplishments have currently culminated in significant contributions in each of the major business areas—marketing, finance, and production—where he has shown an ability to coordinate, leading to a business recovery.

His potential was recognized early in his career (1964–1965), as evidenced by his superior's comments. Apparently lacking opportunity for growth consistent with his abilities, the candidate moved to another job. The period 1965–1969 embracing two jobs was not productive enough to warrant detailed description, and the résumé states only that the subject moved up to larger responsibilities.

It was more important for this applicant to expand upon his accomplishments where they were most important than to list all lesser accomplishments. When you have important things to say about yourself, omit the insignificant ones.

EXAMPLE OF CHRONOLOGICAL RÉSUMÉ WITH SUMMARY PAGE

366 Sliderule Street
Snake River, Ill. 60606

Home (312) 123-3220
Office (312) 012-6543

R E S U M E

of

<u>HARRY E. GOETHALS</u>

<u>SENIOR EXECUTIVE</u>

***   Accustomed to emphasizing <u>profit</u> in the P. & L. responsibility.
Experienced in all areas of business management with record of
reversing losses and achieving turnarounds for major corporations.

***   Background in heavy industrial products, air conditioning, air
purification. Record of reorganizaing marketing, production and
finance to increase profits more than 100% involving millions of
dollars.

***   Able to assume responsibility for design and construction of
complete manufacturing facilities, to staff, train and put into
production. Starting from scratch brought new chemical facility
to breakeven within 14 months of startup and to R.O.I. of 22%
within 26 months.

***   Creative in new product design and in product revisions to
gain new markets (up to hundreds of millions) and increase
established markets.

***   Age 42, M.S. and B.S. degrees in Engineering, married.

HARRY E. GOETHALS   PAGE 2

<u>1968–Present</u>   WORTHINGTON-STARRETT CORP., Elgin, Ill.

<u>1972–Present</u>   VICE PRESIDENT and GENERAL MANAGER of Engineering Divi-
sion of $\$\frac{1}{2}$ billion heavy industrial machinery, air conditioning, turbines, decon-
tamination equipment manufacturer for utilities, industrial plants, U. S. and
foreign governments, ranging in cost from $250,000 to $10 million. Division
volume approximately $50 million. Report to Group V. P. of parent Company.
Supervise four Vice Presidents of Marketing, Construction and Engineering and
Finance. Responsible for engineering and construction of special projects as
described above with accountability for profit and loss.

Achievements include:

- recovery of Division from a $2 million loss to a $1 million profit within a
  year by contract renegotiation and reorganization of Department to operation
  on a project basis.
- developed standard designs for the most commonly used utility turbine, added
  15% to profitability and 27% to sales volume.
- assigned individual profit and loss accountability to two Marketing V. P.s.
- laid plans for broadening sales base by potential billion dollars by designing
  relatively inexpensive standard decontamination installation for industrial
  waste.
- established target dates for each project with monthly monitor report.

<u>1968–1972</u>   VICE PRESIDENT, MARKETING for $80 million Refrigeration
and Air Cleaning Division. Reported to Division President. Directed field
force of 105 and headquarters staff of 21 including Sales Managers and Engineers. Administered annual budget of $3.5 million.

Achievements included:

- turning an annual loss of $800,000 into a profit of $2.5 million in the first
  year of this assignment by analysis and elimination of unprofitable accounts.
- changing emphasis of salesmen from price and volume to profit; revised compensation to relate to profit instead of volume; in second year of operation
  Division earned $10 million.
- assigned engineers to marketing managers in specific areas with mutual responsibility for meeting objectives; increased sales 20%.
- redesigned certain air conditioning specifications to meet growing demand for
  smaller but powerful industrial units; increased volume 28% in two years.

<u>1966–1969</u>   AIRTEMP DIVISION OF IG CORPORATION.

GENERAL MANAGER of wholly owned subsidiary of European Division. This new
Company produced industrial gases and air cleaning equipment in Geneva, Switzerland with storage depots in Germany, Belgium, Holland and Sweden. Responsible
for: construction of new $8 million chemical process plant with 25,000 hp connected
load consumed in three large compressors and process piping and distillation; hiring
and training personnel; profit and loss.

Accomplishments:

EXAMPLE OF CHRONOLOGICAL RÉSUMÉ WITH SUMMARY PAGE

HARRY E. GOETHALS   PAGE 3

- reached breakeven point within 14 months of startup.
- R.O.I. of 22% within 26 months in the face of established competition by giant
  and well-established companies.
- trained Swiss national as successor.

1962-1966   ATMOSPHERICS, INC., Industrial Park, Cal.

MANAGER of Western Region of $50 million manufacturer of electrostatic air clean-
ing equipment for industry. Responsible for: regional profitability; administration
of $3 million budget; distribution; union negotiations; all construction projects.

Accomplishments:

- planned and supervised $17 million new plant construction.
- installation of computerized truck load scheduling; reduced costs $500,000.
- increased sales 31% in two years.

1957-1962   McKENNA & CO., Menlo Park, Cal.

SENIOR CONSULTANT with nationally known management consulting firm serving
largely industrial clients. Started as Trainee, successively, Junior Consultant,
Consultant, Senior.

Assignments included:

- advisor on loan to NASA with responsibility for analyzing (classified) engineering
  for space exploration.
- engineering consultant to major manufacturer of gas turbines.
- analysis of rare earth production for major West Coast facility. Recommended
  procedures which were implemented with savings of over $500,000 annually.

MILITARY SERVICE: U. S. ARMY, Sgt.

EDUCATION:

M.S., Industrial Engineering, University of Pennsylvania, University Park, Pa.
B.S., Mechancial Engineering, Rensselaer Polytechnic Institute, Troy, N. Y.

EXTRA-CURRICULAR ACTIVITIES:

Class President, Senior and Sophomore years. Captain, Lacrosse. President,
Engineering Honor Society.

HOBBIES: Herpetology, model railroading.

PERSONAL DATA: Born 3/3/32, married, three children, excellent health.
                    Willing to relocate.

REFERENCES AND FURTHER DATA ON REQUEST

DISCUSSION

Chronological Résumé with Summary Page. The résumé shows Mr. Goethals to be experienced in all the major departments of management and skilled in leading and coordinating them to attain corporate goals.

The subject gives his title, specifies company size and nature of business, describes his responsibilities, and lists his achievements. He immediately indicates possession of an all-around ability in product engineering, and marketing leadership, high financial awareness, and skill in exercising controls to assure adherence to programs once they have been started.

Marketing competence is established by accomplishments in the position preceding his present one, and his handling of marketing responsibilities suggests that he is ready for greater responsibilities.

Engineering and production experience was utilized in the Airtemp position, which also included P. & L. responsibility.

Engineering, analysis and planning, and marketing experience was gained at Atmospherics.

The basis for this career was established in a good school: consulting. This profession provides an unexcelled education for anyone who approaches each assignment as a learning process. Consulting has been a springboard for many top executives.

Education and extracurricular activities all support the portrait of a man of promise. Industrial engineering is of course the broadest of the engineering disciplines.

EXAMPLE OF CHRONOLOGICAL RÉSUMÉ WITH SUMMARY PAGE WITH VARIATION

275 West 50th Street
Harper's Ferry, N. Y. 10069

Home (212) 543-7890
Office (212) 765-4321

R E S U M E

of

<u>JOHN BROWN BODEE</u>

<u>EXECUTIVE SALESMAN</u>

***   Approximately 15 years experience with leading company in marketing, regional sales management and personal sales.

***   Record of success in achieving national recognition for type, quality and volume of sales produced; received bonuses and awards; more important - produced outstanding profits.

***   Experienced in hiring and training salesmen, developing quotas and objectives, formulating and implementing marketing and sales strategies and techniques.

***   Enjoy excellent contacts among key personnel of major companies. Recognized for establishing and maintaining productive relationships and experience in customer/public relations; capable public speaker.

***   Thirty-seven years old, married, Bachelor of Arts degree with honors; postgraduate work in Psychology.

***   <u>In short</u>, consistently achieved quotas over a period of eight years; increased sales by 400%; boosted profits proportionately.

<u>FOR FURTHER DATA PLEASE SEE FOLLOWING PAGES</u>

EXAMPLE OF CHRONOLOGICAL RÉSUMÉ WITH SUMMARY PAGE
WITH VARIATION

JOHN BROWN BODEE   PAGE 2

* <u>Record of success in achieving a 400% increase in sales as a result of effective
sales management</u>.

1960-Present   ABC CORPORATION, Freeport, N. Y.

A major producer of business machines and data processing equipment.

<u>1968-Present</u>

As SALES MANAGER, Office Products Sales and Data Entry Sales, in the Brooklyn
and Queens area, responsible for:

- supervision and training of six salesmen.
- development of schedules, strategies and techniques to develop leads and increase sales. Brooklyn and Queens have relatively few large customers. It
  was, therefore, necessary to tap the potential smaller market. This was done
  and the region generated 10% of nationwide sales.
- continued personal selling and won sales bonuses year after year; became one
  of the highest producers in the company.
- participated in the establishment of sales quotas and product mix; developed
  promotional programs.
- systematically and effectively converted customers from low profit items to
  higher profit items.
- instituted a regional policy to require cash deposits on orders, substantially
  decreasing cancellations. So dramatic were results that this became standard
  company policy.
- maintained a "get tough" collection policy without sacrifice of good will or
  cordial public relations.

* Other experience in maximizing sales through modern sales management techniques:

<u>1960-1968</u>   ABC CORPORATION, Boston, Mass.

As SALES MANAGER, supervised a group of salesmen and achieved sales quotas
every year for eight years.

- conducted continuing market surveys to determine customer needs.
- worked closely with key personnel of customers and potential customers to
  maintain sales of accessories and supplies, upgrade equipment and provide
  corporate technical and maintenance services.
- tripled personal earnings.
- designed retail accounting equipment that ultimately resulted in multi-million
  dollar sales.

* <u>Demonstrated talent for industrial and consumer sales; achieved countrywide
leadership</u>.

EXAMPLE OF CHRONOLOGICAL RÉSUMÉ WITH SUMMARY PAGE
WITH VARIATION

JOHN BROWN BODEE   PAGE 3

<u>1958-1960</u>   IBM CORPORATION, New York, N. Y.

As ACCOUNT MANAGER/SALES REPRESENTATIVE achieved sales quotas each year
and was responsible for:

- development of an outstanding sales record; substantially contributed to division's leadership on a countrywide performance basis.
- gained such major accounts as Railway Repress, Texacto, American Canning and
  others.

<u>1955</u>   GROLIERE CORPORATION

Sold encyclopaedia door-to-door throughout New York, New Jersey, Massachusetts,
Connecticut, Rhode Island, Vermont, etc., (part-time while attending college).

Finished seventh out of 1,000 sales people in a national 20-week contest.

* <u>Military Service:</u>

<u>1953-1955</u>   UNITED STATES NAVY

Served as Instructor at the U. S. Naval Academy at Annapolis. Received special
commendation for class' overall proficiency, then the highest in Academy history.

* <u>Education:</u>

<u>1958</u>   UNIVERSITY OF GEORGIA

Received Bachelor of Arts degree; attained Dean's List in the senior year.

<u>1969-1974</u>   NEW SCHOOL FOR SOCIAL RESEARCH

Completed several courses in Psychology which contributed to my understanding
success in sales activities by developing my understanding of human relations.

At college, played varsity football, lacrosse, was Sports Editor, worked summers
during college.

* <u>Personal Data:</u>

37 years old, married, one child, excellent health.

<u>REFERENCES AND FURTHER DATA ON REQUEST</u>

DISCUSSION

Chronological Résumé with Summary Page. The résumé deviates from the norm by using a final omnibus paragraph, starting with ''In short,'' to list the most important assets and by using headlines to emphasize the outstanding factor in each position listed chronologically. Either variation, or both, can be used. Headlining can be effective in pulling a résumé together, provided that the headlines are informative, relevant, and important. They should add to a résumé, rather than being just excess words.

Mr. Bodee's personality comes through in the use of punctuation, quoted phrases, and relatively informal language imbued with a sense of excitement.

The body of the résumé suggests ability to study markets and make changes in marketing approaches, as needed. It suggests strong personal sales talents, sales department organization competence, profit consciousness. There are the aggressiveness, assurance, and knowledge necessary to call on giant accounts and make sales. There is the quality of leadership.

The summary page is effective in giving a special dimension to the subject apart from that obtained from the material in the body of the résumé.

This is a salesman who sounds like a salesman. He would undoubtedly receive invitations for interviews upon submitting this résumé.

The Functional Résumé

The *Functional Résumé* organizes work experience by function, such as general marketing, management, production, finance, or their subfunctions. Chronology is disregarded. To facilitate comparison, we have refashioned one of our *Chronological Résumé* examples into functional form.

The *Functional Résumé* stresses the scope of experience, much as does a summary page. It has the disadvantage of not relating accomplishments to the pertinent company or companies. Most employers are familiar with other companies, especially in the same industry, and take company affiliations into account when judging accomplishments. The same experience is more impressive if gained at a widely known company than at an unknown company.

The writer of a *Functional Résumé,* not being hampered by chronology, can easily change emphasis or camouflage past experience. This is advantageous in cases in which past job experience is best explained in a personal interview, rather than in writing. We reiterate that the main purpose of a résumé is to gain an interview; it is not a substitute for an interview.

The *Functional Résumé* tends to be shorter than the *Chronological Résumé.* The examples that follow have been further shortened to avoid monotonous repetition. Both the *Functional Résumé* and the *Functional-by-Company (Institution) Résumé* are well regarded by institutional recruiters.

EXAMPLE OF FUNCTIONAL RÉSUMÉ

HERCULE PARROT
375 Broadalban Road
Clinton, N. C. 12345
(177) 277-3777

SENIOR EXECUTIVE experienced in all areas of general management.

SUMMARY OF QUALIFICATIONS

Record of consistent profit contributions amounting to millions of dollars in general management, marketing and production in the U. S. and internationally; accustomed to autonomous multi-division responsibility. Equipped to use all management techniques to accomplish company objectives.

EXPERIENCE

GENERAL MANAGEMENT Accomplished seven divisional turn-arounds leading these divisions from high five-fgure losses to six-figure profits in periods ranging from three months to two years.

PRODUCTION Successfully engineered and produced four new products of complex technology supervising Manufacturing Manager, Controller, various engineering disciplines and marketing department.

MARKETING Conceived and implemented new marketing plan which broadened distribution and increased volume 27%, increased profits 9%.

FINANCE Instituted new financial controls and procedures; increased cash flow 19%; improved R.O.I. 13%; set objectives for and achieved financial ratios which were the envy of the industry.

TECHNICAL BACKGROUND Intimately familiar with the metal-working industry and with sophisticated machinery and equipment in a broad area of manufacturing.

EXAMPLE OF FUNCTIONAL RÉSUMÉ

EMPLOYMENT HISTORY

1970-Present   LEAF MANUFACTURING DIVISION, BRF., INC., Winston-Salem, N. C.

1967-1970   THOMAS & SESSIONS, Springfield, Mo.

1963-1967   W. H. THOMPSON & CO., Harrisburg, Pa.

1953-1962   VANADIUM METAL WIRE WORKS, Pittsburgh, Pa.

MILITARY SERVICE

Captain, U. S. Air Force, 1941-1943.

EDUCATION

B. S., Engineering, 1949, University of Pittsburgh, Pittsburgh, Pa.

Graduate work in Business Management at Northwestern University, Evanston, Ill., and Michigan State, East Lansing, Michigan.

COMMUNITY ACTIVITIES

Chairman, Board of Directors, National Hospital, Winston-Salem, N. C.

Chairman, Community Chest, Winston-Salem, N. C.

Member, National Presidential Committee to Study Government Options.

HONORS

Winston-Salem Citizen-of-the-Year Award.

HOBBIES

Tennis, golf, shooting (National 12 Bore Champion).

PERSONAL DATA

Born 3/31/28, married, two children, excellent health, willing to relocate.

REFERENCES AND FURTHER DATA ON REQUEST

DISCUSSION

Functional Résumé.   The Parrot résumé is included to show the *Functional* style as well as to illustrate that it is possible to make a strong presentation in a short form.

This résumé, however, did not spring full grown as shown. It is the result of considerable rewriting, reduced from about 4 pages.

Mr. Parrot has had a highly successful and productive career. He first wrote, in sequence, a detailed chronological history of his employment. This required 10 pages of closely written material. He boiled this down to 4 pages in the chronological form and used it successfully to get interviews leading to a position.

Within a year he discovered that the position did not, in fact, give him the promised autonomy of responsibility, and he left the company. Since in his new job search he planned to approach many of the same companies to which he had written so recently, he did not want to circulate the same résumé. The new résumé, written in a different form is shown here. It has just been circulated, so that the results are unknown.

EXAMPLE OF FUNCTIONAL RÉSUMÉ

Ten Meadows Lane
Gladstone, N. J. 07070

Home (201) 123-4567
Office (212) 000-1000

R E S U M E

of

<u>MARK KETTERING SLOAN</u>

OBJECTIVE: GENERAL MANAGER, VICE PRESIDENT MARKETING OR PLANNING

GROUP VICE PRESIDENT:

Profit and loss responsibility for company with total volume of $30 million. Company was acquired by expanding conglomerate. Restructured sales organization; opened new markets; established new quantity price schedules; reversed static sales trends to achieve 8% sales increase in one year.

MARKETING, FINANCE, PRODUCTION, GENERAL MANAGEMENT

Took leadership of design and development, introduced new product with a sales potential of $5 million within three years.
Implemented forecasting techniques leading to immediate deliveries instead of 6-8 week delays.
Reduced accounts receivable collections from 90 days to average of 30 days.
Instituted five-year plan to modernize obsolete tooling and eliminate OSHA and pollution violations.
Reduced production costs by $250,000 leading to product modernization.

VICE PRESIDENT CORPORATE PLANNING:

Responsible for short- and long-range financial planning for billion dollar insurance company including acquisition and diversification program.
Completed $250 million acquisition using tax loss carry forwards.
Introduced "management by objective" to replace previously uncoordinated planning (company had failed to use accumulated $3 million loss carry-forward).
Obtained stock exchange listing expanding market for company stock leading to improved implementation of acquisitions program.
Set up stock option incentive program for company executives.

VICE PRESIDENT MARKETING:

Set up and implemented marketing program for new bank-sponsored international credit card.
Gained acceptance of major department and specialty groups (Bloomington's, March's, United, Associated) creating billions of dollars in billings.

EXAMPLE OF FUNCTIONAL RÉSUMÉ

VICE PRESIDENT MARKETING:
Test marketed new areas of activity, including insurance with gross margins above 50%. Implemented successful campaign.
Organized 20,000 application box locations; received 173,000 new collections for cards.
Eliminated errors in billing by improving imprint method; reduced billing errors 50% and correspondence 83%.

SALES MANAGER:
Established new, 25% higher sales objective for manufacturer of metal parts by comprehensive sales analysis. Implemented planning for restructured territories, new market penetrations, reduced sales percentage cost. Increased sales 18% in first $1\frac{1}{2}$ years.
Changed marketing emphasis to high-profit items; increased profits 4% within two years.
Changed marketing structure from organization by product to organization by industry.

ASSISTANT DIRECTOR SALES, ADVERTISING:
Evaluated markets for major chemical company with wide and diversified distribution.
Charted industry trends; set up budgets; forecasted sales; recruited; recommended new marketing strategies.

EMPLOYMENT HISTORY:
1971-Present Universal Co., New York, N. Y.
1967-1971 Volcan Life Insurance Co., Hartford, Conn.
1964-1967 First International State Bank, New York, N. Y.
1959-1964 All Metal Products Co., White Plains, N. Y.
1952-1959 Hercules, Inc., Wilmington, Dela.

MILITARY SERVICE:
U. S. Army 1950-1952. 1st Lt. Artillery.

EDUCATION:
M.B.A., Harvard Graduate School of Business Administration, Cambridge, Mass., 1949.
B.A., Cornell University, Utica, N. Y., 1947.

HOBBIES:
Tennis (Junior Olympics earlier), platform tennis (ranked in first ten until three years ago).

PERSONAL DATA:
Born 3/29/26, married, three children, excellent health.

REFERENCES AND FURTHER DATA ON REQUEST

DISCUSSION

Functional Résumé. Mr. Sloan's experience is well suited for the *Functional* form because it is divided among the four elements of corporate management.

His experience has been good, encompassing both large and small companies. For maximum growth in the business world it is helpful to comprehend the differences in problems facing small and large companies. One learns to assess the relative values of rigid and fluid organizational structures. Furthermore, many very large companies are made up of small components, and executives unaccustomed to small operations are often ineffective in their management of such smaller units.

In writing his résumé Mr. Sloan was careful to select interesting career highlights while suggesting to the reader talents in professional management techniques: the economic evaluation of tooling; the use of past tax losses; management by objective; sophisticated executive compensation; positive environmental correction; industrial safety programs.

Contributions to volume and profit increases are emphasized to complete the image of an achievement-oriented applicant.

Education is excellent; hobbies are interesting and therefore worth mentioning.

The Functional-by-Company (Institution) Résumé

The Functional-by-Company (Institution) Résumé lists functions for each employer. In this respect it is superior to the *Functional Résumé*. However, the listing of functions performed for a company need not be chronological, which, though a bit misleading to the reader, may be of advantage to you. Keep in mind that a résumé is an evaluation of you. In taking "poetic license" with your chronology you may improve your résumé and gain an interview, during which discrepancies can be explained.

Preceding comments aside, the *Functional-by-Company (Institution) Résumé* is well suited for teachers and professors and is well received by academic recruiters. Examples follow, including one for the educational area.

EXAMPLE OF FUNCTIONAL-BY-COMPANY
(INSTITUTION) RÉSUMÉ

100 Accomplishment Way   Home (123) 456-7890
Erewhon, Minnesota 12345   Office (098) 765-4321

R E S U M E

of

HORAC ALGERIO

EXECUTIVE

SUMMARY OF QUALIFICATIONS

Experienced in all areas of management: marketing, production, finance and multi-division operations. Record of consistent profit contributions in identifying and developing new markets, in creating more effective advertising themes, in reducing manufacturing costs and lead times, in reducing inventories, increasing cash flow and doubling price of common stock in a period of 12 months under adverse market conditions.

EXPERIENCE

1964-Present   GENERAL LEISURE PRODUCTS CO., INC., Winona, Minn.

1971-Present - PRESIDENT and GENERAL MANAGER with P. & L. responsibility for $100 million leisure products manufacturing division of $600 million conglomerate. Report to parent company President. Supervise four Vice Presidents of Marketing, Manufacturing, Human Resources, Planning, Finance and R. & D. Department.

R. & D.
- led R. & D. team in development of new concept in grass-mowing equipment.
- made innovation in merchandising and advertising home snow-removal machine.

MANUFACTURING
- utilized technology developed in mowing machinery to manufacture snowmobile which captured first place in Alaska race test.

MARKETING
- selected and partially financed new wholesale organization to concentrate on Company family of products.
- increased volume from $60 million to $100 million in four years.

FINANCE
- increased value of AMEX-listed stock from six to $12\frac{1}{2}$ in 1974, based on earnings multiplication.
- reduced inventory by one-third leading to substantial increase in R. O. I.

EXAMPLE OF FUNCTIONAL-BY-COMPANY (INSTITUTION) RÉSUMÉ

<u>1969-1971</u> - VICE PRESIDENT, MANUFACTURING.

<u>MANUFACTURING</u>
- consolidated manufacture of motors in one plant heretofore distributed among four plants around the U. S.
- closed least efficient manufacturing plant; utilized space for needed new warehouse.
- reorganized flow of production for motors, building own specialized automated equipment; reduced lead time from six to three months and manufacturing cycle from two months to two weeks.
- restyled mowers, snow removers, electric garden tools: developed with R. & D. new concept in electric grass shears which became nationwide best sellers and contributed $6 million of profitable new volume.

<u>1967-1969</u> - GENERAL MANAGER, Caracas, Venezuela.

<u>MANUFACTURING</u>
- recognized application of new technology to manufacture of small horsepower motors; increased plant productivity by 30%; technology adopted in three U. S. plants with similar results.

<u>GENERAL MANAGEMENT</u>
- met with government officials to gain "favored manufacturer" status in Venezuela leading to lower export duties.
- expanded distribution to Colombia and Brazil with consequent doubling of volume.

<u>FINANCE</u>
- reorganized accounting procedures; speeded corporate monthly reports by ten days each month leading to quicker identification of problem areas and increase in profits from 6% to 15% before taxes.

<u>MARKETING</u>
- conducted market research leading to distribution of wider group of U. S. manufactured products in South America with only minor changes in styling.

<u>1964-1967</u> - SALES MANAGER for U. S. and South America. Responsible for sales development.

<u>SALES</u>
- studied marketing procedures in the U. S. and South America.
- studied company potential for new products in areas of competence.
- increased U. S. sales 25% through new system of regional profit centers and improved training methods.
- switched main distribution efforts from traditional outlets to newer forms of distribution.
- increased sales in South America 15% and recommended change in product mix which led to accomplishments previously mentioned.

<u>1958-1964</u>

AVERILL & HARRIMAN COMPANY, INC., Dellmore, Ill.

VICE PRESIDENT, MANUFACTURING for small ($40 million)

EXAMPLE OF FUNCTIONAL-BY-COMPANY (INSTITUTION) RÉSUMÉ

manufacturer of marine motors. Responsible for:

- complete manufacturing operations and R. & D. Department.

Accomplishments:

- set up new production line using new automatic equipment.
- cleared out accumulated inventory of excessive parts and raw material.
- conducted cost studies leading to 11% reduction in costs.
- conducted value studies; made decision to purchase fasteners and other components at a saving of 16% in raw material costs in addition to above.

Invited by executive search firm to consider position with General Leisure Products and accepted.

1955-1958   AUTOMOTIVE PARTS, INC., Jackson, Mich.

ASSISTANT PLANT MANAGER (one of seven) for $100 million manufacturer of small parts for BIG-3 automobile manufacturers.

Learned automatic and automated production methods with one of most advanced companies in the industry.

MILITARY SERVICE: U. S. ARMY AIR FORCE, 1952-1955. Captain. Served in Korea.

EDUCATION: B. S., Engineering, California Institute of Technology, Pasadena, Calif., 1951. Graduate work in Business Management, 1952, Stanford University, Stanford, Calif.

COMMUNITY ACTIVITIES: Chairman, Board of Directors, National Hospital, Winona, Minnesota.

Chairman, Community Chest, Winona.

HONORS: Winona Citizen-of-the Year Award.

HOBBIES: Tobogganing (National Two-Man Champion), skeet, trap, cross-country skiing.

PERSONAL DATA: Born 3/31/31, married, three children, own home, excellent health.

REFERENCES AND FURTHER DATA ON REQUEST

DISCUSSION

Functional-by-Company (Institution) Résumé. The Algerio résumé illustrates how career progression can be effectively expressed using a combination of the *Functional* and the *Chronological* styles.

This applicant started in production, moved quickly to another company utilizing the production skills learned earlier, and became head of manufacturing for a medium size company. Here he demonstrated good management skills in all areas of production. He moved again to a position involving marketing to round his experience and immediately showed talent in this field, advancing quickly to general management of the company's South American division and two years later to the vice-presidency of the headquarters plant. By this time his ability in each position gave such strong indications of the highest qualities of leadership that he was appointed president of the company with results that made a strongly favorable impact on the company and its stockholders.

There was apparently nothing to which he turned his hand that did not benefit from his leadership. His character and ability were recognized in his community by appointments and honors. He took time out from a busy job schedule to work for the community, thus broadening himself and adding to the image of his company.

This is a capsule illustration not only of excellent management but also of career planning, in which the subject determined to make himself knowledgeable in all areas of management. You may here recognize a parallel to another famous career.

EXAMPLE OF FUNCTIONAL-BY-COMPANY (INSTITUTION) RÉSUMÉ

110 Lake Road
Chicago, Ill. 60606

Home (000) 000-0000
Office (100) 200-3000

R E S U M E

of

FELIX BAMBERGER

RETAIL EXECUTIVE

EXPERIENCE:

1954-Present   ASSOCIATED MERCHANDISING ORGANIZATION, Chicago, Ill.

1964-Present

MERCHANDISE
MANAGER:

Represent major department stores nationally with volume exceeding $2 billion in product selection, pricing, promotional planning, budgeting, forecasting, vendor liaison, profitability planning.

Created programs adding tens of millions of dollars to existing volume.

Led office in finding new sources of supply, in gaining style leadership, in buying exclusives and in revamping departmental layouts to achieve better traffic patterns.

Credited with playing leading role in forging position of elite store leadership for group within the Organization.

Fully inculcated in the mathematics and methods of profitable retailing.

1954-1964   ARWRONG BUYING OFFICE, Chicago, Ill.

MARKET
REPRESENTATIVE:

Conducted market research, reported; established group wholesale programs internationally for:

Developed
Wholesale
Programs

Books
Stationery
Notions
Furniture

EXAMPLE OF FUNCTIONAL-BY-COMPANY (INSTITUTION) RÉSUMÉ

Housewares
Budget Floor

Gained additional profitability for stores.

Increased Stores' Volume	Increased volume in Books, seven times. Increased volume in Stationery, three times. Increased volume in Housewares, three times. Increased volume in Furniture, two and one-half times.

Added more than $30 million of increased sales to group.

Published Catalogs — Initiated, developed and managed Spring Merchandise Catalogs for Notions, Stationery, Sporting Goods, Furniture for nine years.

Extensive Overseas Buying Trips — Made nine trips to Europe and the Far East purchasing over $20 million of new merchandise as leader of buying group.

<u>1950-1954</u>   MARSHALL, DAYTON & CO., Chicago, Ill.

BUYER   Assistant to Divisional Merchandise Manager: Books, Accessories, Stationery, Smallwares.

<u>EDUCATION:</u>   <u>B.B.A.</u>, New York University School of Retailing, New York, N. Y., 1950.

Dean's List.

<u>MILITARY SERVICE:</u>   U. S. Army Air Force, 1942-1946. Captain. Navigator. Trainer.

HONORS: National Buyer Award 1962

National Retailer-of-the-Year Award 1972

<u>PERSONAL DATA:</u>   Born 3/15/22, married, two children, excellent health.

<u>REFERENCES AND FURTHER DATA ON REQUEST</u>

DISCUSSION

Functional-by-Company (Institution) Résumé. In his long association with one company Mr. Bamberger operated within two functions: most recently as merchandise manager and earlier as market representative.

The style of résumé he chose is logical for his experience, emphasizing achievements in the two areas concisely but effectively.

The subject's activities and accomplishments are so typical of retail operations that any retail executive reading this résumé would immediately understand exactly what Mr. Bamberger can do.

Since he is probably known personally or by reputation by most retail executives nationwide, there is no need to elaborate on background.

It is for these reasons that such a résumé can be very brief without losing effectiveness.

Note the use of much white space to enhance readability.

EXAMPLE OF FUNCTIONAL-BY-COMPANY
(INSTITUTION) RÉSUMÉ

27 Avalon Avenue
Holyvail, Colo. 00000

Home (123) 456-7890
Office (123) 100-2000

CURRICULUM VITAE

ARTHUR BEDIVERE

Objective:
Administrative position with non-profit institution: university or foundation where there is an opportunity and a need for enlightened planning.

Qualifications:
Twenty years of experience in university planning and administration, counseling and teaching; with a record of success.

Education:
Ed.D., Columbia University, New York, N. Y., 1955.
M.A., Higher Education and Administration, University of Chicago, Chicago, Ill., 1951.
B.A., Cornell University, Ithaca, N. Y., 1949.

Honors:
Who's Who in American Education, 1966-Present.
Honorary Ph.D., McGill University, Montreal, Quebec, 1973.
Bronze Star, South Korea, 1952.

Publications:
Philosophies of Curriculum Planning, Silver-Burdett, 1973.
(See also under Experience, 1972-Present).

EXPERIENCE

1972-Present

PLANNING
OFFICER
and
ASSISTANT
to the
PRESIDENT

University of Burdette, Col rado Springs, Colo.
University was founded in 1965, has an enrollment of 1800, projected to rise to 3400 by 1980. There is a faculty of 270, projected to be 500 by 1980.

Studied demographic, political, economic and environmental influences upon the future of the University. Met with Federal and State government officials and with private corporations and individuals to explain plans and objectives and to raise money.

Provided plans for full program: administrative and academic objectives, functional responsibilities, space needs, budgets, forecasts, faculty expansion and detailed plans for a new College of Humanities and College of Medicine, the latter to be associated with Vail Memorial Hospital, a 500-bed acute general hospital with complete facilities.

Act as alter ego for the President of the University.

ARTHUR BEDIVERE   PAGE 2

1966-1971   Rangers University, New Bedford, N. J.

DEAN   Reorganized and enlarged liberal arts curriculum to accomodate
of   large increase in student body resulting from transition of Uni-
MEN   versity from a small private college to a State University.
                   Created a work-study program originally funded at $100,000, in-
                   creasing to $½ million over a period of four years.

                   Introduced wider range of business subjects leading to new ac-
                   credited degree, B. S. in Business Administration.

1962-1966   New York State Department of Higher Education, Albany, N. Y.

STATE   Visited all state colleges and universities; studied curricula,
EDUCATION   programs, facilities, enrollment. Made recommendations lead-
SUPERVISOR   ing to expansion of State universities and two-year colleges in
                   upstate cities and towns.

                   Findings were published in 1975 under the title, The Changing
                   Structure of Education in America, published by John Wiley &
                   Sons, New York, N. Y. (2nd edition, 1975, third edition,
                   1976).

                   Received annual award of American Education Association, 1976,
                   for contributing most to education in 1975.

1959-1962   Governor Dummer Academy, Newburyport, Mass.

INSTRUCTOR   Teacher, Social Sciences and Football Coach for first prepara-
                   tory school established in the U. S.

1956-1959   Board of Education of the City of Boston, Boston, Mass.

VOCATIONAL   Participated in official program to evaluate the effects of in-
COUNSELOR   school mental hygiene units in junior and senior high schools
                   subject to changing social situations.

                   Established initial plans for possible need to integrate black
                   and white pupils arising from ethnic neighborhood considerations.

                   Recommended evaluation of teacher effectiveness among a group
                   of twenty disparate elementary schools to assess quality of ed-
                   ucation.

Military Service: U. S. Army, 1952-1953. 1st. Lt.

Hobbies: Court tennis, squash racquets (A), bridge.

Personal Data: Age 45, married, three children, two attending college. Excel-
                   lent health. Will relocate.

REFERENCES AND FURTHER DATA ON REQUEST

DISCUSSION

Functional-by-Company (Institution) Résumé.

This administrative officer (Bedivere) has had continuous progress. He was fortunate to be appointed to a study group early in his career, which gave him a broad background in educational procedures and planning, providing the foundation for his continuing development and leading to his educational contributions.

The *Functional* style of résumé permits a natural emphasis on the career sequence starting with vocational counselor, and proceeding through instructor, state education supervisor, and dean to his present position. This provides an effective presentation.

Publication of well-received books, honors, and interesting hobbies all contribute to create a portrait of an individual who would give significant leadership anywhere in his chosen field.

Administrative abilities are documented by indicating his detailed and careful planning, his use of budget discipline, and the breadth of his currently successful assignment. Fund raising activities and negotiations with government officials and wealthy potential contributors emphasize his personal status and suggest the level of responsibility he is equipped to undertake.

The Harvard Résumé

The *Harvard Résumé* is widely used because it has been broadly publicized and some readers immediately associate it with the Harvard Graduate School of Business Administration. The form is good and presents an excellent appearance. It is characterized by narrow margins, a rather informal approach to descriptions of experience, and an expanded personal data section to include information that many writers would consider to be extraneous.

The delineation of responsibilities and accomplishments is not so clearcut as in the *Chronological* and other forms of résumé because they are not presented separately.

The form suffers a little from its widespread use, which makes so many executive résumés seem stereotyped.

The *Harvard Résumé* is usually chronological, but differs enough in presentation of data to be entitled to a name of its own. Examples of the *Harvard Résumé* follow.

<u>RESUME</u>

JAMES CONANT
107 Bannister Road
Mission, Kansas 65432
(123) 456-7890

<u>OBJECTIVE</u>

A general management or marketing opportunity where broad background in consumer and industrial products would be valuable. Major experience includes:

- P. & L. responsibility.

- General management, sales management and field sales experience.

- Extensive attainments in wide range of markets and in new product development.

<u>EXPERIENCE</u>

Jan. 1973   ROVER AND BOYES, INC., Harrison, Mo.
  to
Present

Residential division of above, an independent sheet metal contractor, with annual volume in the range of $12 million, serving residential, commercial and industrial markets.

<u>Vice President</u>

Formed and autonomously manage this new division concentrating on the residential market. Sales were increased by 100% in first two years while getting new division organized; earned a profit from beginning, amounting to 12% before taxes in second year.

Developed and implemented an overall business plan: market analysis; order forecasting; production plan; man-power needs and recruiting; training; P.&L. forecast; facilities and equipment; capital expenditure and operating capital requirements.

Recruited and trained over 300 people.

Developed product changes, standardized production and standard costs to achieve 16% reduction in product cost.

JAMES CONANT
PAGE 2

Developed consumer financing plans with St. Louis and Kansas City banks to support expanded sales activities.

Took the organization into new product areas to expand markets and eliminate seasonal weaknesses.

1970
to
1973

HUBERT SELBY DIVISION OF LAMBERT, INC.

A $5 million manufacturer of mechanical equipment for commercial and industrial use.

<u>General Sales Manager</u>

Handled all sales through 23 independent U. S. dealers and 35 overseas distributors; with staff of five. Orders were increased in weakening markets which had previously shown a decline.

Earnings were increased through: price increases; reducing expenses through strict budget applications; implementing product cost reduction programs to obtain lower costs in a period of rising prices.

Also made changes in representation; set up new dealers; instituted new training program for all dealers retained; redirected advertising.

1956
to
1970

THE MACARTHUR COMPANY, Truman, Mo.

A $100 million manufacturer of plumbing equipment for residential, commercial and industrial use.

<u>Manager, Dealer Development</u>, March 1969 to April 1970.

In charge of all Division dealer activities to sell commercial and residential plumbing supplies. New dealers were established through company financing and long range plans for growth. This involved management of internal staff, regional staff, and local offices in recruiting and training qualified personnel to own and operate dealerships. It also involved development of management skills to support business startup at a profit. The organization grew from 30 to 60 dealers, and the sale of products from $40 million to $50 million.

<u>Manager, Dealer Distribution</u>, March 1967 to March 1969.

JAMES CONANT   PAGE 3

Managed three sales districts in the development of a dealer organization. This involved market analysis, recruiting and training. Sales increased from $2 million to $3 million.

<u>Manager, Market Research</u>, 1964 - 1967.

Headed a marketing group to promote and sell all types of plumbing products in the Industrial and Wholesale markets. Supervised marketing departments and research department. New marketing strategies and sales opportunities were created through new product and system ideas.

<u>Sales Engineer</u>, 1963 - 1965.

Assigned to increase market share, profitability, and new product development. Developed marketing strategy, coordinated sales and bidding methods and trained field sales personnel.

<u>Field Sales Engineer</u>, 1956 - 1963.

Sold all types of plumbing products to apartment owners, architects, contractors, industrials, wholesalers and dealers. Increased sales 230% during this period.

1952   U. S. NAVY
 to
1956

Assigned to Destroyer, South China Sea. Lt. Commander.

<u>EDUCATION</u>

B. S., 1955, University of Missouri

<u>PERSONAL</u>

Born October 12, 1933 in the small town of Hackett, Arkansas where father owned and operated a retail hardware store for more than 40 years. Married childhood sweetheart who attended University of Missouri during two of my undergraduate years. We have five lovely children including two sets of twins. I am 6'4" in height, weigh 230 lbs. and played varsity football during my last three years at the University. Remain in excellent health.

REFERENCES AND FURTHER DATA ON REQUEST

DISCUSSION

Harvard Résumé.   The Conant résumé features continuing career development from field sales to general management. You will note that achievement started with increases in territory sales. Management was impressed and gave the subject the opportunity to get similar results in a more responsible position. Success here led to market research management and finally to management of all dealer activities. Opportunities apparently did not come fast enough, and Mr. Conant moved to another company. Soon he changed employment again to obtain general management experience, so that now he is equipped for P.&L. responsibilities in addition to those in marketing. The business biographies of successful people are replete with illustrations of the desire to learn leading to employment changes—sometimes at a temporary financial sacrifice but usually to one's ultimate benefit in terms of greater success.

The *Harvard* form of résumé expresses this career exceptionally well. Note the expanded comments under personal data.

The Creative Résumé

The *Creative Résumé* lacks a commonly recognized form. Instead, the writer *creates* his own form. *Creative* in this sense does not necessarily mean a better résumé, but one different from the norm. Its quality and effectiveness, as always, will depend on the writer's skill.

The creativity in a *Creative Résumé* may consist in paragraphing, layout, decoration, color, method of folding, or drastically different writing—in rhyme perhaps, or with illuminated capitals, or bearing graphic forms and symbols.

Nor is a *Creative Résumé* necessarily associated with the creative professions. An artist, writer, editor, photographer, stylist, decorator, actor, musician, entertainer, entrepreneur might be drawn toward this style of résumé, but others might use it as well. Actually, too great a departure from the norm turns a résumé into a brochure.

Examples of the *Creative Résumé* follow. The Cowles résumé is creative in its method of paragraphing and its objective appraisal type of presentation. To that extent it is different and effective. The Ray résumé has an unusual appearance and an interesting format.

EXAMPLE OF CREATIVE RÉSUMÉ

145 Harrison Avenue   (212) 456-9876
Rye, New York 12345

R E S U M E

of

<u>IRENE COWLES</u>

<u>MAGAZINE EDITORIAL DIRECTOR - EDITOR</u>

Qualifications:

Twenty five years of successful experience as Editorial Director with unusually broad responsibilities embracing three successful magazines with largely female readership; and as Executive Editor, Managing Editor, Features Editor, Assistant Editor in reverse chronological order; with three different publishers.

Publishers Weekly said: "The most knowledgeable woman's editor in the field." (June 1973)

Magazine Writer's Digest said: "Miss Cowles has helped more aspiring writers than anyone we know." (Jan. 1970)

Magazine Guild said: "Miss Cowles has identified her markets and hit them in the bull's eye; without question one of the most talented editors in her field." (Nov. 1968)

Objective evaluation by Corporate Development Committee on Executive Evaluation:

Competent in all areas of manuscript selection and purchase, production, control, organization and administration, wide author contacts and excellent reputation for judgment; decisiveness and creativity.

Possesses ability to lead, supervise, train and gain loyalty and dedication of staff. Oriented to profitable operations.

Sensitive to ethical, editorial and reader needs; capable of bringing together to gain optimum circulation and to make adjustments quickly as need appears. (Dec. 1970)

Employment History:

1955-1974 - National Publications, New York, N. Y.

1949-1955 - Hillside Publishing Company, New York, N. Y.

1948-1949 - Rex Magazine Company, New York, N. Y.

Education:

B. S., Journalism, University of Syracuse, Syracuse, N. Y., 1947.

Personal Data:

Single, excellent health, no dependants. Willing to relocate.

<u>REFERENCES AND FURTHER DATA ON REQUEST</u>

<u>CHARLENE RAY</u>

<u>EDITOR</u>

*T*wenty-five years of successful experience as Editorial Director with unusually broad responsibilities embraching three successful magazines with largely female readership; and as Executive Editor, Managing Editor, Features Editor in reverse chronological order; with three different publishers.

*P*ublishers Weekly said: "The most knowledeable woman's editor in the field." (June 1973)

*M*agazine Guild said: "Miss Ray has helped more aspiring writers than anyone we know." (Jan. 1970)

*M*agazine Writer's Digest said: "Miss Ray has identified her markets and hit them dead center; without question one of the most talented editors in her field." (Nov. 1968)

*C*ompetent in all areas of manuscript selection and purchase, production, control, organization and administration; wide author contacts and excellent reputation for judgment, decisiveness and creativity.

*P*ossess ability to lead, supervise, train and gain loyalty and dedication of staff. Oriented to profit.

*S*ensitive to ethical, editorial and reader needs; capable of coordinating all elements of publishing to gain optimum circulation; and of making quick adjustments if necessary.

*E*mployment
History:

National Publications, New York, N. Y., 1955-1974.

Hillside Publishing Co., New York, N. Y. , 1949-1955.

Rex Magazine Co., Topeka, Kans., 1948-1949.

*B*s., Journalism, University of Syracuse, Syracuse, N. Y., 1947.

*P*ersonal data: single, excellent health, no dependents;

EXAMPLE OF CREATIVE RÉSUMÉ

21 Old Bond Street
Greenwich, Conn. 00000

Home (861) 300-0000
Office (212) 100-0000

R E S U M E

of

<u>SERAPHIM PEI</u>

<u>INVESTMENT MANAGER</u>

I have been associated with my present company for 23 years.
Name of company will be furnished on request.

Comprehensively trained and competent in money management. Accustomed to handling an investment volume of $3 billion annually for one of the world's largest financial institutions with operations conducted in the U. S. and Swiss funds.

- currently manage investments for 13 pension funds.

- widely acquainted among banks, brokers and financial companies.

Expert in searching out and finding high safe yields, new investment opportunities in the U. S. and Europe.

- portfolios include or have included commercial paper, treasury bills, C.Ds., municipal and corporate bonds, stocks selected for both short- and long-term.

- achieved 3% increase in value of investments during 1974; previously achieved gains in portfolio values up to 55% in several successive years.

Experienced in all financial reporting, forecasting, controls.

- prepare cash flow projections and analyses for other divisions: real estate, industrial mortgages, commodity, stock and bond departments.

- prepare departmental budgets and budget consolidations; advise with respect to budget implementation.

- prepare reports to Federal Reserve, S.E.C. and Company officers relating to all operations.

SERAPHIM PEI   PAGE 2

Responsible for development of new forms and methods of making calculations saving hundreds of man-hours per month.

- designed new bank instruction form for collection of sinking fund payments; saved 72 man-hours per month.

- recommended use of computer for calculating interest yields (formerly made on desk calculators); saved 48 man-hours per month.

- set up new controls for fund transfers from European agents to achieve increased interest earnings amounting to $150,000 annually.

Earlier as Executive Assistant maintained mandatory security valuation records. Developed method of expediting daily calculations to achieve immediate portfolio evaluations at each half hour of stock exchange day. Instituted Telex system for domestic and overseas reporting hooked up to computer.

- analyzed daily Telex readouts.

- assisted State examiners.

- supervised coupon cutting department with staff of 40.

- kept all investment records, records of collections and payments.

- supervised delivery of securities.

- instructed banks re collections.

Served in the U. S. Army 1949-1952, 1st Lt. Assigned to Korea prior to opening of hostilities. Given mission to infiltrate behind lines to make intelligence assessment of North Korean buildup for evaluation of future intentions. Awarded Silver Star. Promoted to Captain.

Educated at University of Denver, Denver, Colo. Graduate work completed at Columbia University, New York, N. Y. Academic background and experience strongly based in Accounting, Finance and Economics.

Hold M.B.A., International Finance, and B. S., Accounting and Economics.

Age 46, married, two children, excellent health. Will relocate.

<u>REFERENCES AND FURTHER DATA ON REQUEST</u>

DISCUSSION

Creative Résumé. The Pei résumé utilizes a general statement paragraph to describe competence or experience, followed by indented sentences providing specific examples. It departs from this formula at the end when earlier experience is detailed.

The entire presentation is different from any standard résumé form and therefore comes within the classification of *Creative Résumé*.

The reader gains a clear picture of the candidate's competence in handling financial affairs. The résumé begins with the most important activity—the investment of funds. Next, suggests that considerable acumen was used in selecting safe havens for capital maintenance at a time when equities were in a decline and most investors were suffering severe capital losses. The expertise was acquired on the sound foundation of extensive experience in financial analysis and reporting.

Education and earlier experience all support an evolutionary career, which should be attractive to an employer.

The form of the résumé strongly suggests that it is the personal expression of the subject.

The résumé also indicates that this man, though he has had only one position in his entire business career, has never lost his forward momentum and will probably continue moving forward with new and perhaps larger responsibilities.

The Narrative Résumé

The *Narrative Résumé* can be a pleasing variation from formal presentations. You might use this format if you write well, including about the difficult topic of yourself, or if your background is unusual, with perhaps a strong academic foundation. The *Narrative Résumé,* because of its relative rarity, can have extra impact. Remember, however, that it will appeal to some résumé readers only.

The form is exceptionally suitable for the *vita brevis* (''short life'') type of description of one's lifework. Personal statistics and imformation about education, military service, hobbies, and the like can be woven into the narrative or given in a separate section.

The disadvantages of the *Narrative* form could be lack of unity, coherence, and compactness. There is also the ever-present difficulty of narrating one's personal and professional life history sufficiently objectively.

EXAMPLE OF NARRATIVE RÉSUMÉ

100 Auditorium Street   (890) 321-6666
Salt Lake City, Utah 54321

RESUME

<u>JOHN PETER</u>

<u>PERSONNEL DIRECTOR/MANPOWER DEVELOPER</u>

Born September 30, 1939, single, excellent health. Residence and travel in Belgium, France, Tanzania, Kenya, Holland, Germany, Switzerland, Italy, Tunisia, Morroco, Ivory Coast, Uganda.

Educated as follows:

<u>M. Divinity</u>, <u>M. R. E.</u>, 1965, St. Christopher's Seminary, Becton, N.Y.

<u>B. A.</u>, 1960, University of Notre Dame, South Bend, Ind.

Post Graduate:

1967, 10 months, Sociology, Louvain University, Belgium.
1966, 12 months, Sociology, Anthropology, Social Research, Princeton University, Princeton, N. J.
1964 (summer), Social Change, Social Psychology, Princeton University.
1963 (summer), Anthropology, Cross Cultural Research, Loyola University, Baltimore, Md.

Languages include: French, Spanish, Kisukuma, Kiswahili.

Hobbies include: scuba diving, mountain climbing, any racquets game.

Employment experience:

1967-1974, International Catholic Charities, New York, N. Y.

1962-1967, Extra-curricular activities while studying included: art exhibits, community relations and marriage counseling, labor negotiation, consulting, initiation of dramatized TV programs on humans relations nationally televised on Channel III, New York City.

I give the preceding statements first because they are the raw data forming the platform for my life to the present and can be tied up in a neat little package and set aside.

In 1967, acting as Program Developer, Sociologist and Personnel Director for the Overseas Division of the International Catholic Charities, I conceived the idea of researching two African church organizations of 7000 members to ascertain the level of their functional efficiency. I was authorized to carry out such research and as a result suggested a program utilizing sociological techniques to provide

JOHN PETER   PAGE 2

job enrichment and stronger support of the Division by the organizations studied.
My report was read with some skepticism but nevertheless the thesis was finally
accepted and I was appointed to implement the suggestions made.

Essentially my suggestions involved a program of personnel reformation and membership education to serve as a model for other branches which would ultimately
involve as many as 75 organizations with 60,000 members and 500 supervisory
personnel. I spent seven years in Africa on this project in the following activities:

- clarifying the objectives and roles of leaders through re-expression in communications and seminars.
- developing a personnel policy embodying employee relationships.
- conducting role-playing sessions and strategy meetings to help bring solutions
  to administrative problems and improve interpersonal relationships.
- periodic evaluation of activities to assess their effectiveness.

I published the following articles during this period:

    Restructuring Pastoral Programs
    Catechetical Program
    Youth Study Program
    Attitudes in Marriage
    Aspects of Communication Between Church and People
    Attitudes of Youth Toward Christianity and Marriage
    Attitudes of Adults Toward Christianity and Marriage
    Training Manual for U. S. and African Organization Personnel

These publications were made in English and appropriate African languages.

As a result of these and related activities, we enjoyed a 50% increase in membership, the program was implemented in 35 additional organizations, relationships
between local and overseas personnel were improved, tensions among U. S. workers in Africa were alleviated, medical care was bettered and a library for school
children was established.

I am not sure what you may think my education and experience fit me for, but I
wish to leave the Church to embark upon a career in business.

I think my best contributions would be made in the area of personnel, although I
would be willing to take any position which would be effective for you while giving me the opportunity to establish a new career.

My qualities include an understanding of and liking for people, some creativity,
practical experience in working with people, a good education and an ability to
conceive and implement progressive plans.

<u>REFERENCES AND FURTHER DATA ON REQUEST</u>

DISCUSSION

Narrative Résumé.   John Peter spent about 30 years of his life in study and service contributing greatly to the expanded usefulness of his organization. At the end of that period he made a reappraisal and, deciding that such service need not be a lifelong commitment, chose to try employment in the private sector. This career change required an evaluation of his past to determine the areas in which he might be most effective. His experience in dealing with people logically suggested the areas of personnel or manpower development.

Being a competent, well educated writer, but lacking business experience, Mr. Peter selected the *Narrative* form, thus notifying the reader that his was an unusual situation calling for a different approach to the job market.

As expected, the subject's obvious interpersonal communications skills, combined with an innovative mind, resulted in a successful résumé that appealed strongly to selected readers. Though without the discipline present in more formal résumés, it has the coherence, unity, logical sequence, and interest needed to make it a compelling document.

EXAMPLE OF NARRATIVE RÉSUMÉ

V I T A

of

HENRY GEORGE DITMARS

For 20 years I have been associated in various capacitie with
such institutions as Newark Museum (Newark, N. J.), Metropoli-
tan Museum of Art, New York, N. Y., Mellon Museum of Natural
History, P·ttsburgh, Pa., Yates Museum, London, England, as follows:

Director, Curator of Fine Arts, Curator of Ancient Ceramics, Direct-
or of Special Services, Program Planner, Assistant to the Director.

I have traveled extensively in South America, Europe, the Balkans,
the Mediterranean and Aegean Islands individually and leading
groups in archeological exploration funded by the National Geographic Society. Five years ago I was President of the Explorers
Club.

I have been responsible for the following, some with national attention:

> Showing of French Impressionists at the Metropolitan Museum
> of Art drawing the largest public attendance ever experienced
> at this museum.

> Purchase, at auction for $9 million, the famed painting by
> Buardicio, Venice Beneath the Sea.

> Arrangements with the French Government and the Louvre for
> the traveling exhibition to 27 museums around the U. S. of
> Roman bronzes and statuary of the first millennium A. D.

> Supervised the razing, shipping and reconstruction and res-
> toration of the Temple of Zeus from Piraeus (Greece) to its
> present home in the Mellon Museum requiring two years of
> study and planning.

EXAMPLE OF NARRATIVE RÉSUMÉ

I am currently Director of the new Museum of Fine Arts in Kansas City, Mo. where I aided in raising $37 million for construction and purchase. I am responsible for assembling all of the works currently on display. The new Museum has received wide publicity in the media and has been acclaimed for purity of design and discrimination and elegance in content attracting visitors from all over the world.

I have told my Board that for the immediate future the direction of the Museum will be more administrative than creative and I am looking for a new post where my particular combinations of experience and talents can be used in a culminating effort of achievement in the public interest.

I am a graduate of the New England School of Fine Arts, <u>B.A.</u> and attended the Harvard Graduate School of Business Administration, <u>M.B.A.</u> graduating with distinction and majoring in Museum Administration.

My age is 45. I am married to a lovely wife and am proud of our three children, two of whom are now attending college.

Publications include:

<u>Museum and Public Participation</u>, Lippencott Press, 1970.

<u>Heavenly Taste</u>, Scribner's, 1968.

<u>Greek Exploration: Story of a Dig</u>, University Press, 1964.

Your suggestions as to any suitable activities for me within your knowledge will be appreciated. I have notified the Kansas City Museum of my planned departure in six months from this date.

Very truly yours,

George Henry Ditmars
10 Hades Street
Hot Springs, Mo. 00000
Tel. (000) 987-0101
    (000) 783-1010

DISCUSSION

Narrative Résumé. Mr. Ditmars is well educated and has published widely and successfully in the world of art. He therefore chose the *Narrative Résumé,* which is well suited to the individual with an unusual background. In fact, it is difficult to see how this kind of career could have been expressed adequately within the more formal confines of another résumé style.

As would be expected, Mr. Ditmars starts by describing his background and career progression. He mentions his travel, which plays an important part in his acquisition of knowledge. He then proceeds to give examples of some of his achievements to let the reader know the scope and size of his responsibilities. Education and publications are provided. The résumé may be used as a letter by the addition of the complimentary close or that may be omitted.

Mr. Ditmars is of course a composite of many different people. There could hardly be one real person such as Mr. Ditmars.

The Professional Résumé

The traditional "learned professions" are law, medicine, and theology. More broadly, a professional is one who has special knowledge enabling him or her to advise, guide, or instruct others. Teaching is a profession, as is any vocation requiring extensive specialized educational preparation, such as accounting, engineering, or military science.

A *Professional Résumé* therefore places initial emphasis on academic qualifications for the profession. Any other form can serve to present the balance of the information, except the *Narrative.* The most appropriate forms, however, are the *Chronological Résumé with Summary Page* and the *Functional Résumé.*

EXAMPLE OF PROFESSIONAL RÉSUMÉ

134 East 34th Street   (212) 323-5454
New York, N. Y. 10017

R E S U M E

of

EPHRAIM TUTT

ATTORNEY

OBJECTIVE: Association with law firm in general corporate and
                     securities areas, including litigation.

SUMMARY OF   Awareness of legal needs of business with ability
QUALIFICATIONS: to provide clear answers and effective remedies for
                     corporate legal problems, including litigation when
                     necessary. Intimate knowledge of the Securities
                     Act of 1933 and Exchange Act of 1934; the rules of
                     the major stock exchanges; private placements, lost
                     securities, arbitrations. Fully familiar with tax and
                     securities laws and accounting procedures. Effective
                     in client relationships.

                     Admitted to practice in New York State and New
                     Jersey.

EDUCATION: B. A. degree, Princeton University, Princeton, N. J., 1963.

                     J. D., University of Michigan School of Law, Ann Arbor,
                     Mich., 1967.

PERSONAL DATA: Age 30, married, two children, excellent health.

FOR FURTHER DATA PLEASE SEE FOLLOWING PAGE

EXAMPLE OF PROFESSIONAL RÉSUMÉ

PROFESSIONAL EXPERIENCE:

1973-Present   WILD, SPENCER AND KING, INC., New York, N. Y.

ASSOCIATE with law firm.

Provide services to clients with wide range of problems but with particular concentration on broker-dealer and specialist problems, controversies involving securities laws, sometimes leading to litigation, registrations of public offerings with S. E. C.

- personally and successfully represented clients before N. Y. Stock Exchange, American Stock Exchange and S. E. C. involving disciplinary matters.

- successfully completed and closed a public offering for a corporation formerly privately owned.

- prepared broker-dealer applications for N. Y. S. E. membership.

1969-1973   HORNBLOWER, BIDDLE CO, New York, N. Y.

ASSOCIATE HOUSE COUNSEL for major Wall Street Investment Firm.

- won arbitration involving large client of firm.

- approved many Rule 144 sales.

- successfully prosecuted or defended Firm position in connection with customer claims.

- aided in drafting a compliance manual for firm; completed compliance inspection of branch offices.

1967-1969   MIDWEST STOCK EXCHANGE, Chicago, Ill.

INVESTIGATIVE ATTORNEY

- investigated violations of member firms and their personnel of Exchange rules and regulations and of other regulatory agencies.

- prepared charge memoranda for prosecutions which led to disciplinary action by the Exchange.

- reviewed law suits and arbitrations to find if any violations existed.

REFERENCES AND FURTHER DATA ON REQUEST

DISCUSSION

Professional Résumé. In a *Professional résumé* different approaches must be used for different objectives. For example, a doctor wishing to be considered for a state, municipal, or federal position or a hospital administrative position must describe administrative capacities in addition to medical competence. A thorough background search may be necessary to find a platform for administrative excellence in an otherwise purely professional (specialist) career.

Attorney Tutt's problem was to make a dignified presentation that would at the same time support his objective. Some of his more interesting activities were described to give the reader a chance to evaluate his experience level and potential.

Legal cases are often highly complex and legal language is exact. A résumé in the legal profession must therefore avoid too much detail. Competence must be suggested rather than explicated. Emphasis is on results rather than responsibilities and methods.

The Accomplishment Résumé

The *Accomplishment Résumé* lists accomplishments without reference to dates and companies and without regard for a chronological order. It is often used by individuals who wish to disguise age, length of experience, employment gaps, lack of progress in recent jobs, job-hopping, and other matters that are easier to explain in person during an interview than in writing. Do not let these reasons dissuade you from using this form if you like it, however. Some nonprofit executive employment services favor this style. The elements of the *Accomplishment Résumé* are the following:

1. Name, address, and telephone number.
2. Summary of qualifications.
3. List of accomplishments (the most important are given first).
4. List of companies by whom employed (no dates).
5. Military service (no dates).
6. Education (no dates).
7. Hobbies, professional memberships, community activities, and honors (no dates).
8. Personal data (omit age).

Two examples of the *Accomplishment Résumé* follow.

EXAMPLE OF ACCOMPLISHMENT RÉSUMÉ

221-B Baker Street   (123) 456-7890
Sherlock, Va. 54321

<u>JOHN MILTON</u>

<u>OPERATIONS EXECUTIVE</u>

* * * Experienced manager with proven record of accomplishments in creating profits and often innovative
solutions to corporate problems representing tens
of millions of dollars.

* * * Record of progress to increasingly important responsibilities in every employment. Accustomed to working with and leading staffs in improving systems and
procedures, in developing harmonious labor relations,
in organizing projects for most efficient completion.

* * * Excellent in written and oral communication with
wealth of experience in construction, maintenance,
site selection, leasing, facilities planning, display,
floor layout, contract negotiation, organization of
diverse departments involving multi-million dollar
programs.

* * * Experience in the activities enumerated has been
world-wide.

<u>FOR FURTHER DATA PLEASE SEE FOLLOWING PAGE</u>

JOHN MILTON   PAGE 2

<u>ACHIEVEMENTS</u>:

Cost saving of $1 million in one year using reduced level of personnel and no loss of efficiency.

Completed $50 million construction project in five months with four general contractors saving Company from financial difficulty.

Saved $35,000 annually by devising new method of inventory control.

Set up central purchasing for ten units saving 13% on annual purchases of $12 million.

Planned, coordinated and supervised a multi-million dollar construction project with cost saving of $183,000 and bonus to contractor for beating deadline by two weeks.

Planned new housewares department (100,000 sq. ft.) for increased traffic and improved merchandise visibility without loss of business during reconstruction, using in-house labor.

Saved 12% in electricity and fuel in group of 37 nationally-known department stores saving more than $3 million in annual costs.

Reduced cost of new two million sq. ft. warehouse 25% with creative planning.

Reduced insurance costs for a three million sq. ft. building by a program of continuous maintenance.

Consolidated insurance on a national basis at a cost saving of $10 million over a period of two years.

Devised new security methods that reduced shoplifting and other causes of loss by 75% with a resultant saving of $13 million.   And more.

The preceding accomplishments were achieved for the following companies:

Great Atlantic and Caribbean Coffee Company, Vice President.

The International Insurance Companies, Vice President for Operations.

Allied Retailers, Incorporated, Buildings Manager.

Hughes Construction Company, Field Engineer.

<u>EDUCATION</u>:   <u>B. S.</u>, Rice University, Houston, Texas

<u>PERSONAL DATA</u>: Married, 3 children, excellent health. Willing to relocate.

<u>REFERENCES AND FURTHER DATA ON REQUEST</u>

DISCUSSION

Accomplishment Résumé.   The material in the Milton résumé was condensed from another résumé of about four pages to two for purposes of illustration. It suffers from a lack of relationship between achievements and employers and lack of explanation of work methods (such as determining the flow of information from the point of sale to the computer, making time studies of jobs, and so forth), which would have added greatly to an understanding of this man's value and the reasons for some of his assignments. Nevertheless, it is effective in presenting a man whose every assignment has been so successful that an employer in need of such skills would be inclined to interview him.

Actually the original résumé, written in *Chronological* form, was very impressive. A broadcast letter summary elicited replies from 70% of the companies approached—an unusually high percentage. Not all replies, largely from the top officers, resulted in interviews, but they provided a base for aggressive follow-ups, leading to personal interviews.

The résumé is reproduced here because it has been successful in gaining employment and may have application in specialized situations. The general rule is—if one approach does not work, use another.

The operations executive in this résumé was utilized in many ways outside of the usual responsibilities of his job classification. The résumé therefore indicates considerable versatility, judgment, and imagination.

EXAMPLE OF ACCOMPLISHMENT RÉSUMÉ

100 Satellite Way   Home (201) 123-4567
Wigwam, N. J. 07111   Office (212) 321-9876

<u>BUSINESS BIOGRAPHY</u>

<u>SAMUEL MORSE BELL</u>

OBJECTIVE: Opportunity to contribute hundreds of thousands of dollars in cost
savings and communications improvements for major corporation offering appropriate opportunity.

Communications Executive with a history of cost savings of nearly $2 million and
improved systems for "Big 8" accounting firm, major brokerage and "Fortune 500"
companies.

As COMMUNICATIONS and MANAGEMENT SPECIALIST for international public accounting firm:

- conducted an analysis, designed and placed in operation an international system
  of voice and teletype service superseding existing system, for rapidly growing
  commodity exchange. Achieved a saving of $10,000 per month.

- developed voice and data communications program for worldwide minerals import-
  ing company resulting in a cost reduction of $75,000 annually.

- designed network of voice communications for large conglomerate utilizing WATS
  and Tie line services and interconnect systems; made operating improvements;
  reduced costs $375,000 annually and improved communications.

- modified switchboards and telephone systems of major New Jersey bank reducing
  costs $27,000 a year.

- created and implemented clerical cost reductions for billion dollar insurance
  company involving restructuring organization, rescheduling work, utilizing teletype; saved company more than $270,000 annually with strengthened manage-
  ment control, reduction and reassignment of clerical personnel and greater employee productivity.

As VICE PRESIDENT and COMMUNICATIONS MANAGER for internationally known
brokerage firm with 300 branches in the U. S. and around the world:

- planned first comprehensive international communication system linking all
  branches using computer switched private line teletype providing split-second
  quotations for all markets in any part of the world. Participated in increasing
  revenues over $100 million.

- set up and put in operation frequency division multiplexing systems between
  New York and Houston and New York and Toronto saving company $30,000 an-
  nually.

EXAMPLE OF ACCOMPLISHMENT RÉSUMÉ

- designed and implemented CRT report entry system replacing teletype equipment; with saving of $63,000 annually.

- developed communications system incorporating national odd lot quotations leading to current new planning in odd lot transactions.

- held P. & L. responsibility for newly created communications profit center offering services to major brokerages in the U. S.; achieved profits exceeding $1 million within one year.

As COMMUNICATIONS SPECIALIST for major manufacturer of household electrical appliances:

- designed and implemented first 76D4 teletype network linking U. S. and overseas offices for instant communication. Identified actual savings of $50,000 and intangible contributions to operating efficiencies of several hundred thousand dollars.

- planned and implemented use of advanced telephone design with annual saving to company of $37,000.

- introduced tandem dial network with computer hookup.

As SPECIAL DEVELOPMENT REPRESENTATIVE for telephone company Long Lines Department:

- sold brokerage firms, manufacturing companies, department store groups (Macy's, Federated, Allied) cost justified communications systems leading to savings of more than $\frac{1}{2}$ million for participating companies.

Achievements related were accomplished with:

- Anderson, Touche and Morehouse, New York, N. Y. C.P.A. firm.
- Merrill, Lehman, Hornblower, Inc., New York, N. Y.
- General Selectric Co., Endicott, N. Y.
- Continental Telephone Co., Boston, Mass.

MILITARY SERVICE: U. S. NAVY, 1st Lt. Assigned to destroyer <u>Hammerslough</u>, Mediterranean duty. Executive Officer two years.

EDUCATION: <u>M.B.A.</u>, University of Chicago, Chicago, Ill.
         <u>B.A.</u>, University of Michigan, Ann Arbor, Mich.

MEMBERSHIPS: National Association of Communications Engineers
         American Telecommunications Society

PERSONAL DATA: Married, three children, excellent health.

<u>REFERENCES AND FURTHER DATA ON REQUEST</u>

DISCUSSION

Accomplishment Résumé.   Mr. Bell is sensitive about his age, which is 62. His résumé is therefore designed to eliminate all date references. His appearance and vigor belie his years, and it is hoped that his many accomplishments will lead to an interview, even though a résumé reader may suspect that the omission of dates is done for the purpose of obscuring them.

It is illegal for an employer to discriminate in hiring because of age. The decision not to hire because of age can often be cloaked in terms of other, purely capricious, factors, however. Though many older people could make a tremendous contribution to any business, there is a definite business bias against hiring them. High insurance and pension costs are one reason, as is the difficulty in assimilating some older persons.

For this reason some advisors recommend that an older candidate use any means to gain an interview. They suggest that the omission of all dates from a résumé removes age clues and therefore improves interview opportunities. The style of the Bell résumé is that suggested by such advisors.

IDENTIFYING YOUR ACCOMPLISHMENTS

Many job applicants find it difficult to identify accomplishments that they consider to be worthy of writing about. Doing their jobs day by day, they fail to recognize that the accumulation of daily tasks results in achieving certain goals, such as expedited work flow, more timely reports, improved customer service, reduction in complaints, greater productivity, and better morale.

Almost everyone has accomplishments if he will search for them. All the résumés shown as examples were seemingly about very successful individuals. Actually this is not so. Some have been unsuccessful in their careers to date. Some found it difficult to discover accomplishments without hard digging. Accomplishments can be culled from avocations as well as vocations. The following list may help you to identify yours. You:

- Increased profits.
- Increased sales.
- Improved work efficiency.
- Saved money.
- Reorganized.

- Reduced staff.
- Earned additional income (for employer).
- Improved competitive position of company.
- Devised new products, improved existing products.
- Expanded markets.
- Arranged financing (for company).
- Increased value of corporate securities.
- Trained.
- Solved problems.
- Contributed new ideas.
- Reduced overdue accounts.
- Reduced inventory.
- Increased turnover.
- Improved financial reporting.
- Found acquisitions.
- Reduced taxes.
- Improved management reporting.
- Reduced employee turnover.
- Used cost-saving purchasing techniques.
- Discovered better copy theme.
- Introduced better filing system.
- Increased typing speed and accuracy.
- Relieved boss of administrative details.
- Planned better meetings.
- Improved employee morale.

The list of things you may have done is almost endless. Occasionally your avocational accomplishments may be more important than your vocational achievements, providing a better means of evaluation. For example, one young man, employed by a large retailer, was unhappy with his slow progress through the various levels of responsibility. In his spare time he played tennis and belonged to a well-known tennis club, where he accepted the task of selling advertising, and publishing a program for an important annual tennis event. By analyzing such pertinent data about club members as income, age, and sex and effectively presenting the resulting figures and conclusions, he sold much more advertising than had any other chairman in the past. He did this job for three years, each year exceeding the results of the previous year. A brief description of his extracurricular activities was included in his résumé, leading to a new career in advertising that he found to be more challenging and more interesting, as well as better paying, than had been his career in retailing. Many people have found new careers based on their extracurricular interests when seemingly stymied in their regular jobs. Find and express all your accomplishments wherever you find them.

EFFECTIVE SHORT RÉSUMÉS, LETTERS, AND ADVERTISEMENTS

All résumés and letters need not to be long and detailed. Here are examples of some very short ones that would get results. (Addresses, full names, and some other details would ordinarily also be included.)

An Advertisement
Available to enforce and lead "One World" concept. Now have gun. Will travel.

Alexander the Great.

A Letter to Heads of State
Willing to work way up through the ranks (starting level: general)

Cleopatra

An Example of the Telegram Approach
Lending Urgency to Application for Employment
Seek third chance with employer who has substantial investment in army and navy.

Napoleon

Letter to Watergate Committee
Now know answer to "What is Truth?" Willing to exchange for modern poison antidote.

Socrates

Direct Solication Letter
(to Harold Robbins, Author)

Dear Mr. Robbins:

I do not believe that my career was adequately expressed. Sales have fallen off. Would you undertake to rewrite my life?

Sincerely,

Moll Flanders

Letter to Civil Liberties Union

Gentlemen:

Demand new trial

Lizzie Borden

London Times, Personal
Wanted: wealthy woman for support and companionship.

Don Juan

Brief, Informal Application for Employment
Gracie Mansion
New York, N.Y. (zip)

My Dear Mr. Mayor:

Although I have been in upper Mongolia for some time (classified), I am now fully recovered and have read about your fiscal problems. I am now on leave from British M.I. Have had, as you know, wide official discretion to "liquidate," and have worked in New York City. I could save you millions of dollars in trial costs; possess my own equipment. References can be supplied by millions of readers worldwide, incuding heads of state.

I am available at once. Please also give my regards to the Governor when you see him.

Address me care of "M."

Cordially,

James Bond 007

Letter of Resignation

CONFIDENTIAL TO
John Smith, President
Alpha Beta Kappa Co.
Red Hill, S.D.

Dear Jack,

Have $30 million company funds in my personal checking account. My contacts are refusing to accept any more payments. Two have been shot. Have decided to resign from ABK. Will let you know my future whereabouts at a later date, perhaps. In the meantime, do not worry; will not disclose existence of fund; have transferred it to Switzerland. I have set fire to the plant; all records are destroyed. You will be able to take a good write-off.

You have always been a genius in marketing. Suggest you create new selling plan.

I have just bought a large diamond from Richard Burton for Mary who joins me in sending best regards to you and Jane.

You know who

WRITING THE RÉSUMÉ

Follow these six basic steps in writing your résumé:

1. Assemble the raw data (from your answers to our analytical questionnaire).
2. Refine the data (initial draft).
3. Select the most relevant data.
4. Translate the data into suitable language. Your sentences and paragraphs are the building blocks that you can move around to fit your chosen résumé form.
5. Select your résumé format.
6. Write your résumé.

The key to a successful résumé is the analysis and listing of your responsibilities and achievements in an orderly manner. That is, you must know about yourself: what you were or are supposed to be doing, what you actually did or are doing, and the effect of your actions on your own work, your section, your department, your division, and your company or organization

The analytical questionnaire presented below will help you to organize this type of information about yourself. It has been carefully prepared to make you think about yourself, to recall to your mind activities that you may have forgotten, and to help you focus on the important aspects of your vocational life. First you must recall; then you must express your recollections. It is easier to express yourself properly after you have accomplished the first task of remembering and writing down the things you have done. This first writing can be informal—put down words, phrases, and sentence fragments, which will provide the basis for proper exposition when you start to wite your résumé.

1. Your name, address, and home and office telephone numbers.
2. Titles of jobs desired, if possible. If you cannot supply them at this time, briefly *describe* the job you want. Identify several jobs by assigning to them the letters A, B, C, and so on, using the same code in Question 3 below.

    Turn to Question 11 and answer it before ansering the questions that follow.
3. Qualifications that you believe you should have for the jobs A, B, C, and so on, listed in Question 2. (Most data should be in answer to Question 11.) *For example,* your answer to Question 2 is "sales manager," you might answer the present question as follows:

    a. Appraise pricing and distribution policies.
    b. Recruit and train sales staff.
    c. Maintain distributor liaison.
    d. And so on.

    Now *underline* the qualifications you have *and* list any other qualifications you feel you should have for the jobs you desire.

4. Your age, marital status, number of children, home ownership, car ownership, and so on.
5. Military service

   a. Dates, branch of service, rank.
   b. Special training, courses, responsibilities.

6. Education—dates, schools, academic degrees, and proficiency in languages.
7. Major and minor courses. List courses relevant to the jobs desired. State your class standing if possible. Describe scholarships, awards, and honors.
8. Extracurricular activites at school (sports, jobs, social activities, etc.).
9. Hobbies and your degree of proficiency in them, travel (if extensive), memberships in societies and community activities.
10. A summary of your employment history. *Work backwards,* giving the last job first. Use three columns to assemble the following information:

    Dates of beginning job and
    leaving job (years only)   Company and address   Job titles

11. For each job listed above, starting with the *last* job, give the following data. Treat each position or important assignment with the same company, or with important clients of your employer, as though it were a separate and distinct job. Answer *each* question carefully.

    a. Job title.
    b. Dates of beginning and leaving job (by transfer to another company or by promotion or change within a company).
    c. Name of company and division or department within company.
    d. Description of what the company makes, sells, or does.
    e. An indication of size of company—by sales volume, number of employees, number of plants, and number of branches or stores, for example.
    f. The title of the person for whom you worked (president, foreman, sales manager, etc.).
    g. The number of persons you supervised (if any).
    h. The kinds of employees you supervised (engineers, clerks, etc.).
    i. The types of equipment you used (or that was used under your supervision) and for what purpose. This will be relevant for such jobs as production manager and computer executive, but irrelevant for others.
    j. Your responsibilities. Describe them briefly but fully; give facts, rather than abstract generalities. Consult page 46 under "Experience" before answering this question.
    k. Your accomplishments. Describe them briefly but specifically.

- The problems you were faced with.
- What you did about them.
- What you achieved and how.

This is, what did you see that needed to be done, what did you do about it, and what happened as a result? Do not list mere claims, such as ''I increased sales.'' Give facts: ''I found that sales were only $150,000. I made a market survey and determined that the market needed a ''widget.'' I introduced a new line of widgets. I trained salesmen by doing X Y Z. Sales increased in six months by $50,000.'' Such an analysis is important. You need it in your résumé if you are to stand out from other job applicants. It will also reassure you that you are qualified for the job you want, in addition to refreshing your memory and providing valuable *rehearsal and training* for your job interviews.

12. References: name, title, company, address, and telephone number (and extension). Do not include references in your résumé; assemble them for use at interviews.

ANSWERING THE ANALYTICAL QUESTIONNAIRE

The two sample answers to this questionnaire appearing below illustrate what you should *not* do. Here is how one man answered Question 11:

1972-present (name of company). AREA SUPERVISOR. Began February 1972 as restaurant manager in failing unit. The unit started to show profit after four weeks. I was promoted to supervisor of two units after three months. In the following months I was given the entire Maryland area to supervise (five units). A new type of concept was developed, and I was picked to bring it into a profitable operation. At that point the larger volume (Philadelphia) units were given to me to supervise. At my request, I was moved to the New York area as supervisor in July 1973. Since that time I have opened three large volume units for the chain, both in New York and in Pennsylvania. All of the six units now under my supervision gross $1 to $1.5 million per year.

This very successful man needed much prodding before supplying additional information vital to his case. In the final résumé below the portions with data initially not disclosed are underlined. Prod yourself for the type of detail that, as just demonstrated, can turn a poor résumé into an effective one. What did you see that needed to be done? In this case the corporation was in need of profitability. What did you do about it? In this case the man created better cost concepts. What happened as a result? In this case the units became profitable.

1972–present (name of company)

AREA SUPERVISOR for a rapidly growing, limited menu, full service, $30 million AMEX-listed restaurant chain with 30 locations; earlier single unit manager. Responsible for New York and Pennsylvania area supervising six $1 to $1½ million units each with a staff of 60 to 90 people.

— Indoctrinated company with new cost concepts which have contributed significantly to rapid growth from nine units in 1971 to 30 units currently.
— Reduced food cost from 40% to 35%.
— Opened three large volume units: hired, trained complete staffs, installed systems.
— Accustomed to exercising controls through analysis of computer printouts daily on food, liquor, payroll. Trained managers in use of cost analyses.

Earlier managed failing unit; turned it from loss to profit in four weeks by exercise of proper controls, by establishing incentive system, and by gaining cooperation of employees. Personally contributed to success of 15 of existing 30 units and set standards for entire operation.

In our second example of how *not* to answer the analytical questionnaire the subject took a shortcut. The result again was the omission of vital information.

1. John Abrams, 367 Pasadena Ave., Pasadena, Calif. Home (123) 456-7890. Office (321) 654-0987.
2. Sales manager.
3. a. Style of line.
   b. In charge of all shipping.
   c. Distribution of goods to the factory—what goes into work at the machines.
   d. Production.
4. 36—married—3 children—own home and car.
5. U.S. Naval Reserve 1956–1964—2 years active—6 years reserve.
6. High school graduate—4 years—with some college.
7. Academic.
8. Worked in speciality shop—worked in bowling alley. Sports—bowling, football, baseball, horseback riding.
9. Horseback riding, photography.
10. Seventeen years in the employ of Toni Co., 1958–1975.
11. a. Sales manager.
    b. 1958–1975.
    b. 1958–1975.
    c. $45 week to $560 week.
    d. Sales department.
    e. Ladies' ready-to-wear.
    f. 35 employees—$4,500,000.00.
    g. President.
    h. Supervised up to 10 employees.

   i. Salesmen, shipping clerks, production workers.

   j. Sewing machines, cutting machines, taping machines.

   k. Making sure all machines were running in proper order. Responsible for putting them in proper order if not working. Selling, getting orders by phone out of town. Getting merchandise from the factory in time to ship goods. Getting piece goods in on time as per delivery order. Consistently, I had to be after these people to get the goods I needed to run the business in a proper manner.

   l. In the 17 years I was with the company, I worked up from delivery boy to sales manager. The achievement of being able to book $1.0 to $1.21 million a year.

The man omitted the following important information:

1. Business increased from $2 million to $3.5 million during his tenure.
2. The business was discontinued because of the owners' retirement.
3. The company had a sales showroom in conjunction with the factory, where he accomplished a lot of selling to out-of-town buyers.
4. He was in charge of purchasing, inventory control, and sales forecasting and was production manager in addition to being sales manager.
5. He supervised seven salesmen operating nationally and reported to the president.
6. His association with buyers was such that he could book large orders by telephone.
7. He was an excellent salesman himself, in addition to successfully managing a sales organization.
8. He personally sold to most of the major Los Angeles and other West Coast department stores and was responsible for getting business from such national accounts as Sears, Ward, and Penney.

The final résumé, with all information included, follows.

REVISED RÉSUMÉ OF JOHN ABRAMS

367 Pasadena Avenue
Pasadena, Calif. 12345

Home (123) 456-7890
Office (321) 654-0987

R E S U M E

of

<u>JOHN ABRAMS</u>

<u>SALES MANAGER-APPAREL</u>

* * *   Seventeen years experience in apparel field with one company, for last ten years as Sales Manager responsible for increasing multi-million dollar business by 75%. Owners retired and business was terminated.

* * *   Close associations with leading Buyers of women's dresses and pants suits all over the U. S.; experienced in selling to department and specialty stores, chains, giant national retailers and in maintaining productive contacts with major buying offices.

* * *   Effective trainer and leader accustomed to managing national sales organization. Management versatility led to expanded responsibilities including production, purchasing, shipping and assistance in styling and pricing in addition to marketing.

* * *   Excellent personal salesman with ability to get and retain customer loyalty and write business either by personal calls or by telephone with hundreds of leading buyers across the nation.

* * *   Capable of bringing additional volume and profit to any Women's Wear Manufacturer.

<u>FOR FURTHER DATA PLEASE SEE FOLLOWING PAGE</u>

JOHN ABRAMS   PAGE 2

BUSINESS EXPERIENCE:

1958-1975   TONI COMPANY, 3015 Wilshire Blvd., Los Angeles, Calif.

SALES MANAGER for $4.5 million manufacturer of Women's Apparel with show-room and factory at above address; sold nationally to department and specialty stores, chains and such giant retailers as Sears, Ward and Penney. Supervised seven salesmen and Production Manager. Reported to President. Owners decided to retire and business was terminated.

Responsible for:

- developing increased sales through leadership and training of seven sales-men and personal selling.

- sales forecasting, inventory control, purchase of piece goods and trimmings.

- aiding in pricing and styling.

- expediting production as necessary to achieve prompt shipments.

Accomplishments:

- rose from delivery boy to Sales Manager with earnings increases to 12 times starting salary.

- increased volume 87%; opened scores of new customers; developed existing customers.

- personally accounted for sales of $1.0 million to $1.25 million annually to leading accounts across the country.

- improved turnover by rigid inventory controls.

- curtailed price increases by creative piece goods purchasing.

MILITARY SERVICE: 1956-1964, U. S. NAVAL RESERVE. Two years active duty; Airman 3rd Class.

EDUCATION: Three years at University of California at Los Angeles.

EXTRA-CURRICULAR ACTIVITIES:

                  Worked while attending high school and college; participated in football, lacrosse, bowling, riding.

HOBBIES: Riding, photography.

PERSONAL DATA: Age 36, divorced, three children.

                  REFERENCES AND FURTHER DATA ON REQUEST

TYPING THE RÉSUMÉ

Start the summary page approximately 1 inch from the top of the page, typing your home address at the left margin. Your home (and business) telephone number is typed on the same line at the right margin. Margins should be at least ½ inch wide.

The word "RÉSUMÉ" typed in uppercase letters is centered 5 or 6 lines below the last line of the address. Double space and write the word "of" in lowercase letters (centered). Double space and center the name in uppercase letters. Double space again and center in uppercase letters the position title or objective.

Triple space and type a dividing double line to separate the heading from the body of the summary page.

Triple space and indent each paragraph, setting it off with triple asterisks.

Center paragraphs on the page, with triple spacing separating single spaced paragraphs.

Leave three or more spaces (depending on the position on the page of the last paragraph) before centering the phrase (in uppercase letters) "FOR FURTHER DATA, PLEASE SEE FOLLOWING PAGES."

For the résumé itself allow 1 inch from the top of the page, before typing your name in uppercase letters at the left margin. The page number, indicated by an uppercase PAGE and an arabic numeral, is placed on the same line at the right margin.

Triple space before the first category, "EXPERIENCE." Each category is typed in uppercase letters.

Double space and type date of employment of last job at left margin. Company name and address are typed in uppercase letters on the same line at approximately the center of the page.

Double space and start the job description, with the job titles in uppercase letters. The body is single spaced with double spacing between paragraphs and categories.

After the last category and description, triple space and center the phrase, "REFERENCES AND FURTHER DATA ON REQUEST," in uppercase letters.

Choice of margins, positioning of headlines, paragraphing, use of dashes and asterisks, and spacing are largely aesthetic matters.

THE COVERING LETTER

Your résumé, when mailed, should be accompanied by a covering letter. It should be dated. The covering letter is a way of introducing yourself, saying what you want, and asking for an answer. Keep it brief, quickly leading to that all important document—your résumé.

It is approprirate to write a special covering letter for any résumé being sent to someone you know or with respect to a job about which you have some knowledge. You can adjust a covering letter to fit a particular person or job while a résumé cannot be that frequently revised. Address such a special letter to a specific person, with the proper title, address, and salutation.

For a general mailing a general letter is suitable. Though it is always better to address a letter to a specific person, the salutation ''Dear Sir'' or ''Gentlemen'' is acceptable in a general letter. Filling in a name might be impossible in a printed letter because of the difficulty of matching typefaces.

Your covering letter identifies you:

After 14 years as sales manager of a major company in the lighting industry during which time I was instrumental in increasing sales 27%, I am now qualified for full marketing responsibilities in or outside this industry. My résumé discloses the nature and depth of my experience.

It asks for an interview:

I would like to discuss with you how I can be productive for your company while at the same time creating a satisfactory career for myself.

It requests an answer:

I look forward to your reply.

Sincerely,

John Smith

A covering letter may also serve as a summary of qualifications if they do not appear in the résumé. We suggest, however, that the covering letter be kept informal and brief, letting the résumé convey your message.

Type the covering letter on a sheet of 8½ by 11 inches, or 7 by 10 inches if the letter is short. Name and address, appearing at the top, can be engraved, in raised letters, printed, or typed. Engraved or printed stationery is preferred, but not essential if you are short on money or time (getting stationery printed can take several weeks).

A résumé that is weak because one's accomplishments cannot be suitably expressed, can be strengthened by a covering letter describing latent abilities, aspirations, and personal qualities that have no place in the résumé itself but might help to obtain an interview.

Unsolicited letters should be addressed to the most appropriate individual within a company (see p. 157 for a list of sources):

1. In a small company it is usually the president or owner who makes or approves all employment decisions.
2. In a larger company send middle management inquiries to the executive in charge of your departmental area (sales, finance, production) or to the personnel director.
3. For a position at the entry level in a medium size or large company address your letter to the personnel director.
4. If you know someone in the company you are approaching, send your letter to that person.
5. If you are an upper level executive with unusual qualifications use a broadcast letter instead of a résumé with covering letter and address it to the top executive or one of the top executives by name.
6. At the clerical level send your letter to the attention of the personnel department.
7. If your case is unusual (you are changing careers, for example) or if you have special credentials (education, background, military career) that you think would be of interest to a top executive, send the covering letter and résumé to him or her. Your letter will be routed to the proper department head.
8. If you are interested in working in a particular department, send your covering letter and résumé to the head of that department, rather than the personnel department.

When addressing a corporation, use the salutations "Dear Sir" or "Gentlemen." When addressing an individual, use his or her name and title, as shown below. Information about unusual forms of address can be found in most dictionaries.

Mr. John Smith, President
Roland Smith Co., Inc.
1 Bridge Street
Cohama, Nevada

Dear Mr. Smith:　　　[or]　　　Dear Sir:

Roland Smith Co., Inc.
1 Bridge Street
Cohama, Nevada

Gentlemen:　　　[or]　　　Attn: Mr. John Smith

Mrs. John Smith, President
Roland Smith Co., Inc.
1 Bridge Street
Cohama, Nevada

Dear Mrs. Smith: [or] Dear Madam:

Ms. Eleanor Smith, President
Roland Smith Co., Inc.
1 Bridge Street
Cohama, Nevada

Dear Ms. Smith:

In typing your covering letter, place the date three lines below the last line of the letterhead (the heading containing your name and address), slightly to the right of the center of the page.

Start the address four or five lines (or more if the letter is short) below the date, at the extreme left margin.

Salutation starts on the third line after the address.

Double space before typing the body of the letter. The letter text is single spaced, with double spacing between paragraphs. When completed, the body of the letter should be centered on the page, with all margins being equal.

Double space between the body of the letter and the complimentary close. The complimentary close should be aligned with the date.

The name (aligned with the complimentary close) is typed five spaces below, allowing sufficient room for the signature.

Reference initials of the writer are indicated on the same line as the typed signature at the extreme left margin, typed in uppercase letters.

Examples and a layout of a covering letter appear below. The first letter is typed with a *block margin,* that is, without indentations. *Indented* margin means that the first line of each paragraph is indented.

Dear Sir:

My work as Controller for a $20 million division of a "Fortune 500" company has resulted in profit contributions through innovative planning and cost savings amounting to hundreds of thousands of dollars annually.

I am thoroughly grounded in accounting, finance and economics.

My resume is enclosed.

I can provide effective management for a growing company in need of creative financial leadership.

May I discuss employment possibilities personally?

Your reply will be appreciated.

Sincerely,

Dear Sir:

I am the Sales Manager of a $30 million corporation in the durable goods field. I have been responsible for doubling our company's share of market in a period of five years.

My resume is enclosed.

I am qualified for full marketing responsibilities as a personal interview will help to disclose.

Your company is one for which my abilities would be of special value. May I talk with you about possible mutual interests?

I look forward to your reply.

Sincerely,

THOMAS JEFFERSON, IV
Monticello, Va. 10000

July 21, 1975

Dear Sir:

I have just graduated from the University of Maine with a B. S. in Architectural Engineering and some practical experience in remodeling university buildings and in some small new construction.

I hope to become associated with a Boston architectural firm.

My resume is enclosed.

May I have an appointment with you to discuss my qualifications?

I look forward to your reply.

Sincerely,

TJ

Thomas Jefferson, IV
(123) 456-7890

THE BROADCAST LETTER

The broadcast letter is a special type of employment application letter that is widely circulated to top company executives, rather than the personnel department. Its role derives from the fact that more than 80% of available jobs are never advertised and must be tracked down by mail.

When using the broadcast technique, whether for résumés or for letters, you judge the effectiveness of your mailing by the percentage of response, as would be the case with any mail order product. A response (inviting you to an interview) of 2% is fair; 15% is excellent.

Broadcasting is one of the quickest and most effective ways of finding a position. Send out at least 100 and preferably as many as 500 broadcast letters. The broadcast letter is used in such cases as the following:

1. Your career level makes it appropriate to bypass the personnel department.
2. Your talents and experience may have special appeal to a company executive.
3. Your special abilities may cause an executive to employ you now for a position that will actually become available only later.
4. Your qualifications might exactly meet the requirements for a position that the company has been unsuccessfully trying to fill for some time.
5. Your unusual qualifications may be particularly appreciated by a particular executive.
6. You might be well and favorably known at the top executive level of many companies.
7. Your qualifications might lead to an executive reorganization, making a place for you that did not exist until your letter acted as the catalyst to initiate such action.
8. Many top executives, including chief executive officers, like to be made aware of the availability of certain kinds of people.
9. Recruiting an executive by way of a broadcast letter can save a company thousands of dollars in search fees.

The use of a résumé in such cases would nullify your objective—résumés are almost automatically routed to personnel departments. Your broadcast letter might lead to requests for your résumé, which, sent at this point, serves the positive function of satisfying the company's affirmative interest in you.

By using the broadcast letter approach you are not depreciating the personnel department. Many personnel departments do not handle the employment of personnel at higher levels where the subtleties of character and required expertise are difficult to gauge. Employment ideas, amorphous at first, often may be formed only after an interview. Many corporations do not even list employment directors by name in the standard directories.

Fit your broadcast letter on one page. It is really a summary of a summary. It is easier to write this letter if you have a good résumé from which to extract the information.

Start the letter by identifying yourself and your field of specialization:

I have 15 years of successful, progressive experience in marketing management in the pharmaceutical and health care fields with a $100 million company.

State your objective:

I want to become associated with a medium size company or a division of a large company in the Southwest or Midwest where I will have complete marketing responsibility and opportunity for growth to general management.

List some of your accomplishments:

In six years I increased regional sales of pharmaceutical and health care products from $9 million to more than $30 million while maintaining or improving profitability.

Recruited, trained, and led a sales force of 60 salesmen, 3 field assistants and 7 district managers.

Three of the 7 district managers under my leadership were awarded "Manager of the Year" recognition.

Indicate special qualities:

I have been a successful salesman. I have trained scores of salesmen and managers to sell and manage effectively. I am innovative, motivated, and dedicated and possess the quality of leadership to a degree that has made my region first among all company regions in four of the last seven years. I am experienced in budgeting, forecasting, advertising, promotion, and compensation administration.

Give favorable statistics:

M.B.A.; B.A. in marketing; age 35; married.

Ask for an answer:

I would like a personal interview to discuss my potential for contributing to your company and opportunities for me to grow within your company. I look forward to your reply.

Examples of broadcast letters follow.

EXAMPLE OF A BROADCAST LETTER

350 Riverside Drive   Home (212) 123-4567
New York, N. Y. 10075   Office (212) 321-1000

John D. Oyler

Gentlemen:

I have had twenty years of experience with large international oil companies in
the following areas:

- estimating exploration and drilling costs.

- organizing equipment, people and materials for new exploration and drilling and forecasting capital needs.

- budgeting operations and projecting cash flow; monitoring progress.

- evaluating drilling results; changing procedures if needed.

- controlling wild wells.

- presenting programs to prospective investors.

During this period I have made profit contributions running to millions of dollars
resulting from correct equipment selection, cost economics, risk/reward calculations,
recruiting and training, contractor supervision and onsite controls.

My experience has been worldwide from drilling rig operator to managing engineer.

I have been responsible for budgets up to $600,000 per day.

I have a reputation for innovation, sound planning, safety, harmony in working relationships at all levels and with foreign governments; accurate hydrocarbon assess-
ments.

The experience related has been with Gulf and Mobile.

My education consists of the following:

M.E.A., Engineering Administration, Cornell University, Ithaca, N. Y., 1960.

B.S., School of Mines, Oklahoma City, Okla., 1955.

Additional graduate work in Automation and Electrified Lease Operations and
in Computer Systems.

Age 42, married, three children, excellent health. Willing to relocate.

References and further data are available upon request.
May I discuss employment with you?

Very truly yours,

EXAMPLE OF A BROADCAST LETTER

(000) 123-4567

Thomas Watson
90 Numbers Way
Easton, Pennsylvania 00000

Dear Sir:

With ten years of progressive experience in data processing, currently department manager, I am qualified for similar responsibilities in a larger company.

My experience includes systems planning, systems analysis and programing. For the last five years I have supervised a staff of 20 in preparing a management information system that has given management new and more timely data leading to substantial growth and improved efficiency. Experience includes NCR 390 and IBM advanced third generation equipment.

Some accomplishments include:

- epitomization of massive reports to a brief document providing top management with all data in a relatively few pages: total profit, profit by division, sales, inventory finished and in process, forecast, accounts receivable, accounts payable, all compared with five preceding years.

- reduction of payment time from 60 days to 15 days through more rapid invoicing.

- production control records that have helped reduce inventories by more than $1 million annually with a goal of $2 million now in reach.

- analysis of sales by customer by product leading to new corporate objectives.

I have been given a series of problems to solve, by management, and commended for providing expeditious answers while reducing machine time by 20%.

My education includes M.B.A. in Computer Science from New York University School of Business Administration and a B. S. in Business Administration from Dartmouth's Tuck School.

My age is 32, I am married, we have three children. I am in excellent health. Relocation would present no problem.

If you have a suitable opening with opportunity for general management I would appreciate an interview.

Sincerely,

EXAMPLE OF A BROADCAST LETTER

MARKETING EXECUTIVE

Gentlemen:

With 15 years of successful experience in marketing management for major companies, involving power tools, and a record of consistent progress from salesman to manager of a $30 million region, I am a qualified marketing executive.

Among my accomplishments:

- over a period of six years increased regional sales from $9 million to nearly $30 million while staying well within profitability guidelines.
- recruited, trained and led a sales force of 60 salesmen with two field assistants and seven district managers.
- of seven district managers under my leadership, two ranked first and second nationally with the first awarded recognition as "Manager of the Year".
- planned effective promotions and advertising on the way to achieving the sales increase described.
- successfully promoted 25 of my salesmen into corporate positions in various areas: Product Planning, Marketing, Regional and District Management.
- upon assignment to important Atlanta District, brought it from fifth to first place in sales and earnings and won "Manager of the Year" award.
- earlier developed district which ranked last in sales to fourth position nationally.
- as salesman, was routinely among top salesmen in the U. S., winning sales contests and earning numerous awards.

I am an effective innovator, sales leader and trainer, with a solid background in modern management techniques and concepts, banking and finance. B. S., Business Administration, age 40, married, two children, own home, excellent health.

I seek a position as Director of Marketing or General Sales Manager for a medium-size corporation in the tool industry.

If my qualifications are of interest to you, I would like an opportunity for a personal meeting.

Sincerely,

REWRITING AND RESUBMITTING
THE RÉSUMÉ

Résumés, covering letters, and broadcast letters are sensitive writings. The change of a word, a sentence, or a paragraph, a different order of presentation—all influence their effectiveness. If your writing has not elicited positive responses, review and *improve* your presentation material. Edit it several times until you seem to have just the right method of expressing yourself for maximum response. Advertising agencies test copy in the marketplace to find out what themes and presentations bring the greatest attention and readership. You may have to do the same with your writing. There are thousands of cases in which slight changes have converted unsuccessful résumés or letters into winners.

You may send a rewritten résumé to the same companies that received your original one without fear of having worn out your welcome. Many individuals have had the experience of obtaining no response from their first mailing, but receiving many requests to come for interviews from subsequent résumés.

STEP TWO: USING YOUR RÉSUMÉ

Once you have your résumé in hand, you are ready to use it to gain interviews. This chapter discusses what you should do with your résumé—whether you should pass it on in person or send it by mail, when to substitute a broadcast letter for a résumé, and so on. Sources of jobs are described, and suggestions given for evaluating your job competition and following up on résumé mailings.

The basic rule to follow in searching for a job is to present yourself, personally or by way of a résumé, to as many persons as possible. Among them would be the following:

- **Friends.** "I'm looking for a position. I have written up my qualifications. Here is a copy. Do you know anyone who would have an opening for someone with my qualifications? Do you ever hear of any openings? Can I give you additional copies for distribution? Can you give me any advice?"
- **Acquaintances.** Use an approach similar to that used when speaking or writing to friends.
- **A vice-president or the president of your bank.** Explain who you are and what you want. Describe your qualifications. Conduct a practice interview. Ask for advice. Request the names of others with whom you might have a constructive conversation, ask for a letter of introduction, and follow up the leads given. Leave copies of your résumé for distribution if it seems appropriate.
- **A partner in a large accounting firm.** If you have access to such a person, make use of it. Many large accounting firms act as employment intermediaries between their clients and job applicants.
- **Executive search firms.** If you are in middle or upper management, send your résumé to executive search firms; a personal visit is usually not worthwhile. They will get in touch with you if they have assignments that relate to

your qualifications. There are several hundred executive search firms in the United States and overseas, though you need not write to all of them. See Appendix C for a list of selected executive search firms and for other sources of such lists.

- **Consulting firms.** Such consulting companies as McKinsey and Co. and Booz, Allen and Hamilton also do recruiting. Send your résumé to a few of the largest consulting firms.

- **Competitors.** Your company's competitors may find your expertise useful. Confidentiality must be assured if you are still employed—an employer will not appreciate an employee applying for a job with a competing firm.

- **Trade associations.** Directors or executive secretaries of trade associations often get inquiries from members about the availability of certain types of job seekers. Associations can thus serve as clearinghouses for setting up interviews between potential employers and job candidates. They are usually well informed about their members' businesses. Send your résumé to the appropriate trade association.

- **Trade magazines.** If you know the publishers, editors, or other important staff members of trade magazines, send them your résumé. Ask for assistance in getting placed. Ask for names of people you might meet, and follow up such leads.

- **Employment agencies.** For all positions except at the middle and upper management levels present yourself at several employment agencies. Agencies often need 6 to 12 copies of your résumé for further distribution.

- **Help wanted advertising.** Follow carefully the display and classified help wanted advertisements in your leading local newspapers. The *New York Times* (the Business and Financial Section and the Education section in the Sunday edition) and the *Wall Street Journal* (Tuesday edition) are in a sense the "bibles" of employment sources for middle and upper management executives. The *New York Times* classified help wanted section carries hundreds of advertisements on Sunday but usually for lower level jobs. Scan both newspapers daily. Send your résumé to all appropriate advertisers if requested. Remember that in advertising, employers frequently idealize or exaggerate the qualities they require of an applicant. If the advertisement is within your general competence, answer it. Note, too, that you can, if necessary, reply to an advertisement even as long as two weeks after its appearance. Most employment decisions take many weeks or even months, and employers expect to receive replies for several weeks after advertising.

- **College employment services.** Do not overlook the possibility of getting help from your alma mater. Most colleges and universities have a placement service.

- **Newspaper reports of personnel changes.** Such newspapers as the *New York Times* and the *Wall Street Journal* daily show personnel changes in large corporations. Changes create openings. Corporations making changes are good targets for your letters.

Some older executives make a hobby of helping younger people find positions. They listen for opportunities, passing the information on when requested. Seek among your friends and acquaintances for such people.

EMPLOYMENT AGENCIES

Employment agencies solicit information about job openings from employers and act as an agent between employer and employee. The agency charges a fee for successfully filling a job opening—a week's salary, a month's salary, or more. In some cases the agency fee will come out of your pocket. Or your employer may pay the fee, depending on company policies. In most states employment agencies operate under state licenses.

Since they depend on a large turnover, employment agencies handle mostly lower level positions. Study the advertisements in your local newspaper to find out what kinds of positions are available at what salary levels. Do not list yourself with more than three or four appropriate agencies. You become undesirable from an agency and from an employer point-of-view if you let yourself be "multiple listed," for many agencies have the same job listings. An employment agency will want your résumé. Your discussion with an interviewer should be limited to about 30 minutes. Second and third interviews will probably be a waste of time, unless the agency requests a return visit. If you are looking for a position paying above $25,000 or $30,000 a year, generally avoid employment agencies.

EXECUTIVE SEARCH FIRMS

Executive search firms are retained by employers to "search for" qualified executives for middle and top management positions. Most executive search firms handle positions in all classifications. Some specialize—in finance or retailing, for example. The fee, which can be up to 30% of annual salary, is paid by the employer. An executive search firm or "headhunter" will be useful to you only if it has a search in progress for a person like you at the time your résumé arrives. Repeat your mailings to these firms every couple of months, because their assignments change continuously and they may not retain your original résumé on file. Make an appointment with a "headhunter" executive after he has received your résumé.

Executive search firms are a valuable source of jobs. They prefer to "find" an employed executive rather than one who is unemployed. Before selecting you for client interviewing, they will have you undergo in-depth screening.

Some accounting firms and management consultants also engage in recruiting for clients (see Appendix C).

ADVERTISING SPACE SALESMEN

Publisher's representatives for trade and consumer magazines sometimes know of available jobs. Their association with company managements is often close. One representative kept a file both of individuals available for employment and of companies seeking new employees, not only in advertising or sales, but other areas as well. If your present or past employer is or was served by a publisher's representative, make his acquaintance and talk with him.

Some publishers of business newsletters also act as informal job brokers.

HELP WANTED ADVERTISEMENTS

Many of the help wanted advertisements are "blind"—they do not provide the name of the company that has the job opening. This is usually done to avoid unwanted follow-ups by eager but sometimes unqualified candidates.

In some instances you may be able to identify the company, such as that describing itself as "a leisure products company in Northern New Jersey"—a business directory will disclose that only a few such companies exist in this area. You are one step ahead if you can write directly to a company, avoiding the grouping of your résumé or letter with the scores or hundreds of others received in answer to the advertisement.

BROADCASTING YOUR RÉSUMÉ

Next to personal contacts the most effective technique for finding a position quickly is a mail campaign. It has been well documented that *at least* 80% of the positions available at any given time are never advertised. To publicize your availability, send your résumé, or a substitute such as a broadcast letter, to as many employers as you can.

In a mail campaign you, in fact, make yourself a mail-order product, hoping that some percentage of the companies receiving your résumé will have an opening that fits your qualifications at the time of receiving your material. Responses suggesting an interview will range as widely as 2 to 15% of your total mailing. The average response under normal employment conditions is 6 to 8%; it is lower during recessions. Make your mailing as large as possible, therefore, so as to increase the potential number of affirmative responses. Some replies—from unsuitable geographical areas, from unsuitable companies (after investigation), or for unsuitable positions (for which you are overqualified or underqualified)—will be of no use to you. Give yourself the maximum opportunity to have a choice of possible employers as well as a choice of jobs and responsibilities.

Because of their nature, such campaign mailings to the same companies can sometimes be effectively repeated.

USING LISTS

To conduct a job search campaign by mail you will need to refer to directories and lists of various kinds to develop your personal mailing list. Your list should be tailored as closely as possible to the kinds of companies, geographical areas, and other characteristics that reflect your personal needs or preferences.

The names and addresses of corporations and organizations and the names of their personnel can be obtained from the following sources found in most libraries:

1. Dun and Bradstreet *Reference Book of Corporate Management*.
2. *Telephone directory Yellow Pages* (company and organization names and addresses only).
3. Standard and Poor's *Register of Corporations, Directors, and Executives*.
4. State industrial directories.
5. Industry associations (almost all major industry classifications have one).
6. Thomas' *Register of American Manufacturers*.
7. *Martindale-Hubbell Law Directory*.
8. *Moody's Handbook of Common Stocks*.
9. *The Value Line Investment Survey* (published by Arnold Bernhard & Co., Inc.).
10. *Rand McNally Bankers International Directory*.
11. *Fortune*'s annual supplement listing the 1000 largest corporations (no individual executive names) and other listings.
12. Forbes annual list of 2500 corporations (no individual executive names).
13. *Hardware Age Directory* (published by Chilton Co., Radnor, Pa.).
14. *Pharmaceutical Handbook*.
15. *The Standard Advertising Register*.
16. American Management Association publications (such as Executive Search Firms).
17. *The Literary Marketplace*.

18. *MacRae's Blue Book.*
19. *Standard Rate and Data Service.*
20. *United States Government Organizational Manual.*
21. Trade magazines.
22. *Directory of Foundations in Massachusetts.*
23. *College Placement Annuals.*
24. Association of Consulting Management Engineers (New York City).
25. *The Wall Street Journal* daily list of corporate operating reports.

Standard and Poor's Register of Corporations, Directors, and Executives contains an alphabetical listing of the names of about 35,000 corporations, 300,000 officers, directors, and principals, and 70,000 officers, directors, trustees, and partners. *Fortune* magazine annually lists the 1000 largest industrial corporations as well as the largest financial institutions and the largest overseas corporations. *Stores,* a National Retail Merchants Association publication, annually lists, by volume, the leading department stores. *Forbes Magazine* has an annual listing of 2500 major companies.

If you prepare your own list of companies to write to, make use of the S.I.C. (Standard Industrial Classification) numbers to identify a company's business. Many companies have multiple S.I.C. numbers. The first two digits of the four-digit S.I.C. number show the major industrial group to which a company belongs:

> 01 to 09 Agriculture, forestry, fishing
> 10 to 14 Mining
> 15 to 17 Construction
> 20 to 39 Manufacturing
> 40 to 49 Transportation, communications, utilities
> 50 to 59 Wholesale and retail
> 60 to 68 Finance, insurance, real estate

The last two digits classify each company more closely; for example, 3172 and 3199 refer to leather goods and 2844 to cosmetics. A cross-reference to the main body of the register (Standard and Poor's for example) will then give you the address and size of the company and names of executives. Many fine companies are unexpectedly missing, as are some divisions resulting from mergers. Most lists, as distinguished from directories, do not include location, area code, names of executives, and products. Creating your own list is an arduous and time-consuming task, but the result is invaluable. You may also purchase lists containing the information you need from specialist list companies and other sources such as some of the better résumé writing/career guidance companies.

The executives of the 500 or 1000 largest companies are bombarded with résumés. You might find it worthwhile to address your mailings to smaller, equally fine and growing companies.

The *Yellow Pages* is another good source of local company names, but does not provide names of executives and area codes.

In using lists and "broadcasting" your availability you take the best, quickest, and surest route to employment, other than knowing someone who can place you or having some other "inside track" to a position. Note the following in mailing your material:

- Address your letter or résumé to a specific individual by including the name on the envelope.
- If possible, include the individual's name on the letter as well, though this is not mandatory.
- If you are an upper middle or top level executive or administrator, send a broadcast letter to one of the top executives or to the chief executive officer (by name).
- If you are a lower middle executive earning, say, $25,000 or less a year, send a covering letter and your résumé to the personnel director (by name if possible).
- Make your initial mailing to 200 or 300 companies, or more if possible, in order to obtain a satisfactory number of useful responses.

CHOOSING AMONG COMPANIES

In choosing companies to which to apply for employment, you must consider for which type of company you prefer to work and are best qualified to work.

One factor is company size, which can range from small $1 million to $2 million to very large multibillion dollar concerns. Some large companies are conglomerates, containing many surprisingly small units. Some small businesses are highly profitable, and many are the giants of tomorrow, taking advantage of the continuously emerging new areas of technology.

Large single product companies are apt to be highly structured, with formal channeling (job descriptions) for all functions (some small companies seek to copy the structure). The units of large multidivision companies that allow operational autonomy within their divisions, however, can run the full gamut of management philosophies.

Small companies generally tend to be less rigidly structured, allowing greater participation in more areas. Smaller companies are also more subject to the vicissitudes of the marketplace. Single product companies can be eliminated almost overnight by technological changes. Companies in trouble need better management. You might be able to supply it. There are stories about such companies in the newspapers each day. Many small companies pay salaries that are as great as or greater than those of large companies. Too, smaller companies receive many fewer résumés, so that your résumé is much more likely to be noticed.

All in all, fast-growing smaller companies are among the best targets for employment. Many of the large corporations prefer to promote from within and their major recruiting is at entry levels. If you are at or near the entry level, major corporations are your primary source of employment. The smaller companies, however, do not have a reservoir and *must* hire from outside at *all levels*.

To identify rapidly growing companies watch the quarterly and annual reports in such major newspapers as the *New York Times* and the *Wall Street Journal,* which usually compare current and previous periods. Refer also to the *Business Periodical Index* under "Growth Companies." Magazines like *Forbes, Fortune,* and *Business Week* contain quarterly listings and other regular information.

In choosing among companies, consider also their business philosophies and practices to the extent that you can do so. Some companies are highly promotional and base their continuing progress on "gimmicks." Others are slow and solid, looking toward a small but measured growth each year.

Advertising agency executives often work under great pressure, as do airport flight managers. Retail store hours are long. The brokerage business is a bad one to be in during a recession. Banks have good vacation schedules, but poor pay except at top levels. Some companies and managements are unethical. Some have a reputation for rapid employee turnover. Some are productivity oriented, while others are less demanding.

Consider the conditions under which you do your best work. Working for a company whose policies are basically incompatible with your temperament or principles will not only make you unhappy, but probably ineffective.

Keep in mind, too, that some corporations and institutions unfortunately operate under ethnic or religious restrictions, employing only Jewish, or only Catholic, or only Protestant employees in all except clerical positions. If you are disqualified by a restriction of this type, avoid approaching such companies. On the other hand, if you are qualified, make such companies prime targets in your job search.

In searching for a new job, you need not necessarily confine yourself to your own experience. Generally an individual who was successful in one position can be productive in another; *experience* does make it easier and quicker to adapt to a new position in a similar area, however.

Retail department or chain store experience is difficult to apply in a totally different field. Retail store ownership does not particularly qualify one for other positions. One might, however, become a salesman for a supplier to similar stores; a hardware store proprietor might make a good hardware wholesaler's salesman or buyer.

Financial responsibilities at any level would be applicable to nearly any business. The financial specialist has a broad employer spectrum upon which to draw.

The salesman of intangibles might not be happy selling hard goods. The hard goods salesman might not like intangibles (insurance, stocks, funds, systems). A salesman is strongly related to the markets with which he is familiar, and most firms, hiring a senior salesman, will prefer to employ individuals with experience in their markets.

A production manager is usually best related to those companies that use similar manufacturing methods. Manufacturing is divided into different worlds by special technologies: capital equipment, electronics, small metal parts, plastics, automation, steelmaking.

The qualified generalist is fortunate in being able to fit in anywhere. *Experience* in a special area adds an extra dimension to these qualifications, however.

EVALUATING YOUR JOB COMPETITION

The job market is highly competitive. Scores or hundreds of individuals may compete for one position. For example, an attractive advertisement for a senior marketing executive in a Tuesday edition of the *Wall Street Journal* elicited the following response:

Number of answers	310
In the New York area	186
Outside the New York area	124
Résumés received	294
Letters receives	16
Applicants who are employed	257
Applicants who are unemployed	19
Not clear whether employed or unemployed	34
Salary stated	198
Salary not stated	112
Undergraduate degree	180
Master's degree	80
Doctoral degree	7
No degree	43

Obviously, your résumé, your covering letter, and your interview must be as perfect as you can possibly make them in order to stand out among those of other job applicants.

FOLLOW-UP TELEPHONE CALLS

If your résumé or broadcast letter has not brought a response within 10 days, telephone the person to whom you sent it (at least in the immediate area). Ask if your material has been received. Request an interview.

HANDLING INTERVIEW TRAVEL EXPENSES

When you receive an invitation to visit for an interview requiring expensive travel, expect that the company will reimburse you. In such a case, do not go to the interview if the company refuses to cover your expenses.

CHAPTER 6

PLOYS FOR EMPLOYMENT

Interviews can be obtained in many ways in addition to those already discussed. Some of these techniques have been the subjects of complete books or feature articles in major magazines. Again, a technique that has been successfully used by one person may not be effective for others. No single procedure can guarantee that you will attain your objective—a good job. You must walk on many avenues.

The ideas that follow are a miscellaneous collection of suggestions offered for your personal evaluation and selection. As you consider these ideas, you might think of others that fit your needs even better or you might modify and adapt them to your particular situation. Opinions about the usefulness of a procedure will differ. For example, one method that is sometimes suggested involves gaining an interview with a company's top executive on the pretense of writing a book or an article about the company. The idea is to explore problem areas, bone up on possible answers, and return later with suggestions and a simultaneous application for employment to provide the suggested remedies. Such an approach would be this writer's idea of how *not* to go about getting a job, but any ploy (no play on words intended) that works is good.

THE PERSONAL ODYSSEY

A method used to obtain employment is to draw an itinerary and drive from city to city, trying to gain personal interviews with preselected companies. Though successful for some, this approach obviously is time-consuming, expensive, and often frustrating.

An interesting report about one executive who used this method appears in *Fortune* (Anne Chamberlin, ''An Executive Odyssey: Looking for a Job at Fifty-five,'' *Fortune,* November 1974, p. 192).

"ADVICE" VISITS

Ask friends and acquaintances for letters of introduction to high level executives whom they know. Use the letters to introduce yourself. At the meeting describe your situation and ask for advice. Does the executive know of fast-growing companies where recruiting is active? What industries have the greatest potential for growth? What would the executive do when looking for a position? Ask him or her for letters of introduction and repeat the pattern. Conversations of this kind sometimes create a rapport, leading to employment by the "advisor's" company.

THE "HIGH-POWERED RIFLE" APPROACH

Tailor your presentation to a particular industry or company if you know it well or are sufficiently motivated to learn about it:

- Obtain a copy of the company's latest annual and IO K reports from a broker, the library, or the company (by mail). Study them carefully to develop ideas about your possible contribution to the company.
- If the company or its product is readily accessible, pay a visit. To learn about a consumer goods company, for example, visit some of the stores in which the products are sold. Note the packaging, display, breadth of line, quality, price, and competition. The store proprietor or a salesperson can tell you how well the products are selling and whether the company's policies are sound, its salesman is well-regarded, and the profit margin is suitable.
- Visit the area banks to ascertain, if possible, the financial industry's attitude toward a local company.
- If the company is a large one, look particularly for divisions that may not be contributing their proper share to corporate profits.
- Try to find a friend or acquaintance who knows someone who works for the company and arrange to talk with that person. Learn as much as you can about the company's policy, standing, growth, and employee attitudes; obtain the names of executives.
- Use the data you have thus obtained to write a presentation describing the contribution that you think you could make to the company.

RELOCATION

Do not place a handicap on your selection by your unwillingness to relocate. If getting a job is more important than geographical location, be willing to go anyplace where opportunity exists. There may be no job for you near your present home, while the perfect position may be available in Squedunk, U.S.A.

Keep an eye on population changes. Thus between April 1, 1970, and July 1, 1975, the population has been increasing faster than the national average of 4.8% in the South and the West, but slower than the national average in New York, New Jersey, Pennsylvania, Michigan, Ohio, and other industrialized northern states, with New York and Rhode Island actually losing population. The largest population increases occurred in the following states:

		Population gain*
Arizona	25.3%	449,000
Florida	23.0%	1,566,000
Nevada	21.1%	103,000
Alaska	16.3%	49,000
Idaho	14.9%	107,000
Colorado	14.7%	324,000
Utah	13.8%	147,000
New Mexico	12.7%	130,000
Wyoming	12.5%	42,000
Hawaii	12.3%	95,000
New Hampshire	10.9%	80,000
Arkansas	10.0%	193,000

Not all of the large percentage increases signify sufficiently larger populations, hence greater opportunities, but they do indicate trends. The following states show less significant changes in population:

		Population gain
Oregon	9.4%	196,000
Texas	9.3%	1,038,000
South Carolina	8.8%	227,000
Montana	7.7%	54,000
Georgia	7.4%	738,000
North Carolina	7.2%	365,000
Tennessee	6.7%	262,000
Maine	6.6%	61,000
California	6.1%	1,214,000

* All the data on population in this chapter are from U.S. Census Bureau, *Population Estimates and Projections,* Series P-25, No. 615, December 12, 1975.

The time to take advantage of shifts in population is at the beginning of your career. Upward changes in population usually mean increased business opportunities, higher land and property values, improving living conditions, and bigger incomes. Of course the *kind* of population is also important; Florida and Arizona may be attracting more older people, for example.

The population figures have the greatest impact when compared by sections:

		Population gain
Northeastern states	+0.8%	400,000
North central states	+1.9%	1,076,000
South	+8.4%	5,301,000
West	+8.7%	3,040,000

Note that Florida and California are showing decelerating growth. California's growth in the seventies, for example, is only one half of that in the sixties.

The population figures become very significant when projected for another five years, affecting the whole marketing approach of most corporations. In absolute terms these population increases mean the addition of major new cities to selected geographical areas.

SOME UNUSUAL APPROACHES

Just as the market for products is a segmented one, so is the market for people. There are so many places to which you can apply for work nationally that a different approach can be made to groups of potential employers. Consider the following:

- **Humor.** Although most people will be turned off by humor, a small percentage might be attracted by it. It is only necessary to get *one* response that turns out to be the one you want.
- **Frankness.** I am an ex-convict; I am 62 years old; I have lost all my money in the stock market and must continue to work; I am handicapped; my career has been unsuccessful to date for reasons that may be my own fault; I have special talents of use to a limited number of companies.
- **Aggressiveness.** You need me more than I need you (describe why); I know your business like the palm of my hand; I can create a new area of business for you.

These are not conventional approaches, but one of them might work with somebody. Try the conventional approaches first—and then try a few unconventional ones.

I know one employer who hired an executive because he sent a handwritten résumé. It would not work once in a hundred times, but it did succeed for this particular job seeker.

Try the unusual approach with some employers while pursing a more conservative course with others. The job market is very large!

UPPER MANAGEMENT JOB SEARCH

If you are searching for an upper or even upper middle level job in management, try to meet with the chief executive officer of the company, or another top officer.

You will need fortitude to withstand rebuffs or even to gird yourself to approach the chief executive officer, but persistence combined with a good presentation of your case will often succeed, provided that you have the qualifications.

Overcome any fear you might have in approaching an executive of high standing and authority—his or her position adds the additional dimension of symbol of office to the facts of accomplishment. Remind yourself that people are just people no matter what their rank they, too, are fearful, or nervous in new situations, or have problems and reactions much like yours. It is well to put things in perspective. Life is short. Rebuffs can have no serious effect on your career, whereas obtaining one or two meetings out of a hundred tries may change the whole course of your life for the better.

Approach the executive first by way of a broadcast letter and a telephone follow-up, if necessary; or appear personally without an appointment; or deliver your résumé after original contact; or make use of mutual friends and acquaintances. Push yourself into taking the first step and continue to push at each successive step as much as is necessary until you gain your objective. Be prepared for the interview when you finally obtain it.

WRITING

You might consider writing an article or series of articles about some aspect of your specialty and submitting it for publication in an associated trade magazine, or in other communication media.

Relevant publication will lend you authority and give credence to your claims to be able to make important contributions to some area of corporate profitability. Writing of this kind is hard work, requiring research to supplement your own knowledge. Select a subject and limit your writing strictly to it. Nor is it always easy to gain editorial acceptance for your writings, but the publicity attending publication can be invaluable in opening new doors to employment.

Topics about which to write abound. Write about a new method of marketing in your industry; the use of financial ratios to pinpoint superior management; new production techniques; display methods; packaging successes; the selection and use of an advertising agency; or better industry cooperation. These are all themes in which most executives are interested.

ADVERTISING

In general, advertising is not a very successful way of finding a job at the managerial level. There are exceptions, however. You might be the exception. Advertising one's availability *is* a method of finding a position.

Many interesting advertisements for positions wanted appear in newspapers around the country. You will find it worthwhile to see which ones interest you the most, which ones stand out. You might even ask the advertisers what success their advertisements produced; most will be glad to tell you.

Advertise in a trade magazine in your area of work. Potential employers usually read their advertisements more closely than those in newspapers.

One reason why advertising for positions has often not paid off is that it is overwhelmed by the mass of help wanted advertising. Also, executives, generally speaking, do not have time regularly to review employment wanted advertising. Weigh the cost of advertising against other methods:

- The cost of a display advertisement in the Business Section of the *New York Times* (*Sunday*) is $89.60 per inch.
- The cost of an advertisement in the Classified Section is $73.78 per inch.
- The cost of a display advertisement in the *Wall Street Journal* is $83.30 per inch.

Every major city has newspapers that feature business news, with some influence in the job market. The *New York Times* and the *Wall Street Journal* however, are "bibles" for employers seeking employees, and for employees seeking employers no matter where they live or want to work.

SUMMARY

To sum up, the word to describe your search for work is *exposure*. Your job search is of critical importance to you, and you need to use every device that might lend you assistance. We have tried to provide as many suggestions as possible. All have worked for some, but not all can be utilized by any one person. Some are more appropriate to one individual than to another. Some may have the advantage of getting results quickly, thus eliminating the need to run the gamut of all possible maneuvers.

In any event, make your job search a tour de force in which you use every weapon at your command. Your opponent may be more easily overcome than you expect.

STEP THREE: PREPARING FOR YOUR INTERVIEW

We hold the résumé to be an essential document at any job level—in both outlining your qualifications *and* preparing you for an interview. Your résumé should therefore be the best possible expression of your attributes. Base your oral presentation to a prospective employer on what your ré*sumé* says. Many of the world's best orators have learned their speeches by heart. Memorize your résumé. Learn to talk about yourself unhesitatingly, accenting your greatest talents.

Teach yourself to recall and discuss each sentence of your résumé. Have each sentence also serve as a topical reminder for additional exposition as necessary. Prepare for an interview as you would for a speech that *you will deliver without notes*. It should not be obvious that you have memorized your résumé—your statements should seem spontaneous. The structure of your résumé, if properly prepared, should serve to keep an interview within the framework of the areas in which you have the greatest experience and the most to offer. Discussing oneself fluently, unhesitatingly, and relevantly at a job interview is a skill that everybody can acquire, though some with less effort than others. The kind of preparation described here will, more than anything else you can do except interview practice, eliminate the nervousness that frequently spoils an interview.

The interviewer will expect you to describe what you have done and can do in the context of your work. For example, if you are applying for a position as field sales manager with a hardware manufacturer, you are expected to know the most important hardware wholesalers around the country and their buyers and executives, to be cognizant of the need to sell to dealer cooperatives as well as retail mass merchandisers for effective distribution, and to have budget experience.

As a production executive you would know, for example, how to process and finish forgings, stampings, and castings. You would know something about metallurgy, toolrooms, the various engineering disciplines and their responsibilities, time and piece work rates, labor relations, and perhaps purchasing.

A qualified financial executive would have thorough accounting preparation, knowledge about financial statements, pension and profit sharing expertise, perhaps investment experience, and almost certainly computer management skills.

Because what you are expected to know constitutes so important a part of what you will talk about, at an interview, we provide a list of selected job responsibilities in Appendix B. Review the job responsibilities about which you may be questioned and prepare yourself accordingly.

The lower your level in management the more detailed the knowledge you are required to show within your specialty. The higher your level the more you deal in ideas rather than in specifics.

PERSONALITY

Personality can greatly affect a job interview by creating, or not creating, a rapport between interviewer and candidate. A highly trained interviewer will screen out this factor because a seemingly favorable personality can hide ineptitude. Some individuals have become accomplished actors in their job search, obtaining new positions easily only to lose them when employers discover their lack of qualifications. If your interviewer attempts to irritate you to evoke an angry response, do not permit yourself to react. Act as if you do not recognize the interviewer's attempt. Stall, if necessary: "I am not sure I understand what you mean," "I don't think I have expressed myself properly," or "Let me review this subject"—anything to give you time to collect your thoughts and provide a calm, reasoned answer to diffuse and defuse the atmosphere. A question that is insulting, however, should be acknowledged by you—respond sharply, if you wish, but without losing composure.

Personality, of course, may be used to great advantage. If you have a personality to which other people respond with warmth and friendliness you have a great gift that should be used to its fullest.

Some people have obvious personality defects. Such defects can be corrected by competent psychologists. If *you* know someone with a serious personality defect, alert him or her about it, thus saving, or perhaps creating, a career. Some people elicit antagonism upon first meeting, so that familiarity, which might erase the first impression, never occurs.

One of the reasons for a bad first impression is lack of interview preparation. If you are troubled about interviews, getting training in interview techniques from a competent professional counselor might be among your best investments.

TYPES OF INTERVIEWER

Many interviewers are not good interviewers. Since expert and understanding discussions with a job applicant require a breadth of experience possessed by very few professional recruiters, higher level management positions are usually handled by upper level executives knowledgeable in the applicant's specialty. Such executives are not necessarily equally experienced in interviewing. Those who are most capable in *hiring,* as apart from interviewing, will put you at your ease as quickly as possible both for their and your benefit.

The lower levels of management have their share of small-minded people. Accept this as a fact of life. Keep in mind your abilities and qualifications, refusing to be disconcerted by the many types of interviewer you will meet when seeking employment. For example:

1. The interviewer may seemingly show no interest in you—briefly greets you, never smiles, says little, wants you to talk, listens without comment or expression, and permits no rapport. This may be an overexperienced interviewer who has listened to very many applicants, is a little bored, and may be jealous of the many newer employees who have passed by in the company hierarchy. This method of interviewing makes most interviewees nervous. They lose their poise and talk too much, often impulsively blurting out fatuous. Do not permit your interviewer the advantage of shattering your assurance. State the facts of your experience and accomplishments. When you have concluded, force the interviewer to ask for any further information needed by remaining silent. You are not trying to win a popularity contest, and you will gain greater respect by exercising restraint than by becoming flustered.

2. The interviewer may greet you, start talking—usually about the company or personal matters—and continue to talk for 30, 45, or 60 minutes, giving you no opportunity to discuss the purpose of the meeting.

    This interviewer is trying to know and understand you by osmosis. You may think that an hour-long interview places you in a favored position among the candidates—usually it does not. Let your interviewer talk at length, but be sure that you have presented your story before you leave.

3. The interviewer answers the telephone a dozen times during the interview with you. This is rude. You might reasonably conclude that such an individual feels insecure and is probably too low on the executive ladder to have calls held. Keep your equanimity. Tell your story even if parts of it must be repeated for the interviewer to obtain the complete picture. You can take notes on your progress while your interviewer is talking on the telephone.

4. The interviewer is very friendly, is very interested in you, and listens to you as if every word of yours were a pearl. Such an approach makes you expan-

sive, and you are soon revealing things about yourself that you ordinarily keep secret and that have no bearing on your job quest. This was the interviewer's intent. Few people can erect an adequate guard against this kind of seeming empathy, and reveal too much. Keep a sharp rein on your reactions. Be friendly, but keep to your predetermined interview plan.

5. The interviewer takes comprehensive notes about everything you say. This will not be a good interview. Reading your résumé would have been more productive. What can you do? Upset the interviewer's program by asking questions about his or her job, the company, the people you might be working for, the salary, or anything else pertinent to your visit.

6. The interviewer belittles you: assumes a superior attitude, uses some exotic words that you may not understand, and tries to undermine your self-confidence. Remain unaffected. Ask for the meaning of the word you did not understand—what did it mean in the context of the conversation? Such an unexpected reaction will help to put the interview on a better footing. The interviewer may even be unable to define exactly the unusual word or complicated management concept thus interjected in the conversation.

"CATCH" QUESTIONS

On the job your interests and those of your employer merge. During your job search, however, your interests and those of a prospective employer are in opposition until a mutual understanding has been reached. Asking unexpected "catch" questions is one method that a skilled interviewer will use to find out about you. Be prepared for them, and have your answers ready. Why did you leave your last position? Why do you want to leave your present position? What do you think you could contribute to this company?

Review the examples of interview questions given in the next section with your wife, sweetheart, brother, father, friend, or, best of all, a professional advisor.

EXAMPLES OF INTERVIEW QUESTIONS

About Your Job Attitudes

1. What are your short-range objectives? Long-range objectives?
2. What do you look for in a job?
3. If we employed you, how long would you stay with us?
4. What new goals or objectives have you established recently?
5. What position do you expect to have in five years?
6. How would you describe personal success?

7. Do you not feel that you might be better off in a (larger) company? (Smaller) company? Different type of company? Different job classification?
8. Why do you want to work for this company?
9. If you had a choice, which job and company would you choose?

About Your Attitudes toward the Position You Are Applying For

1. What interests you most about the position we have? The least?
2. What can you do for us that someone else could not do as well?
3. Why should we hire you?
4. How long would it take you to make a contribution to this company?

About Your Previous Position

1. In your present position, what problems have you identified that had previously been overlooked?
2. What did you learn in your present position?
3. How would you evaluate your present company?
4. Why are you not earning more at your age?
5. Why do you want to leave your present position? Why did you leave your present position?
6. What do you think of your boss?
7. What features of your previous jobs have you disliked?
8. Describe a few situations in which your work was criticized.

About Your Social Attitudes

1. How do you feel about members of minority groups? Majority groups?
2. What is your attitude toward working for a woman? For a man?

About You

1. Can you work under pressure and deadlines?
2. What kind of salary do you think you are worth?
3. What is your biggest strength? Weakness?
4. If you could start over again in your career, what would you do differently?
5. Will you be out to take your boss's job?
6. How would you describe your personality?
7. What do your subordinates think of you?
8. What makes you believe you have top management potential?
9. Tell us all about yourself.

10. What was the last book you read? Movie you saw? Sporting event you attended?

About Your Management Philosophy and Job Approach

1. What is your philosophy of management?
2. Do you prefer staff or line work? Why?
3. How have you changed the nature of your job?
4. Have you ever fired anyone? Why?
5. Have you hired people before? What do you look for when hiring someone?

About Your Accomplishments

1. Are you creative? Illustrate.
2. Are you analytical? Illustrate.
3. Are you a good manager? Illustrate.
4. Are you a good leader? Illustrate.
5. Have you helped increase sales? Profits? How?
6. Have you helped reduce costs? How?
7. What are your five biggest accomplishments in your present or last job? Your career so far?

Offbeat Questions

1. Why have you been out of work so long?
2. What other positions are you considering? What companies?
3. Are you interested in causes? If so, what kinds?
4. What do you think of the business outlook over the next year or two?
5. What do you think of the present investment climate for an individual investor?
6. Do you think that busing schoolchildren is good or bad?
7. Do you believe in capital punishment?
8. Do you think that parents generally are too permissive (not permissive enough) in raising their children?
9. Do you think, from your experience, that labor unions were good or bad for (a previous employer)?
10. Do you think that welfare expenditures are too high (too low)?
11. Which senator (or congressman) do you most admire and why?
12. Would you be willing to work for a homosexual?
13. Do you plan to be married?
14. What activities, outside of your work, do you engage in?

Possible answers to such questions are reviewed in the next chapter.

STEP FOUR: CONDUCTING YOUR INTERVIEW

Many books have been written about interview techniques. The subject is almost inexhaustible, involving philosophy, psychology, psychiatry, aptitude testing, common sense, and the variability of interview conditions. Here we present the basic considerations to make extensive further research unnecessary.

Who controls the interview? The answer is moot. Interview control is not an objective on either side. Rather, the objective is to exchange views between the interviewer who is the buyer and the interviewee who is the seller. The interviewer controls the interview when leading the conversation to desired topics. The interviewee controls the interview when discussing abilities and job qualifications with the greatest eloquence and knowledge.

In a sense you—the job applicant—are in control whenever you know what you are talking about and can express your knowledge properly. Hence our emphasis here on preparing for the interview—before appearing for the interview consider how you will conduct yourself, the types of people you might meet, and the kinds of questions you might be asked.

Be certain that you can answer questions. You may think that you are knowledgeable in your area of competence only to find that an explanation requires specific data that you may have forgotten or an in-depth understanding of the subject that you lack, having thought about it only in a general way. For example, one seasoned executive talked about his career as ranging through staff and line jobs. When asked how he distinguished between them he floundered in his answer. The effectiveness of an interview is lowered when such situations occur.

In this chapter we discuss a wide variety of questions and give suggested answers to prepare you for your job interview. Whatever your answers to the interview questions given here, be sure that you have thought about them beforehand and are *prepared*.

THE OBVIOUS FACTORS

Neatness obviously is important at an interview. Writings on looking for employment used to discuss personal appearance in great detail. Not only does the reader of this book not need such fundamental instructions, dress styles have become so flexible and variable as to defy specific instructions. Casual dress, long hair, beards are common and appear even at the board room level. Dress as your life-style dictates as long as you conform to the accepted standards of neatness and cleanliness.

BEGINNING THE INTERVIEW

The beginning of the interview depends on how it came about—by way of a broadcast letter, a résumé, a mutual friend or acquaintance, cold canvassing, an executive search firm, an employment agency, answering an advertisement, a casual conversation, or a book or article that you wrote:

1. **A broadcast letter.** *You* open the conversation, thanking your host for seeing you and explaining why you approached him.
2. **A résumé.** *You exchange* greetings and let the interviewer carry the conversational ball at the beginning.
3. **A mutual friend or acquaintance.** *You* open the conversational gambit. "Mr. Smith (your friend) thought that my qualifications might be of interest to your company or that you might be able to give me some advice with respect to (finding employment; finding new employment). To save a little time, here is a copy of my résumé."
4. **Cold Canvassing.**   Same approach as in situation 1.
5. **An executive search firm.**   You should have been intensively reviewed, in person, by the search firm, and both you and the prospective employer should have been thoroughly indoctrinated about each other. The conversation may start at a social level and develop naturally into the more important aspects of mutual suitability.
6. **An employment agency.**   Let the *interviewer* start and conduct the conversation. Your credentials have already been supplied.
7. **Answering an advertisement.** *You* start the conversation by explaining why the help wanted advertisement was of special interest to you.
8. **A casual conversation.**   Let your host open the conversation. If the meeting is the result of your pressure more than his, however, take over the initial conversation.
9. **A book or an article that you wrote.**   The conversation will proceed naturally and mutually based on the common interest in your writing.

In general, let an interviewer do most of the talking in the beginning. A good interviewer, unless your qualifications are suspect, will in fact try to put you at ease by talking about the company, the weather, mutual interests, mutual friends, or any other topics that produce no strain. Also, by listening to your interviewer you will gain ideas about how best to express yourself. Many people have talked themselves into a job only to continue talking too long and talk themselves out of it.

SENSE OF HUMOR

When appearing for an interview leave your sense of humor at home. Many interviewers either have no sense of humor or do not wish to have it injected in a job-related conversation. Furthermore, what one person considers to be funny may seem inane to someone else. Nothing is more harmful to an interview than the use of humor out of place. This is true in most business situations, except among peers. Stockholders, for example, do not wish to hear humorous remarks from their managers. One reason why good jokes in speeches are so well received is that here they are not a part of the normal business give-and-take.

EXAMPLES OF ANSWERS TO INTERVIEW QUESTIONS

The most common interview question is, "Why did you leave your last job?" or "Why are you thinking of leaving your job?". Be prepared with *your* answer and be honest. Many answers will be self-explanatory. Your company might have been acquired by another company, in which event the employees of the dominant company will be given preference. Loss of business or profits requires layoffs. A new manager, brought into a company from outside, might want a new staff or might bring his own staff. Perhaps you were bored and your work showed it. There are also personality conflicts, internal politics, power plays, family incompatibilities, and nonconformance to a corporate pattern. *Basically, any separation is due to someone else's being preferred for your position.* Even a separation caused by loss of business indicates that you, in your job, could not influence the loss in a manner favorable enough to justify your retention. In a viable company some people will always remain.

A personality conflict is a common reason for a job change and is affirmative for you. You recognized a situation and made a decision (or it was made for you). Most people realize that one man's meat can be another man's poison.

In being honest about your reason for leaving a company, you can nevertheless discuss it in as favorable a manner as possible, often turning it to your advantage. If you *were* bored, for example, say that your position lacked challenge.

Be judicious in talking about a former employer. Do not indulge your inclination to castigate the employer, even if deserved, since such a negative attitude will serve as a red flag signal to an alert interviewer: "If this is the way the applicant feels about a former employer, how is he or she going to feel about us?" Instead, speak in general terms about the fact that some people simply do not get along well together and that therefore you are in search of a more compatible situation. Do not allow a negative attitude to destroy an interview.

If you were fired, you can either (1) admit it and explain why or (2) not admit it, say you resigned, and explain why. Most former employers speak about their former employees euphemistically. Firing an employee can be an employer failure, too.

Suppose you were a salesman with a territory. Your territory lost sales, instead of gaining them. You were fired. There could be these reasons for your failure: the salesman who preceded you ruined the image of the company; the company would not make the policy changes you recommended and you became discouraged; essentially you did not like the products you were selling or the kinds of customer you had to call on. Or the company did not reimburse you adequately for your expenses. And so on.

Or you were an office manager who was very hard to get along with. Your subordinates complained, and you were fired. Admit your former deficiences and claim to have overcome them (and make an effort to do so).

You were a research director for a large company; you were fired. If you were really qualified for the position, there must be a very good reason (favorable to you) why you failed. If you were not qualified, you must be honest with yourself and search for a position at a slightly lower level for which you are qualified.

You were a plant manager. You could not attain the production increases required. You were fired. The various processes are sufficiently complicated to be able to find a hundred reasons for the termination that are not your fault.

You were an automobile salesman. You sold very few cars. You were fired. You discovered subsequently from a salesman with whom you had worked how to sell cars when he sold you one. It was one of the great lessons of your life from which you have profited.

You were an alcoholic. You did not carry out your business responsibilities. You were fired. Subsequently, someone in whom you had great confidence helped you. You have recovered from your problem and are now capable of meeting your responsibilities. Explain it.

You had a boss you liked. His boss did not like you. You were forced out of the company. Explain what happened.

You were an advertising manager. You made plans for a promotional campaign involving a lot of paper. The plan was approved and suddenly canceled. You were committed to your printer for special paper and the company was forced to pay for it. You were fired. It should have been a good lesson. Admit it.

You were operating under a budget. Suddenly expenses that you had not foreseen put you well over budget. Important plans had to be curtailed. You were fired. It is hoped that you benefited from the experience. Explain it.

You are a stenographer. Your work is slow and inaccurate. You were fired. Correct your deficiencies, or expect to be fired over and over again.

The question, "Do you prefer staff or line work?" is an interesting one. Make sure you know the difference between line and staff responsibilities. A staff position is one that supports a manager who executes; it is advisory. When a function becomes important enough, a manager will assign an aide to supervise that function. Examples of staff jobs are director of research and development who reports to someone other than the chief executive officer; product manager; corporate attorney; marketing research director, E.D.P. manager; planning director; or any assistant to. A line position is one requiring execution rather than advice. The top manager of any function who makes a decision that is carried into effect is a line manager with respect to that function, but may be staff in his relationship to his superior. Examples of line positions are chief executive officer; vice-president of marketing; vice-president of finance; vice-president of production; salesman; regional manager; divisional manager; sales manager; department manager.

In rising through the corporate ranks, one will hold both staff and line positions. The answer to the question posed is that you prefer any position, line or staff, where you learn more about the company and can contribute effectively and measurably to some facet of management. Ultimately you want line responsibility.

"What are your long-term objectives?" A reasonable answer would be: to develop your own capabilities and learn enough about the operation of the vocation in which you are engaged to make a maximum contribution (to profitability) (to more efficient operation) (to better executive development planning) (to corporate growth) (to better administration) (to improve education) (to gain knowledge) and to continue your development and learning throughout your career, in order to achieve the life-style most consistent with the desires and hopes of your family and yourself at whatever your job level may be.

A short-term objective is to take the earlier steps necessary to accomplish the long-term objective.

"What position do you expect to have in five years?" Whatever your job level, you expect to have a *better* position in five years. You will have a better position if you are promoted or if you bring new ideas and achievements to the same position. You also expect to have a position that is consistent with your ability to contribute to the aims of the organization for which you work; and *you expect to have a continuing learning opportunity.*

If you are not ambitious, you may be happy with the routine of a familiar daily role. There is nothing wrong with this if you understand that the key word is "happy"; however do not express this point of view to a prospective employer.

Below we give a number of possible interview questions and suggested answers to them.

1. "What do you look for in a job?" Personal fulfillment consistent with effective administration.
2. "If we employed you, how long would you stay with us?" As long as you permitted me to learn and advance at a pace consistent with honest objective and subjective appraisals of my ability.
3. "What new goals or objectives have you established recently?" If young, you may have just decided on the career you want. If older, you may have learned that you have greater talents in one area than in another and have now decided to concentrate in this new area. Or your objectives may have been established some time ago and you are still pursuing them.
4. "How would you describe personal success?" Complete fulfillment of one's capacities to develop and contribute.
5. "Don't you feel you might be better off in a (larger) (smaller) (different) type of company or in a different job classification?" If you did have a specific reason for choosing that particular company, explain it. It is a silly question, but do not show that you think so. Ask the interviewer to answer the same question. You might learn something.
6. "Why do you want to work for this company?" This is the kind of question the answer to which would vary greatly according to the kind of position you are looking for. For example, you might want to work for the company just because you need a job and would be willing to work for any company. Or you might want to work for it because you have special expertise that would be particularly effective if put to use. You cannot, of course, give the first reason. Say that you want to work for the company because of reputation, location, growth, substance, opportunity. If seeking an upper level job, you should know the answer from your research.
7. "If you had your choice among companies, what company would you most like to work for?" To answer this question intelligently would require an almost encyclopedic knowledge of corporations and institutions. The best answer is probably, "A company like yours," which leads then to the answers given to the preceding question.
8. "In your present position, what problems have you identified that had

previously been overlooked?'' You will find your answers to this question by a reference to your résumé in which you have expressed your accomplishments.

9. ''What interests you most about the position we have available?'' It coincides with your abilities and interests. ''What interests you least?'' is an inappropriate question to which you could not give any other answer than that you are unaware of uninteresting aspects. A better question would be, ''What aspects of the position are least attractive to you?'' The answer could be too much travel or too many administrative details, but they are aspects that you are willing to accept as a learning prelude to a better position.

10. ''What can you do for us that someone else could not do as well?'' Relate your past accomplishments.

11. ''Why should we hire you?'' Same answer as above. ''How long would it take you to make contributions to this company?'' How old is Ann? You learn quickly; you are experienced; you are professional; you reorganized a section, a department, a business in such and such a length of time. You work as hard as necessary to acquire the particular skills required as quickly as possible.

12. ''What did you learn in your present (or most recent) position?'' This is a good question because your acceptance of continuous learning is a primary element in an evaluation of you. You should learn from every job. When you stop, look for another position. If you did *not* learn anything in your present or recent job, go back to any situation where you did learn something. You may also explain that failure to learn in a recent position is one reason you are seeking new employment. This should not be a difficult question to answer.

13. ''How would you evaluate your present company?'' An excellent company *but* (with respect to you) too small, too large, too structured, too slow in growth, not enough new products, offers limited opportunity, losing business to competition, no employee benefits, poor salary structure, and so on. This should be an easy question to answer. Do not divulge confidential information to a competitive company at this stage of negotiation.

14. ''Why aren't you earning more at your age?'' Opportunity was more important than money. You have learned but the opportunity you sought has not developed as you expected. This is a major reason for wanting to make a change.

15. ''What do you think of your boss?'' Even if he is an S.O.B., do not say so. You respect and admire him for his good qualities. If you do admire him, tell why.

16. ''What features of your previous jobs have you disliked?'' Do not answer this question too hastily. Answer in general rather than specific terms.

17. "Describe a few situations in which your work was criticized." For example:

> It was within my responsibilities, as written in my job description, to establish company terms of sale. I extended our terms from a dating of 30 days to one of 60 days to meet competition and increase business. The (new) president of the company criticized me for making the decision without consulting him even though I had been making the same kinds of decisions for many years.

> I developed a new and needed product. I was criticized because the new product made some other products obsolete.

> I took a job in a factory involving the disassembly of old fire extinguishers. The foreman criticized me for working beyond the normal speed of the production line.

Always try to give examples of criticisms that put you in the best possible light.

18. "How do you feel about people from minority groups?" You are neutral. You would work for or employ any person who is qualified. You would not want to work for anyone less qualified than yourself. Nevertheless the situation of a less qualified individual supervising one who is more qualified is common. You may be in such a situation and now trying to extricate yourself from it.

19. "What is your attitude toward working for a woman (or a man)?" Again, you are neutral and would work for or employ any person who is qualified. You should, however, be fully aware of any bias you might have, so as to be able to correct or handle it with as little detriment to your career planning as possible.

20. "Can you work under pressure?" This is not a good question. People respond to crises in very different ways, handling one crisis with difficulty and another crisis with assurance. Basically one works under pressure according to one's training to meet a particular kind of situation, such as delivering merchandise to a customer or delivering a baby—a crisis or a routine, depending on one's training. The answer to this question is "yes" if the crisis is within one's general competence and experience. The experienced individual who does not know how to handle a situation admits it and seeks time to find a solution.

21. "What kind of salary do you think you are worth?" If qualified for the position, you are probably worth more than the employer is willing to pay. This does not mean that you would not be willing to accept the level of pay offered. The question is without real merit, but gives you a chance to value yourself. A capable executive generates more than 40 times his cost in profits.

22. "What is your biggest strength?" The question is susceptible to a million answers. The ability to see what needs to be done and to do it personally or by delegation. Leadership. Knowledge of the industry. Knowledge of the markets. Knowledge of whatever is the specialty under consideration.

23. "What is your biggest weakness?" Turn this question to your advantage. You are impatient. You want to see a job done quickly and expeditiously and sometimes are critical if you think the work is progressing too slowly. You are apt to say what you think instead of being a "yes" man. This sometimes gets you into trouble with a superior who is intolerant of disagreement. You are stubborn. If you know you are right you maintain your position despite the possibility that by giving up your viewpoint you would make yourself better liked by others. Some will see such traits as weaknesses (lack of diplomacy), but enlightened employers usually like them. In politics one has to compromise but compromise can be the death of business.

24. "If you could start your career over again, what would you do differently?" Perhaps you would not have remained so long with your last, or previous, employer. Possibly you would have been stronger in pressing your point of view. Maybe you would have sought outside advice for a situation that needed an objective approach.

25. "Will you be out to take your boss' job?" In general, yes—with the hope that your boss will also be qualified to move up.

26. "How would you describe your personality?" In general, your personality is one that develops affirmatively in your dealings with other people, as they come to know you better.

27. "What do subordinates think of you?" They either like or dislike you, but always respect you.

28. "What makes you believe that you have top management potential?" Because you have superior insight and foresight, the ability to motivate and delegate, the capacity to get things done, the skill to choose the right people to accomplish the jobs that need doing and to inspire their loyalty, the talent to be right more often than wrong, the willingness to do yourself what you would ask anyone else to do, integrity, reliability, dedication.

29. "Tell us all about yourself." You should have prepared yourself by following our earlier advice to learn the elements of your résumé by heart.

30. "What was the last book you read? Last play you saw?" Such questions are intended to gauge the breadth and nature of your outside interests. Are you a part of the contemporary scene or are you withdrawn into past events and experiences? Advice: expatiate on any outside interests you have, whether in direct answer to the question or not. The question merely attempts to draw you out with respect to your nonvocational activities as a measurement of your total personality. If all of your interests are work-

oriented, you may have a narrow outlook, perhaps be dull, and possibly be a poor manager.

31. "What is your philosophy of management?" Millions of words and thousands of books have been written on this subject. A brief answer might be: efficiency, invention, innovation, alertness to all relevant trends, enlightenment, fairness to stockholders and employees, firmness to withstand what is disadvantageous, management by exception, management by holistic analysis to the degree possible, management to make a profit, management by ethical standards, management by objective. The more you read about and participate in the practice of management, the more eloquently and easily you can speak on this subject.

32. "Have you ever fired anyone? Why?" As a manager, you have probably had this experience. You may have had to fire someone for a reason with which you did not agree. Regardless of the reason, the question is intended to give the interviewer additional information about you and how you operate. Give an example that reflects favorably on you.

    Example: Employee X had been with the company for 20 years. He was an excellent manager in an area where customers could be very appreciative of his subordinates' activities in their behalf which were at the same time beneficial to the company. Some years ago he accepted a small gift from a customer. Subsequently as a matter of policy the company notified all customers that gifts could not be accepted by company employees. It was recently discovered that some of this manager's subordinates were accepting large gifts from customers for special favors that they could extend without the manager's knowledge. You had to fire the manager for two reasons: (1) he had at one time accepted a gift that, as a manager, he should have known not to accept, and (2) as a manager, he should have been aware of his subordinates' activities.

33. "Have you hired people? What do you look for?" You look for individuals who will meet the standards of the position. The standards can vary. Not every individual is qualified for management; not every job leads to the top. Sometimes a position calls for a person who is not highly motivated—a plugger rather than a racehorse. Continuous promotion for every employee is impossible. Some Indians do not become chiefs; some bellhops remain bellhops instead of becoming hotel managers. In answering this question you express your cognizance of the realities of corporate life.

34. "What size of budget are you accustomed to administering?" A manager knows his departmental budget. Inasmuch as a budget is usually dealt with only a few times a year, refresh your memory about budget details before an interview. You should know the percentage of your budget to sales or revenue. You should know the major elements in your budget. In marketing, for example:

    a. Executive salaries and bonuses.
    b. Clerical salaries and bonsues.
    c. Salesmen's salaries and bonuses (commissions).
    d. Media advertising.
    e. Trade advertising.
    f. Displays.
    g. Charge for computer time.

35. "Are you acquainted with the use of PERT and CPM in making management decisions?" PERT (*p*rogram *e*valuation and *r*eview *t*echnique) and CPM (*c*ritical *p*ath *m*ethod) are network techniques that are used to define and improve the sequence of scheduling for such projects as a pilot model plant, the shutdown of a plant for overhaul and maintenance, and the Polaris Weapons Systems, though the notations of the systems differ. Do not get involved in a discussion of these techniques unless thoroughly familiar with their use and method. Suggestion: if the position you want is one that would utilize network techniques, familiarize yourself with them before your interview.

36. "What is the name of the buyer at XYZ Wholesale Company?" If XYZ is a large company that is important to the distribution of the interviewer's company and you are a national or regional sales manager, you will be expected to know the buyer's name. Your degree of familiarity indicates the intimacy of your participation in the sales efforts of your past or present employer. Knowledge of *markets* is important in this job classification.

QUESTIONS YOU CAN ASK

There are a number of questions that you can ask at a job interview:

- May I see a copy of the job description?
- Whom would I be working for and with?
- Where would I appear on the organization chart? (If position is appropriate to this question.)
- What is the growth rate of the company?
- May I have a copy of the annual report?
- If I am productive, what would I have to look forward to in further career development?
- What are your major markets?
- Who are your biggest competitors?
- Who is your biggest customer in this area?

- What qualities do you want most in the position for which you are considering me?
- How soon will you make up your mind about me?
- Would you like to have a list of references? (If the question is not asked of you.)
- What are the employee benefits?
- How much travel would you consider normal for this position?
- Might relocation be required at this time or in the future?

AFTER THE INTERVIEW

Follow an interview with a letter addressed to the individual with whom you talked. Thank him or her for courtesies extended; express your continuing interest; ask for a decision. If there is no response within a few days, telephone your interviewer to find out what is happening; offer to supply additional information or to appear for another personal meeting.

CHAPTER 9

PSYCHOLOGICAL TESTS

The use of psychological tests in employee selection is a controversial subject. While beneficial and even mandatory for a mentally disturbed person and helpful in vocational and career counseling, they are considered by many to be an invasion of personal privacy when used on job applicants. Nor are they error-proof—the experienced testee who knows the value and interpretation assigned to certain answers can deliberately fool or mislead a tester. Furthermore, the essential validity of psychological testing for position aptitude has never been completely established.

I advise job applicants generally to avoid or refuse company-sponsored psychological testing for the reason that it tends to be damaging more often than it is favorable. This may not be always possible.

You must understand why tests are given. Employers are looking for keys to unlock your characteristics and measure such qualities as the following:

- Neurotic tendencies.
- Self-sufficiency (too much–too little).
- Introversion–extroversion, indicating introversion and imagination or extroversion and action orientation.
- Dominance–submission, indicating tendency to dominate others in face-to-face situations.
- Self-confidence, indicating self-consciousness and feeling of inferiority or the opposite.
- Sociability, gregarious or solitary.

In such tests significant differences appear between supervisors or managers and nonsupervisors. Other tests can indicate the following traits:

- Rational balance or tendency to lie, cheat, steal, or act antisocially.
- Emotional instability.
- Depression.

188

- Tendency to daydream.
- Adherence to fixed ideas, suspicion, contempt for others.
- Achievement percentile.

The information that follows is provided to help you in the event that you must subject yourself to testing. Most tests result in a so-called profile of the testee. Some tests require two or three days of examination; others require only a day or a few hours. Most valid testing requires the presence of the subject. Some testing companies will give an opinion or create a profile without meeting the subject.

TYPES OF PSYCHOLOGICAL TEST

Psychological testing includes the following:

- Viewing a series of inkblot designs (in the Rorschach test, for example) and describing their meaning. The responses are then interpreted by a psychologist or psychiatrist.
- Extensive conversations with a psychologist during which you are asked what you think about others: parents, friends, business associates, superiors, yourself, and perhaps current events of important or notorious people currently in the news. Similar tests can also be given in writing.
- Written tests are the most common. Most frequently they have to do with your associating certain words with your character traits. What the psychologist looks for is consistency. You may be asked to check the words in a certain order and then to do it again in a completely different order. It will be helpful if you know exactly what all the words mean, so that you will respond to them in the same way under all circumstances.

  A psychologist may go so far as to discuss with you why you selected each word as appropriate for you. About half the words will be negative and half positive. Naturally you will need to project more positive than negative characteristics. At the same time you cannot appear too perfect. Some apparently negative characteristics can actually be explained positively. For example, being "reserved" is not necessarily a negative trait, nor is being "stubborn," "suspicious," "uncertain," or "impulsive." Moreover, you will interpret many of your characteristics as being positive at some times and negative at others. Unless your answers are reviewed in conversation, a tester cannot recognize your negative answers that are "possibly positive" and may draw invalid conclusions. You are evaluated by both the words you check and those you do not check.

  Test yourself on the list of positive and negative words given below. In a real test situation your instructions might read as follows: "In (a specified number of) minutes check off the words that apply to you. You may check all the positive words (hardly with complete honesty) and not less than 10 negative words." Familiarize yourself with these words, looking up those about which you are not sure—these words may be used in a test to check your consistency, with synonyms substituted for them.

Generally positive

active	economical
adaptable	efficient
aggressive	eloquent
alert	energetic
ambitious	enterprising
analytical	enthusiastic
argumentative	esteemed
artistic	exacting
astute	extroverted
attentive	fair
broad-minded	forceful
composed	forward-thinker
congenial	frank
conscientious	friendly
considerate	generous
consistent	genuine
constructive	good-natured
contemplative	honest
courageous	imaginative
courteous	independent
creative	individualist
cultured	inspiring
daring	intellectual
democratic	intuitive
dependable	just
detailed	keen
determined	kind
dignified	logical
diplomatic	loyal
discerning	methodical
disciplined	modest
discreet	objective
discriminating	observant

opinionated

optimistic

orderly

outspoken

patient

perceptive

perfectionist

personable

philosophical

poised

positive

practical

productive

proud

purposeful

realistic

reliable

resourceful

respected

self-reliant

sense-of-humor

shrewd

sincere

sociable

sophisticated

sympathetic

systematic

tactful

talented

thoughtful

tolerant

truthful

visionary

Generally negative

abrupt

agitator

agnostic

anti-social

arrogant

avaricious

awkward

belligerent

bizarre

bogus

bungler

capricious

clumsy

complacent

conceited

conventional

corrupt

covetous

crafty

deceitful

despondent

discourteous

domineering

easily depressed

eccentric

egotistical

embittered

emotional

excitable

extravagant

fabricator

fastidious

forgetful

fragile

impractical

impulsive

inconsiderate

inconsistent

incorrigible

indifferent

inhibited

irritable

insubordinate

intolerable

introverted	self-conscious
jealous	selfish
lavish	sensitive
lethargic	sentimental
mean	shallow
mutinous	simple
naive	skeptical
narrow-minded	squeamish
negligent	stubborn
obstinate	submissive
paltry	superficial
pessimistic	suspicious
pompous	temperamental
possessive	trivial
pretentious	two-faced
rash	uncertain
repugnant	unobservant
reserved	unreliable
restless	unscrupulous
sarcastic	unsophisticated
secretive	vacillating
self-centered	vicious

Many books have been written about psychological testing. The material is almost inexhaustible. Two books that might be of value to you are William Whyte's *The Organization Man* (Simon & Schuster, New York, 1956) and Martin Gross' *The Brain Watchers* (Random House, New York, 1962).

RELATION OF PSYCHOLOGICAL TESTING TO EXECUTIVE COMPETENCE

Much psychological testing, past and present, depends on measurements: word association, mechanical reactions, clerical, accounting, administrative, technical aptitudes, general information, arithmetic reasoning, analogic reasoning, reading comprehension, personality, and so on. Psychological testing at the managerial level, however, cannot be productive unless it relates to the *functions* of the manager. Before making a measurement we must know what qualities we want to measure rather than using arbitrary measurements because they seem to have some application or are available.

The essential measurements of a manager tend to be abstract. For example, the eight most important managerial attributes are the following:

1. To be right more often than wrong in all business judgments, frequently using the extra dimension of insight.
2. To be able to manage, motivate, and lead others while maintaining harmony among diverse but suitably productive individuals.
3. To be able to act with composure under pressure.
4. To be able to plan both logically and creatively.
5. To be able to act decisively when necessary.
6. To be able to act with subtlety and finesse when they are required.
7. Personal motivation.
8. High personal standards.

Such attributes are difficult to determine and measure. There are not many tests available to assess them. Moreover, such qualities may not appear until they are called for—in the case of many people, never.

Obviously, the best test is past accomplishment, but often accomplishment has not had time to develop and it is potential that must be tested. Who is qualified to make such judgments? Can one impartially judge another person whom he or she dislikes? Does a young manager tend to favor a person of the same age? Is an older manager attracted to maturity—or perhaps to youth? Does a manager groom a successor in his or her own image; if so, is this desirable?

An experienced executive may be more qualified to make such judgments than are all except the finest professional psychologists. An executive who has not operated under conditions demanding these attributes is unlikely to be able to assess them. Each manager is best able to make judgments within his or her own classification, except the production executive who should be limited to judgments relating to technical competence.

THE EMPLOYMENT APPLICATION FORM

Some employers at certain job levels will ask you to fill out an application form and from this material will make a series of surmises about you. It would be well for you to have your résumé with you for reasons that will be apparent as you read what follows.

1. A sloppily filled out application form is a poor advertisement for you. Crossing out words and sentences and rewriting them, perhaps illegibly, shows a careless attitude and possibly a poor memory.
2. If a question requires a narrative answer, the reader will look for coherence, unity, and conciseness. Verbosity is used to conceal weaknesses. If you can copy from your résumé, your answers will be superior.
3. The reader looks for contradictions, unexplained gaps in employment, or

time overlaps. Be sure that your experience chronology is correct and without these flaws. Extended periods between jobs in times of prevailing bad economic conditions will be understood, however.

4. An application that shows too many changes of residence will be suspect. Have a good explanation ready in such a case.

5. Your reasons for leaving your last position will surely be among the questions asked. Be ready to answer this question by prior preparation of a concise and truthful answer. Do not put the blame on others; it makes a bad impression.

6. If you are changing careers, expect to be questioned closely about it. Carefully explain your reasons in your résumé, and refer to these reasons during the interview, so that you can discuss your career switch briefly, plausibly, and pertinently.

7. When filling out an application form you must be prepared to disclose your salary history. If you are planning to accept a reduction in pay, have a very good reason at hand. If, on the other hand, you are seeking a large increase, your qualifications must clearly show that you are worth it. Be prepared.

8. Be ready to explain why you would like to work for the particular company.

SALARY NEGOTIATIONS

SALARIES

Every corporate or institutional position has a salary range. The range can be very wide. The range is different at the job entry period, at job maturity plateau, and the winding up stage (nearing retirement). For example, an administrative sales position with a large corporation might be $14,000 at entry and rise to $24,000 at a maturity or plateau level. It might rise to $26,000 as retirement approaches to afford the incumbent a better pension benefit. If a new employee can manage this position as well as an older one, it is obvious that the older employee is earning too much. At the first sign of recession or any other reasonable cause a mature employee holding the same level of responsibility after 18 or more years is subject to replacement or is pushed into early retirement. This is especially true in corporate life. Promotion becomes a continuing necessity.

Salary ranges are usually plus or minus 20% of median, rising to plus or minus 30% at the highest levels. An offer of employment is usually made at the median minus 20%. In negotiating your salary, therefore, you can seek as much as 40% above the first offer but usually not more than 10% above it because there must be room for future reward if you are on firm ground, that is, if your credentials are excellent and you have no competition superior to you. Negotiation is always a matter of personal judgment based on your assessment of all the factors. At higher levels of corporate remuneration it can be readily seen that the negotiating area may have a spread of $6000 to $25,000 or more annually. Negotiation is easier at higher than at lower levels.

Compensation, whenever possible, should be tied to productivity. This is most easily done in marketing or in any upper level executive position. Marketing compensation can be tied to volume increases. General corporate officers can participate in profitability. It is more difficult to measure exact contributory productivity in finance and production, although it can be done.

Inflation has a great influence on compensation levels. With an annualized

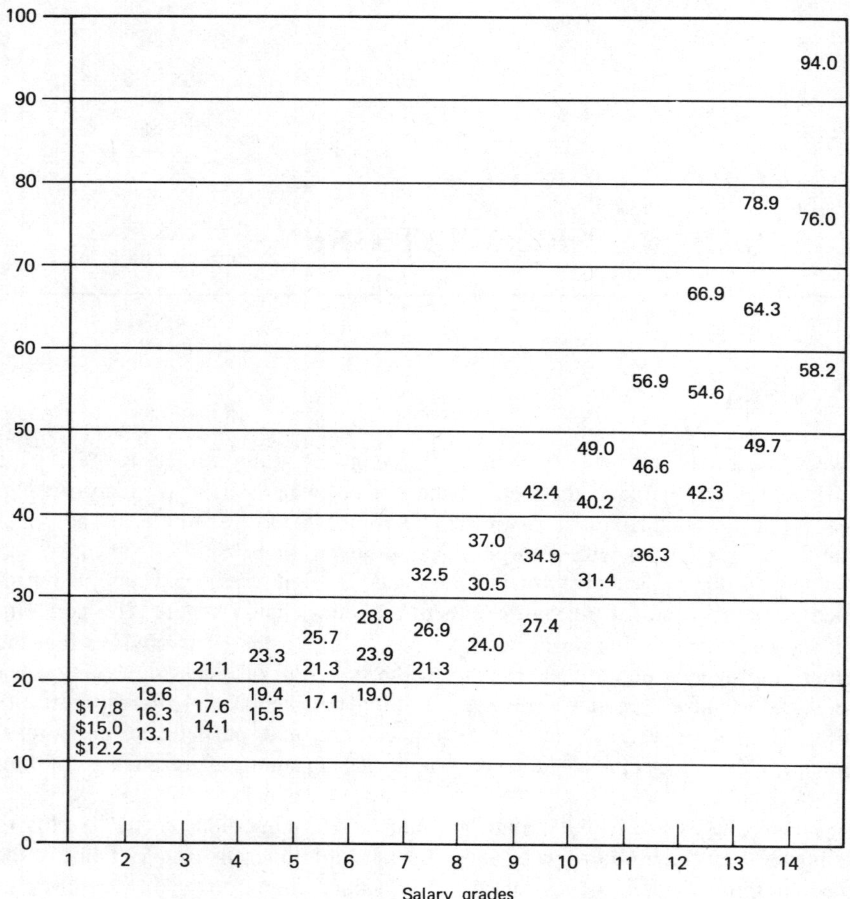

Figure 13   Model of typical management salary structure.

inflation rate of 5% you must have a 5% salary increase just to remain even. Five percent used to be a favorite figure for estimating annual salary changes. With inflation it has now become 10%. This obviously cannot go on forever without great economic damage, but it can be stopped only by government or by a depression. Each of us is concerned with self and cannot afford altruism in the compensation area. What government can or should do is a subject for which we have no space in this book.

Salary levels vary greatly among industries and among employment classifications—even those that appear on the same level in organization charts.

In general you are entitled to at least the lowest level of the salary range for the job grade for which you are applying regardless of your former salary. You might accept the lower range if it is understood that after six months, having demonstrated your capacities, you will receive an increase. If you have excellent qualifications for the position, negotiate for remuneration in the area between the median and the top of the range.

At an entry level you may wish to discount beginning salary in favor of opportunity. One corporation established the following salary practice at the recruiting level:

- Applicants who meet minimum requirements—minimum of range.
- Applicants who exceed minimum requirements—25% above minimum range.

BONUSES

Do not accept a bonus as a large part of your remuneration unless you are in a position personally to influence its size by what you do and are confident that you can achieve the results you expect.

Some employers will set a lower salary level at the beginning of employment with a promise of a bonus at year's end. In effect they reserve the right to assess your performance. If good your bonus will bring your income to what it should have been at employment. If small it constitutes a warning of disappointment in your performance.

To the degree possible a bonus should be based on definite figures—a quota and a percentage over quota, for example; a saving, and percentage after saving. Even under the best conditions it is not desirable to leave the amount of a payment to the discretion of an individual or management—the discretion can be affected adversely by conditions at the moment of decision.

FRINGE BENEFITS

Typical fringe benefits, which have become very costly, are the following:

- Hospitalization insurance (Blue Cross–Blue Shield).
- Major medical insurance.
- Dental insurance.
- Accident insurance.
- Sick pay.
- Pension plan.

- Disability income.
- Life insurance (group plan).
- Vacations/holidays.
- Profit sharing.
- Stock option.
- Employment bonus.
- Sabbatical.
- Company car.
- Country club membership.
- Expense account.
- Moving expenses.
- Purchase of home if transferred.
- Death allowance.

You should have a clear understanding of what your benefits will be. As a rule of thumb, company life insurance should equal annual salary. A pension plan should assure half pay at age 65 for your lifetime (expect some maximum to be imposed at very high salary levels) and a diminished amount (one-third less) for your spouse upon your death for her lifetime.

Make profit sharing a part of your employment package if you are at a level to participate in it; it will show up as a bonus if you are in the marketing division. You can negotiate an employment contract if you are at the proper level and the employing company wants you badly enough. These negotiations are often carried on with the aid of an executive recruiting firm.

Stock options, out of favor at this writing, should once again become very valuable.

A deferred payment plan is an excellent way to reduce taxes if your salary is high.

It is better to know the perimeters of your benefits in advance, even though you will probably be limited by the existing company policy. A few top level executives can sometimes break all the rules.

For everyone, decision-making is the most difficult of actions. Whether or not to accept an employment offer is no harder for you than is the decision to employ you by the manager who makes the offer. Competence, interpersonal relationships, the measurement of future company and individual growth are intangibles impossible of scientific measurement.

Your decision, important to your future, may also affect the future of your employer.

In making this presentation we have tried to take your side as an applicant for employment while at the same time exposing you to all the subtleties of the selection process.

Uncertainty and change are immutable. Our basic advice is to remove uncertainty in your future to the extent possible.

The great majority of companies and institutions grow and prosper. If your judgment is good, you too will benefit accordingly.

RÉSUMÉ LANGUAGE

There are many words, phrases, sentences, and paragraphs illustrative of good résumé writing. Examples of them are given here so that you may become acquainted with the succinct and expressive, yet formal, language of a résumé that has come to be accepted and preferred by recruiters at all levels. The examples are intended only to guide you and to suggest style. Appraise them carefully before choosing a word or phrase that fits you best. Your résumé should be as distinctive as your fingerprints.

ABOUT YOUR EXPERIENCE

consistent record (of progress, growth, achievements, promotion)
demonstrably (successful, capable, effective)
effective
experienced
extensive
intensive
in-depth, comprehensive, of wide scope, wide, broad, diversified, varied
intimate (familiarity with rules, regulations, procedures)
progressive
solid
complete
thoroughgoing
successful

ABOUT YOU

accustomed, used to
an administrator
analytical
broad gauge
(possess) communication skills
competent, capable, able
contest or award winner
contributor
contributory
controlled
a coordinator
dedicated
developer
distinguished
dynamic
educated, schooled, trained
efficient, effective
exceptional (avoid
    ''unexceptionable'')
an executive
a generalist
harmonious
imaginative, conceptual
indoctrinated (with)
ingenious, inventive
innovative, creative
a leader
a manager
motivated
a motivator
multilingual, bilingual
a negotiator
an organizer
outstanding

planner
a producer
reliable
responsible
skilled
a specialist
strategist
stress resistant
student of
a supervisor
talented
a trainee
a trainer
traveled

ABOUT YOUR SKILLS AND ABILITIES

analyze
assist
communicate
conceive (an idea)
contribute
create
create profit, profitability
delegate
develop
economize, save money
implement
innovate
learn
lead
organize, systematize, install
plan
qualify for
recruit
solve problems

supervise, manage, administer
train, indoctrinate, teach
understand
work well with others, work in harmony
write, compose, create copy

ABOUT YOUR ACCOMPLISHMENTS

accomplished
achieved
achieved company or division
  turnaround
contributed
increased, multiplied profit
increased, multiplied sales
introduced new concepts
progressed
reduced, expanded
reorganized
restored profit
saved
sold
succeeded

In the examples below these words and phrases are put to work.

Comprehensively trained in every aspect of procedures.

Product student, market researcher, competition evaluator, sales planner, salesman.

Competent in developing existing customers; in finding new customers; in implementing sales plans; in maintaining customer loyalty.

Single, young, motivated, willing to travel, willing to relocate.

Accomplished in organizing efficient production, in production control planning, and in the effective utilization of the complete range of metal fabricating equipment.

Able to bring effective solutions to complex (mechanical, engineering, financial, marketing, pricing) problems.

Willing to undertake training. Capable of learning. Possess imagination to conceive goals and find ways to accomplish them, quality of leadership, and ability to communicate.

Author of program to expedite critical data to management leading to expansion (other).

Proven skill in defining requirements, procedures, methods, display, and report formats to keep management informed of progress.

Experienced in managing salesmen, training, recruiting, sales planning, utilizing all techniques (audiovisual, flip charts, advertising, contests, tie-ins, advance merchandising) to stimulate sales.

Labor intensive, capital intensive (industry).

Experienced recruiter and trainer of top producers in the industry, consistently sought by competitive firms because of known qualities of leadership and ability to communicate and identify with others.

Ability to analyze and reorganize corporate administrative procedures and use advanced techniques (word processing, communications center, electronic data processing) to achieve greater efficiency at lower cost.

Talent for recognizing better ways to accomplish business objectives through coordination, consolidation, systematization, retraining.

Able to see interdisciplinary relationships and express them effectively.

Credited with novel concepts and creative approaches to the production of scores of recognized 30 and 60 second prime-time TV spot commercials for leading national advertisers.

After 15 years in public service interested in making a career change to the private sector and qualified in personnel, college administration, recruiting, manpower development, general administration.

Six years of secretarial and other office experience as receptionist, bookkeeper, filing clerk, and PBX operator with a variety of service companies: law firm, management consultant, insurance company, advertising agency. Type accurately 60 to 65 words per minute, with skills increasing continuously.

Awareness of legal needs of business and ability to provide clear answers and effective remedies for corporate legal problems.

Broad administrative background as senior executive with giant public authority; special expertise in the planning and operation of major seaports and transportation centers. Competent in negotiation, persuasion, leadership, and motivation. Record of consistent promotion to greater responsibilities throughout career.

Intimately familiar with U.S. markets, business methods, requirements, strategies. Record of creating sales and profits of significant proportions, measured in millions of dollars in diverse industries involving marketing to supermarkets, chains, department stores, government agencies, institutions, wholesalers, using brokers, agents, direct salesmen.

Comprehensively trained and experienced in brokerage and investment banking, in both "front office" and "back office" procedures: portfolio management, daily transactions and administration, cash flow management, Exchange and S.E.C. compliance. Record of profit contributions to employers.

Experienced in establishing effective management information systems; in the expanded use of E.D.P. to provide critical data expeditiously; in cost accounting, inventory control, production control; in reducing lead time; in measuring productivity; in creating controls at all levels of production to identify profit leaks; in applying innovative methods of accomplishing corporate objectives and increased profitability.

Talent for analysis and organization of complex administrative problems. Innovative. Enthusiastic. Ability to train others. Record of important contributions in management, timesaving systems and profit to major multimillion and billion dollar corporations. Record of conscientious application, reliability and loyalty in every position held and ready acceptance or responsibility to get improved results in every assignment.

Experienced in most aspects of insurance, with emphasis in the investigative and adjusting field, which includes extensive legal negotiations, with autonomous discretion from major insurance companies to settle cases at the highest levels. Also general brokerage experience, including solicitation and development of accounts, counseling relative to insurance needs, complex underwriting evaluations, and placement of coverages by various carriers.

Accustomed to complete management responsibilities for accounting and controls, front office, food and beverage, gold course, club house, entertainment, and other facilities; and to financial reporting, profit and cash flow projections; planning and development. Accomplished also in developing convention business, arranging entertainment, providing gourmet food service and high level of other services. Experienced in close analysis of operating figures and correction of trouble areas; in the use of E.D.P. to assist the managerial function.

Successful record as president of own business; formerly director of industrial engineering for multimillion dollar corporation. Experienced in the selection and evaluation of capital equipment needs, production control, rate setting, productivity standards and measurement, systems and procedures, plant layout, incentive plans; in power plant operation.

Record of major contributions in increased revenues, cost savings; in leadership and revitalization of underproductive departments; in research, analysis, and recommendations with respect to feedstocks, tankage, storage, production and marketing optimization, cost control, economics, forecasting, budgeting.

Successful career as financial analyst, securities salesman, knowledgeable in all areas of brokerage including municipal bonds, commodities, underwriting, placements, individual and corporate portfolio management. Competent trainer, leader, developer of manpower. Excellent public speaker, widely experienced in conducting seminars and adult education courses in securities and investment.

Expert in marketing wide range of ethical and proprietary pharmaceuticals and complex electronic health instrumentation products, with in-depth knowledge of markets, sales techniques, training methods. Skilled in communications. Numerous company awards for sales and other achievements.

Accustomed to leading, training, and motivating large staffs and hundreds of employees.

Leader and developer of sales personnel for effective administration of greater responsibilities.

Expert in accommodating promotion programs to regional, trade, and consumer characteristics; in developing innovative packaging to enhance consumer response.

Ability to see what needs to be done, to do it or get it done in a general management capacity.

Exceptionally consistent record of turning loss-operated companies into profit-makers; recently increased sales and production fourfold in less than three years.

Ability to conceptualize and implement broad, complex programs to reach new goals.

Effective market researcher, sales leader, and trainer with expertise in all kinds of packaging and creative sales ideas.

Complete knowledge of the application of graphics to good design with ability to curtail cost.

Demonstrated management ability in national marketing with strong following among chains, discounters, distributors; excellent personal salesman.

School psychologist and counselor, self-starting and innovative.

Record of continuous promotion to positions of greater responsibility; currently holding P.&L. responsibility for multimillion dollar division where sales have tripled and a profit objective has been met. Fully equipped in all aspects of management; in developing management information systems; in full utilization of data processing; in long-range planning and implementation.

Comprehensive experience in the financial and administrative management of huge engineering and construction projects overseas and in the United States involving diverse heavy industrial and military installations; assured their profitable completion.

Extensive educational background and practical experience in human relations, the latter as program developer for nonprofit organization working in South Africa to improve the effectiveness of the organization's structures, human relations, and economic and health conditions of the nationals of Tanzania and Kenya; and of the organization's personnel. Conceived program and assigned to implement it.

TYPICAL JOB RESPONSIBILITIES

Job responsibilities usually are not listed in books on seeking employment. Among the reasons for this are the following:

- You are expected to know the responsibilities of the job for which you are applying.
- Listing unfamiliar responsibilities in your résumé may catch you in your own trap during the interview.
- The use of such ready-made material might result in a mechanical writeup.
- The abridgment of the material negates its value.

We nevertheless review here the activities in certain job classifications. For one, the résumé form we espouse most strongly (*Chronological Résumé with Summary Page*) relies heavily on describing responsibilities and how they were met (accomplishments). Also, our experience has been that individuals sometimes forget some of their job responsibilities unless prodded to remember them. A lack of affirmative response to a r*ésumé* could be caused by the omission of a forgotten but important job function. Futhermore, a job opportunity could be missed for lack of a little advance ''boning up'' in areas where one is expected to have had experience. Finally, the nomenclature of job functions varies from company to company (particularly between very large and small companies). The list below uses generic terms to describe the responsibilities.

Not all companies specify the same responsibilities. R.&D. as well as warehousing and shipping may sometimes be assigned to marketing and sometimes elsewhere. As a vice-president of marketing you would be expected to be familiar with all the elements listed under that heading depending on a company's organizational structure. As a sales manager you would be responsible only for the areas shown under that heading. You will get ideas about other responsibilities, such as product manager, from one or more of the résumés reproduced.

The classifications include most of the duties within the major functions of a company: marketing, finance, and production. Select your area of activity within these categories.

The list also includes personnel, purchasing, retail, data processing, and others selected somewhat arbitrarily; it could have been expanded ad infinitum. We wished to show that, whatever the job classification, your résumé should discuss the responsibilities and accomplishments normally associated with that job. A sales manager, for example, must know the markets of the industry in question.

Use this section as a reminder of your responsibilities, so that you do not omit relevant and important activities with which you should be familiar. Note that the list does not include *all* job responsibilities.

ACCOUNTING

Act as cashier

Adjust entries

Age accounts receivable and accounts payable

Analyze intercompany expenses

Approve petty cash and checks

Bank reconciliations

Budgets, forecasts, and financial planning

Closing entries

Collect from debtors; pay creditors

Consolidate reports for parent company with recommendations as to standing and results of operations of local branches

Correspondence

Dispose promotional items

Examine salesmen's collections and promotional remittances

Examine weekly reports of branch managers and regional offices

Footings

Maintain books of original entry, general ledger, and subsidiary ledgers

Maintain records and control costs of inventory

Posting to the general ledger

Prepare regular payroll

Prepare reversing entries

Prepare taxes

Prepare various supporting schedules

Take off and post closing trial balance

Trial balance

AUDITING

Age receivables and payables

Analysis and evaluation of cash flow, fiscal and interim statements, and projected statements

Analytical audit of books of original entry and records

Analyze turnovers of receivables and payables

Cash counts

Close books

Comparative analysis of sales and financial statements between two or more fiscal periods

Compute breakeven inventory, estimated inventory, and estimated profit or loss

Conduct physical inventory

Confer with company's officers and accountants

Continuous reconciliations

Detailed analysis of balance sheet and P.&L

Evaluate D.&B. ratings

Examine and check other audit reports

Examine bonds, stocks, important documents, contracts

Examine canceled checks and checks being held

Examine notes

Examine shipping documents

Examine pension fund, welfare fund, vacation fund, unemployment fund, education fund, accrual fund

Examine taxes

Financial and accounting analysis of diversified multidivisional corporations

Observe factory inventory flow and operations

Post to general ledger

Prepare entries; journal, adjusting, correcting, reversing

Prepare financial statements with opinions

Prepare, present, discuss, explain reports

Prepare taxes

Prepare various schedules

Send out trade checks and verification

Systems suggestions

Take off trial balance and post closing trial balance

Work on books of original entry

DATA PROCESSING

Applications to inventory, production, accounts receivable, accounts payable,
payroll, sales, shipping, order processing
Budgets
Data centers
Diagnostic systems
Econometric models
Economic models
Educational systems
Forecasting
Hardware, selection of
Leased time
Management information systems
Minicomputer use
Models—financial, marketing, production
Procedural manuals
Programming
Real time
Scientific systems
Softwear, selection of
Training
Utilization, maximum

FINANCE

Acceleration of financial reporting
Accounting
Acquisitions and mergers
Audits and controls
Balance sheets
Bank reconciliations
Bank relationships
Budgets
Capital resource planning

Cash flow
Cash handling
C.P.A. accreditation
Chart of accounts
Compensation
Consolidations
Cost analysis
Credits and collections—bad debt ratios, accounts receivable, aging
Economic correlations
E.D.P. systems
Financing
Financial models
Financial public relations
Financial reporting
Forecasting
Foreign currency fluctuation
Insurance
Inventory control, turnover
Investment
Invoicing systems
Long range planning
Management information systems
Negotiations
New York Stock Exchange, AMEX reports
New York Stock Exchange, AMEX listings
Pensions, fringe benefits, profit sharing plans
Pricing formulas
Profit and loss reporting
Profitability
S.E.C. reports, registrations, prospectuses
Staff training
Taxes
Terms of sale
Training
Underwritings

MARKETING

Sales management
  Budget
  Compensation
  District sales
  Expenses
  Field sales
  Incentives
  Markets
  National sales
  Organization
  Quotas
  Regional sales
  Sales meetings
  Sales planning
  Sales training
  Territory routing
Sales promotion
  Brochures
  Budget
  Circulars
  Direct mail
  Display
  Merchandising
  Packaging
  Presenatations
  Promotions
Public relations
  Budget
  Employee public relations
  Media liaison
  Planning
  Press releases
  Speechwriting

Legal liaison
    Advertising agreements
    Co-op advertising, discounts, pricing
    Sherman antitrust
Computer utilization
Planning
Product management
(marketing in microcosm)
Research and development
    Budget
    Market evaluations
    New products
    Obsolescence
    Old products
    Product evaluation
    Quality comparisons
Advertising
    Agency relations
    Budgets
    Contests
    Copy, copy testing
    Legal liaison
    Media: print, TV, radio
    Production
    Themes
Market research
    Cost projections
    Demography
    Market testing
    New market planning
    Pricing
Forecasting
Pricing (pricing for profit)
Warehousing and shipping
(distribution)

PERSONNEL, INDUSTRIAL RELATIONS, AND MANPOWER DEVELOPMENT

Administration, wage and salary
Arbitrations
Bonding
Budget
Community relations
Computer utilization
Credit unions
Disability
Discipline
Employee orientation
Employee public relations
Employee productivity reviews
Fair Employment Practices Act
Food service
Grievances
Group insurance
Hiring
Interviewing
Job descriptions
Labor negotiations
Legal liaison
Loans
Major medical insurance
Manpower development
Manpower planning
Medical department
Morale
National Labor Relations Board
OSHA (Occupational Safety and
Health Administration) compliance
Policy and procedure
Records
Security

Social functions
Training programs
Unemployment compensation
Unemployment insurance
Welfare and pension plans
Workmen's compensation

PRODUCTION

Automatic equipment
Automation
Budgets
Chemical engineering
Civil engineering
Computer utilization
Construction
Conveyorization
Cost control
Electrical engineering
Electronics engineering
Environment
Industrial engineering
Inventory control
Manpower planning
Mechanical engineering
Metallurgy
New construction, startup
Patents
Personnel
Plant layout
Power
Production control, scheduling,
planning, flow
Purchasing, materials management
Quality control
Quality engineering

Recruiting
Research and development
Space planning
Stampings, forgings, castings,
extrusions
Safety engineering
Systems
Tools and dies
Training
Warehousing and shipping
Waste disposal, recycling

PURCHASING AND MATERIALS MANAGEMENT

Alternate option purchasing
Blanket and annual contracts
Budget
Computer utilization
Economic Order Quantity
(EOQ) purchasing
Economics
Environment
Inventory control
Legal liaison
Make or buy
Market studies
Packaging
Price trend analysis
Shortages
Strikes
Turnover
Value analysis

RETAIL

Acquisition
Administration

Advertising
Branch store administration,
expansion
Budgeting
Buying
Cash flow
Computer utilization
Credit
Departmental layouts
Display
Expansion
Financial planning
Financial reporting
Housekeeping
Inventory control
Leadership
Management information systems
Market analysis
Market changes
Markup, mark-on
Merchandise selection
Merchandising
Open-to-buy
Operations
Promotion
Quality control
Retailing mathematics
Receiving
Security
Shipping
Staffing
Store layout
Systems
Training

EXECUTIVE SEARCH FIRMS

A number of executive search firms are listed below for your convenience (alphabetically by city and state).

CALIFORNIA

FREDERICKS & MARSHALL
P.O. Box 364
Encino, Calif. 91316

BILLINGTON, FOX & ELLIS, INC.
3701 Wilshire Boulevard
Los Angeles, Calif. 90010

BOYDEN ASSOCIATES, INC.
5670 Wilshire Boulevard
Los Angeles, Calif. 90010

CERTIFIED EXECUTIVE SEARCH
CONSULTANTS
9180 East Florence Street
Los Angeles, Calif. 90010

JOHN G. EDMUNDSON & ASSOCIATES
1545 Wilshire Boulevard
Los Angeles, Calif. 90017

ERNEST L. LEON & ASSOCIATES
2330 West 3rd Street
Los Angeles, Calif. 90057

EXECUTIVE RECRUITING AGENCY
1901 Avenue of the Stars
Los Angeles, Calif. 90067

PROFESSIONAL SEARCH
3445 Wilshire Boulevard
Los Angeles, Calif. 90010

VIP AGENCY
3550 Wilshire Boulevard
Los Angeles, Calif. 90010

ZEHNDE AND CLARK, INC.
555 South Flower Street
Los Angeles, Calif. 90017

BECK MITCHELL ASSOCIATES
129 Montgomery Street
San Francisco, Calif. 94104

CADILLAC ASSOCIATES, INC.
44 Montgomery Street
San Francisco, Calif. 94104

ECRIVANT AGENCY, INC.
260 California Street
San Francisco, Calif. 90067

HR RESEARCH ASSOCIATES, INC.
260 California Street
San Francisco, Calif. 94111

ROBERT BLAKE AND ASSOCIATES
1 Embarcadero Center
San Francisco, Calif. 94111

W S & Y CONSULTANTS
1 California Street
San Francisco, Calif. 94111

ALAN HOWARD ASSOCIATES
16055 Ventura Street
Ventura, Calif. 93008

COLORADO

CORPORATE EXECUTIVE SEARCH
1660 South Albion Street
Denver, Colo. 80220

WILLIAM B. ARNOLD ASSOCIATES, INC.
1776 South Jackson Street
Denver, Colo. 80210

DELTA SEARCH LTD.
1200 Lincoln Street
Denver, Colo. 80202

CARL C. WILSON AND ASSOCIATES
1545 Glenarm Place
Denver, Colo. 80202

CONNECTICUT

EXECUTIVE SEARCH CORPORATION
72 Arch Street
Greenwich, Conn. 06830

MASSAR ASSOCIATES
32 Broadway Drive
Stamford, Conn. 06902

GEORGE W. FOTIS AND ASSOCIATES, INC.
170 Mason Street
Greenwich, Conn. 06830

THE PERSONNEL LABORATORY, INC.
733 Summer Street
Stamford, Conn. 06901

ROBERT HELLER ASSOCIATES, INC.
72 Arch Street
Greenwich, Conn. 06830

BOLLES ASSOCIATES, INC.
21 Charles Street
Wesport, Conn. 96880

AHRENS ASSOCIATES CONSULTANTS, INC.
750 Main Street
Hartford, Conn. 06103

STEPHEN D. COINE & ASSOCIATES
19 South Compo Road
Westport, Conn. 06880

MAXWELL GOULD ASSOCIATES
31 Woodland Street
Hartford, Conn. 06105

TODAY'S WOMAN PLACEMENT SERVICE
21 Charles Street
Westport, Conn. 06880

BREITMAYER ASSOCIATES
72 Park Street
New Canaan, Conn. 06840

EXECUTIVE SERVICES
10 North Main Street
West Hartford, Conn. 06107

EXECUTIVE REGISTER
72 Park Street
New Canaan, Conn. 06840

GEORGIA

BOYDEN ASSOCIATES, INC.
Lenox Towers
Atlanta, Ga. 30344

O'NEIL ASSOCIATES, INC.
3390 Peachtree Road Northeast
Atlanta, Ga. 30326

PROFESSIONAL MANAGEMENT SEARCH
47 Perimeter Center ENE
Atlanta, Ga. 30346

VICTOR TABAKA AND ASSOCIATES, INC.
1800 Peachtree Road Northwest
Atlanta, Ga. 30309

HENRY JORDAN & ASSOCIATES
941 Carlisle Road
Stone Mountain, Ga. 30083

ILLINOIS

AMERICAN PERSONNEL CONSULTANTS, INC.
30 West Washington Street
Chicago, Ill. 60602

CADILLAC ASSOCIATES, INC.
32 West Randolph Street
Chicago, Ill. 60601

CHICAGO MANAGEMENT RECRUITERS, INC.
500 North Michigan Avenue
Chicago, Ill. 60605

EASTMAN & BEAUDINE, INC.
39 South LaSalle Street
Chicago, Ill. 60603

HEIDRICK AND STRUGGLES, INC.
20 North Wacker Drive
Chicago, Ill. 60606

A. T. KEARNEY, INC.
100 South Wacker Drive
Chicago, Ill. 60606

LAMSON/GRIFFITHS ASSOCIATES, INC.
20 North Wacker Drive
Chicago, Ill. 60606

LAUER & HOLBRECK, INC.
135 South LaSalle Street
Chicago, Ill. 60603

MAN-MARKETING SERVICES, INC.
2610 Prudential Plaza
Chicago, Ill. 60601

JOHN PAISIOS & ASSOCIATES
332 South Michigan Avenue
Chicago, Ill. 60604

R. M. SCHMITZ & CO., INC.
Prudential Plaza
Chicago, Ill. 60601

THE REYNOLDS RUSSELL ASSOCIATES, INC.
230 West Monroe Street
Chicago, Ill. 60606

SALES CONSULTANTS
332 South Michigan Avenue
Chicago, Ill. 60604

WYTMAR & COMPANY, INC.
10 South Riverside Plaza
Chicago, Ill. 60603

MARIN ASSOCIATES
3796 North Decatur Road
Decatur, Ill. 62521

RICHARD/ALLEN/WINTER
222 Wisconsin Avenue
Lake Forest, Ill. 60045

WINTER, KAHN, NIELSEN, ROSS &
BUCKWALTER
222 Wisconsin Avenue
Lake Forest, Ill. 60045

MENZEL, ROBINSON, BALDWIN & HILL INC.
800 West Central Road
Mt. Prospect, Ill. 60602

PARSONS ASSOCIATES
711 Building, Devon Avenue
Park Ridge, Ill. 60068

THE DAVIS EXECUTIVES
32065 Waterside Lane
Westlake Village, Chicago, Ill. 60607

LOUISIANA

SNELLING AND SNELLING OF METAIRIE
734 Martin Behrman Avenue
Metairie, La. 70124

MARYLAND

CHARLES A. BINSWANGER ASSOCIATES
9800 Planford Road
Randallstown, Md. 21133

MASSACHUSETTS

AEGIS CONSULTING SERVICES, INC.
31 Milk Street
Boston, Mass. 02109

EXECUTIVE AND UNDERSTUDIES, INC.
11 Newbury Street
Boston, Mass. 02116

MANAGEMENT RECRUITERS, INC. of Boston
500 Bolyston Street
Boston, Mass. 02146

NATHAN BERRY ASSOCIATES
29 Commonwealth Avenue
Boston, Mass. 02116

THE HEFFELFINGER ASSOCIATES, INC.
88 Washington Street
Dedham, Mass. 02026

ALAN GLOU ASSOCIATES
P.O. Box 601
Needham, Mass. 02192

PROFESSIONAL PLACEMENT CONSULTANTS, INC.
1268 Main Street
Waltham, Mass. 02154

MARKETING PERSONNEL CONSULTANTS
1 Washington Street
Wellesley, Mass. 02181

ASQUITH & JASON ASSOCIATES
586 Boston Post Road
Weston, Mass. 02193

MAINE

BRESTON AND ASSOCIATES, INC.
1800 Southwest 1st Street
Portland, Me. 04108

EXECUTIVE RESOURCES, INC.
200 Southwest Market Street
Portland, Me. 04111

CORDES AND COMPANY
P.O. Box 172
Sherman Mills, Me. 04776

MISSOURI

BRANDOM PERSONNEL SERVICES
1006 Grand Avenue
Kansas City, Mo. 64106

THE REAGAN COMPANY
4601 Madison Street
Kansas City, Mo. 64112

ALEXANDER NOERPER AND THOMAS
320 Brookes Drive
St. Louis, Mo. 63122

CAREER RESEARCH ASSOCIATES
200 South Hanley Street
St. Louis, Mo. 63105

EXECUTIVE CAREERS, INC.
Pierre Laclede Center
St. Louis, Mo. 63105

GRANT COOPER AND ASSOCIATES
3388 Schuetz Road
St. Louis, Mo. 63141

POTTER, CHRISTOPHER & Long
7777 Bonhomme, Suite 2105
St. Louis, Mo. 63105

NEW JERSEY

KENNETH H. HOUTZ ASSOCIATES
P.O. Box 287
Basking Ridge, N.J. 07920

WERMERT & ASSOCIATES
P.O. Box 114
Hillsdale, N.J. 07642

FORBES ASSOCIATES, INC.
P.O. Box 612 M
Morristown, N.J. 07960

SEARCH CONSULTANTS, INC.
10 Forest Avenue
Paramus, N.J. 07652

GEORGE SULLIVAN ASSOCIATES, INC.
P.O. Box 338
Rumson, N.J. 07760

TERENCE N. FLANAGAN ASSOCIATES
89 Summit Avenue
Summit, N.J. 07901

SEARCH ASSOCIATES, INC.
12 Bank Street
Summit, N.J. 07901

NEW YORK

MANAGEMENT RECRUITERS, INC.
104-70 Queens Boulevard
Forest Hills, N.Y. 11375

WEBSTER POSITIONS, INC.
76 North Broadway
Hicksville, N.Y. 11801

ANTEL, WRIGHT AND NAGEL
230 Park Avenue
New York, N.Y. 10017

BATTALIA, LOTZ & ASSOCIATES, INC.
342 Madison Avenue
New York, N.Y. 10017

BEACH & SILL, Inc.
420 Lexington Avenue
New York, N.Y. 10017

BOYDEN ASSOCIATES, INC.
260 Madison Avenue
New York, N.Y. 10016

BROOKS/GAY & ASSOCIATES, INC.
50 Park Avenue
New York, N.Y. 10016

BURKE AND O'BRIEN AND ASSOCIATES
233 Broadway
New York, N.Y. 10017

BUTTRICK & MEGARY, INC.
160 East 38th Street
New York, N.Y. 10016

CABOT BALLANTYNE ASSOCIATES, INC.
521 5th Avenue
New York, N.Y. 10017

CASE & COMPANY, INC.
30 Rockefeller Plaza
New York, N.Y. 10020

CHERNUCHIN ASSOCIATES
400 Madison Avenue
New York, N.Y. 10017

WILLIAM H. CLARK ASSOCIATES, INC.
292 Madison Avenue
New York, N.Y. 10017

COLUMBIA EDP AGENCY, INC.
342 Madison Avenue
New York, N.Y. 10017

COMMUNICATIONS PERSONNEL, INC.
441 Lexington Avenue
New York, N.Y. 10017

CORRY, HOWE ASSOCIATES, INC.
Time and Life Building
New York, N.Y. 10020

D.A.K. BROWN & ASSOCIATES
50 Park Avenue
New York, N.Y. 10016

ELMER R. DAVIS AND ASSOCIATES, INC.
60 East 42nd Street
New York, N.Y. 10017

THORNDIKE DELAND ASSOCIATES
1440 Broadway
New York, N.Y. 10018

DRAKE BEAM & ASSOCIATES
277 Park Avenue
New York, N.Y. 10017

EINSTEIN ASSOCIATES, INC.
405 Lexington Avenue
New York, N.Y. 10017

ERNST-VAN PRAAG, INC.
135 East 55th Street
New York, N.Y. 10022

FIELD, FREEMAN ASSOCIATES, INC.
51 East 42nd Street, Suite 1800
New York, N.Y. 10017

40 PLUS CLUB OF NEW YORK, INC.
15 Park Row
New York, N.Y. 10038

J. B. GILBERT ASSOCIATES, INC.
11 East 44th Street
New York, N.Y. 10007

P. PAUL GOGGI ASSOCIATES
233 Broadway
New York, N.Y. 10007

THE GOODRICH & SHERWOOD COMPANY
529 Fifth Avenue
New York, N.Y. 10017

J.R. GORHAM & COMPANY
625 Lincoln Building
New York, N.Y. 10017

HALBRECHT ASSOCIATES, INC.
201 East 42nd Street
New York, N.Y. 10017

HANDY ASSOCIATES, INC.
405 Park Avenue
New York, N.Y. 10022

FRANK W. HASTINGS ASSOCIATES, INC.
420 Lexington Avenue
New York, N.Y. 10017

F. P. HEALY & COMPANY, INC.
630 3rd Avenue
New York, N.Y. 10017

HOFF ASSOCIATES
200 Park Avenue, Suite 4421
New York, N.Y. 10017

HOLAHAN-DEAN, INC.
415 Lexington Avenue
New York, N.Y. 10017

WARD HOWELL ASSOCIATES, INC.
122 East 42nd Street
New York, N.Y. 10017

KAHLERT ASSOCIATES, INC.
375 Park Avenue
New York, N.Y. 10022

KENMORE EXECUTIVE PERSONNEL, INC.
405 Park Avenue
New York, N.Y. 10022

E. THOMAS LALUMIA ASSOCIATES
420 Lexington Avenue
New York, N.Y. 10017

ARTHUR J. LOVELEY ASSOCIATES
521 5th Avenue
New York, N.Y. 10017

MARSHALL CONSULTANTS, INC.
360 East 65th Street
New York, N.Y.10021

MCCULLOUGH ASSOCIATES, INC.
20 East 46th Street, Suite 900
New York, N.Y. 10017

OLIVER & ROZNER ASSOCIATES, INC.
One East 53rd Street
New York, N.Y. 10022

ROBERT OLIVER AND ASSOCIATES, INC.
50 Broad Street
New York, N.Y. 10004

OWEN, WEBB ASSOCIATES, INC.
280 Park Avenue
New York, N.Y. 10017

BRUCE PAYNE AND ASSOCIATES, INC.
1275 Time and Life Building
New York, N.Y. 10020

RENE PLESSNER ASSOCIATES, INC.
10 East 53rd Street
New York, N.Y. 10022

HENRY PONZIO ASSOCIATES, INC.
415 Lexington Avenue
New York, N.Y. 10017

RESUME COUNSELING SERVICE
507 5th Avenue
New York, N.Y. 10017

RUSSELL REYNOLDS ASSOCIATES
245 Park Avenue
New York, N.Y. 10017

ROGERS, SLADE AND HILL, INC.
60 East 42nd Street
New York, N.Y. 10017

WILLIAM A. SHARON ASSOCIATES, INC.
515 Madison Avenue
New York, N.Y. 10022

STACK ASSOCIATES
230 Park Avenue
New York, N.Y. 10017

STAUB, WARMBOLD & ASSOCIATES, INC.
919 3rd Avenue
New York, N.Y. 10022

SPENCER STUART & ASSOCIATES, INC.
437 Madison Avenue
New York, N.Y. 10022

JOHN S. STUDWELL ASSOCIATES, INC.
310 Madison Avenue
New York, N.Y. 10017

CLARK TOBY AGENCY, INC.
18 East 48th Street
New York, N.Y. 10017

NELSON WALKER ASSOCIATES, INC.
52 Vanderbilt Avenue
New York, N.Y. 10017

EDWARD WARREN ORGANIZATION
120 East 56th Street
New York, N.Y. 10022

WARREN H. WILLIS, INC.
445 Park Avenue
New York, N.Y. 10022

INDUSTRY SEARCH, INC.
3100 Monroe Avenue
Rochester, N.Y. 14618

OHIO

BOYDEN ASSOCIATES, INC.
1900 Euclid Avenue
Cleveland, Ohio 45215

EXECUTIVE RECRUITERS
26100 Bush Street
Cleveland, Ohio 45227

MANAGEMENT RECRUITERS
1015 Euclid Avenue
Cleveland, Ohio 44115

SALES CONSULTANTS
1015 Euclid Avenue
Cleveland, Ohio 44115

SALESWORLD, INC.
4500 Rockside Road
Cleveland, Ohio 44131

W. L. WYSON ASSOCIATES
12700 Lake Street
Cleveland, Ohio 45244

BADGETT & ASSOCIATES
1221 Tannehill Lane
Cincinnati, Ohio 45226

REYNOLDS AND MORGAN ASSOCIATES
10863 Reading Road
Cincinnati, Ohio 45241

S. K. STEWART AND ASSOCIATES
11306 Southland Road
Cincinnati, Ohio 45240

MELVIN KENT AND ASSOCIATES
250 East Broad Street
Columbus, Ohio 43215

PENNSYLVANIA

ROBERT J. BUSHEE & ASSOCIATES, INC.
P.O. Box 515
Carnegie, Pa. 15106

MOLLAY ASSOCIATES
145 Narbeth Avenue
Narbeth, Pa. 19072

COLE WARREN AND LONG, INC.
117 South 17th Street
Philadelphia, Pa. 19103

ENION ASSOCIATES, INC.
Three Penn Center Plaza
Philadelphia, Pa. 19102

NATIONAL EXECUTIVE SEARCH BUREAU
1700 Market Street
Philadelphia, Pa. 19103

RUNHAM ASSOCIATES
2 Penn Center Plaza
Philadelphia, Pa. 19102

HARRY F. TWOMEY, JR.
1601 Walnut Street
Philadelphia, Pa. 19102

T. WATSON AND ASSOCIATES
1314 Chestnut Street
Philadelphia, Pa. 19107

EXECUTIVE SEARCH CONSULTANTS
9800 McKnight Road
Pittsburgh, Pa. 15237

TOMSETT CONSULTING ASSOCIATES
402 Frick Building
Pittsburgh, Pa. 15219

PACE ASSOCIATES
40 South Richland Avenue
York, Pa. 17404

TEXAS

J. W. BAUDER ASSOCIATES
2665 Villa Creek
Dallas, Tex. 75234

JACK GENTILE & ASSOCIATES
5952 Royal Lane
Dallas, Tex. 75230

WYLIE COMPANY MANAGEMENT
CONSULTANTS
1005 Business Parkway
Dallas, Tex. 75229

EXECUTIVE EMPLOYMENT CONSULTANTS
P.O. Box 19352
Houston, Tex. 77024

ROLNICK-NEWMAN ASSOCIATES, INC.
4615 Southwest Freeway
Houston, Tex. 77027

SCOTTY LEACH AND ASSOCIATES
1212 Main Street
Houston, Tex. 77002

R. J. WAGGETT & ASSOCIATES
1770 St. James Place
Houston, Tex. 77027

WASHINGTON

EXECUTIVE SEATTLE, INC.
220 106th Place, N.E.
Bellevue, Wash. 98004

MANAGEMENT RECRUITERS, INC.
Denny Building
Seattle, Wash. 98121

WASHINGTON, D.C.

JANUS CONSULTANTS, INC.
1212 Potomac Street Northwest
Washington, D.C. 20007

ROSS MACASKILL ASSOCIATES
1660 L Street Northwest, Suite 612
Washington, D.C. 20036

SIMMONS ASSOCIATES, INC.
1054 31st Street Northwest
Washington, D.C. 20007

WISCONSIN

ROBERT E. LARSON & ASSOCIATES
2300 North Mayfair Road
Milwaukee, Wis. 53226

CHARLES PARTHUM & ASSOCIATES
111 East Wisconsin Avenue
Milwaukee, Wis. 53202

CANADA

T. M. MORAN AND ASSOCIATES LTD.
216 Park Avenue
Newmarket, Ontario, Canada

H. V. CHAMPAN & ASSOCIATES LTD.
2 Bloor Street West
Toronto, Ontario, Canada

P. S. ROSS AND PARTNERS
200 University Avenue
Toronto, Ontario, Canada

JAMES W. WESTCOTT AND ASSOCIATES LTD.
43 Eglinton Avenue East
Toronto, Ontario, Canada

WOODS, GORDON & COMPANY
Royal Trust Tower, Box 253
Toronto, Ontario, Canada

ROURKE BOURBONNAIS AND ASSOCIATES
1808 Sherbrooke Street
West Montreal, Ontario, Canada

Lists of executive recruiters are also available from the following groups:

AMERICAN MANAGEMENT ASSOCIATION
135 West 50th Street
New York, N.Y. 10020 (Price: $2.00 a copy)

ASSOCIATION OF EXECUTIVE RECRUITING
CONSULTANTS
30 Rockefeller Plaza
New York, N.Y. 10020

Also, these C.P.A.s have executive search divisions:

COOPERS & LYBRAND
1251 Avenue of the Americas
New York, N.Y. 10020

PRICE WATERHOUSE & CO.
60 Broad Street
New York, N.Y. 10004

ERNST AND ERNST
1300 Union Commerce Building
Cleveland, Ohio 44115

TOUCHE ROSS & CO.
1633 Broadway
New York, N.Y. 10004

HASKINS & SELLS
2 Broadway
New York, N.Y. 10004

ARTHUR YOUNG & CO.
277 Park Avenue
New York, N.Y. 10017

PEAT, MARWICK, MITCHELL & CO.
222 South Riverside Drive
Chicago, Ill. 60606

BUSINESS DIRECTORIES

Driectories provide names of companies. You may wish to consult them in addition to the list given on page 157. They can be found in most libraries, especially business libraries, and cover many companies and large numbers of employees. The two Dun & Bradstreet directories, for example, represent a total of 75,647,000 employees:

Million Dollar Directory	42,583,000
Middle Market Directory	33,064,000
Total	75,647,000

STATE INDUSTRIAL DIRECTORIES

Each state has its own industrial directory, the title usually starting with the name of the state (e.g., *Delaware Directory of Manufacturers*) and usually published in the state's capital or largest city. Note also the following major state directories:

Industrial Alabama, Alabama State Chamber of Commerce, 468 South Perry Street, Montgomery, Ala. 36101.

Buyers Directory of Maine Industries, Department of Economic Development, State Office Building, Augusta, Me. 04330.

Industrial Directory of Massachusetts, Massachusetts Department of Commerce Public Document Division, 116 State House, Boston, Mass. 92133.

Made in New Hampshire, New Hampshire Department of Resources and Economic Development, State House Annex, Concord, N.H. 03301.

Directory of Plants Established under the Industrialization Program, Economic Development Administration, Office of Economic Research, Box 2350 6 P.O., San Juan, P.R. 00936.

Providence Journal Bulletin Almanac, Rhode Island Development Council, Rodger Williams Building, Providence, R.I. 02908.

Prices range from $2 to about $60. A few are free.

GENERAL DIRECTORIES

Dun & Bradstreet Million Dollar Directory, 99 Church Street, New York, N.Y. 10007. This lists approximately 42,000 companies with an indicated net worth of $1 million or more.

Dun & Bradstreet Middle Market Directory, 99 Church Street, New York, N.Y. 10007. This directory lists 30,000 companies ranging in size (net worth) from $500,000 to $1 million as well as their owners and/or officers.

Venture Capital Source Directory, 3rd ed., Capital Publishing Corp., 10 South LaSalle Street, Chicago, Ill. 60603, 1974. It lists about 400 companies that supply venture capital to new businesses.

SPECIALIZED DIRECTORIES

Advertising

Standard Directory of Advertising Agencies, National Register Publishing Co., Inc., 5201 Old Orchard Road, Skokie, Ill. 60076.

National Register Publishing Co., Inc., 5201 Old Orchard Road, Skokie, Ill. 60076. *Standard Directory of Advertising Agencies* (4000 leading advertising agencies in the United States, with key executives, major accounts, and a geographic index).

Who's Who in Advertising, P.O. Box 556, Rye, N.Y. 10580. *Directory (10,000 alphabetically arranged biographical sketches).*

Apparel

American Apparel Manufacturers Association, 200 K Street Northwest, Washington, D.C. 2006. *Directory* (companies and executives).

Automotive industry

Powers and Company, 550 West Fort Street, Detroit, Mich. 48206. *Wards Automotive Yearbook* (companies and executives).

Wards Automotive Year Book, Power & Co., 550 West Fort Street, Detroit, Mich. 48206.

Buying

The Buyers Guide, Inc., 1440 Broadway, New York, N.Y. 10018. *The Buyer's Guide.*

Merchandiser Mass Retailer Buyers, 211 East 43rd Street, New York, N.Y. 10016. *Directory.*

Canada

Canadian Manufacturers Association, 67 Yorge Street, Toronto, Ontario. *Canadian Trade Index* (13,000 companies).

Chain stores—department stores

Chain Store Guide, 2 Park Avenue, New York, N.Y. 10016.

Drug Chains
Department Stores
Discount Stores
General Merchandise/Variety/Jr. Department Store Chains
Hardware/Home Improvement Centers/Auto Supply Chains
Supermarket Chains
Co-op/Voluntary Chains
Restaurant Chains
Food Service Distributors

Chemicals

Noyes Development Co., Park Ridge, N.J. 07656. *Chemical Guide to the United States.*

Coal

National Coal Publications, 2401 Mt. Royal Boulevard, Glenshaw, Pa. 15116 *MacQuown's Directory of Coal Operating Companies.*

Construction

Associated General Contractors of America, 1957 East Street Northwest, Washington, D.C. 20006. *Directory* (major contracting companies by state; key executives).

Directors

Directory of Directors Co., Inc., 350 5th Avenue, New York, N.Y. 10016. *Directory*.

Drugs and pharmaceuticals

Chemical Economic Service, 92C Nassau Street, Princeton, N.J. 08540. *Executive Directory of the U.S. Pharmaceutical Industry* (500 companies, 3000 executives).

American Druggist, 1790 Broadway, New York, N.Y. 10019 *American Druggist Blue Book* (all drug manufacturers).

Executive Directory of the U.S. Pharmaceutical Industry, Chemical Economic Service, 92C Nassau Street, Princeton, N.J. 08540.

Electronic data processing

Gale Research Co., Book Tower, Detroit, Mich. 48226. *International Directory of Computer and Information System Services* (by country and type of service; names of principal officers of each firm or institution).

Education

The American Council on Education, 1785 Massachusetts Avenue Northwest, Washington, D.C. 20036. *Accredited Institutions of Higher Education* (colleges and universities, with names of presidents).

Electronics and electric

Fairchild Publications, Inc., Book Division, 7 East 12th Street, New York, N.Y. 10003. *Electrical News Financial Fact Book & Directory* (700 publicly owned electronics companies, with names of board members and directors).

Electrical News Financial Fact Book & Directory, Fairchild Publications Inc., Book Division, 7 East 12th Street, New York, N.Y. 10003.

Engineering—science

Computer + Technology Information, Inc., 500 Newport Center Drive, Newport Beach, Calif. 92660. *Directory of Advanced Technology Companies* (4000 firms, with product lines and key executives).

Food

Progressive Grocer, 420 Lexington Avenue, New York, N.Y. 10017. *Progressive Grocer's Marketing Guidebook* (supermarket chain stores and major food wholesalers in 79 major cities, with names of key executives).

National Food Brokers Association, 1916 M Street, Northwest, Washington, D.C. 20036. *Directory* (member firms and names of executives).

Thomas Publishing Co., 461 8th Avenue, New York, N.Y. 10001. *Thomas' Grocery Register* (manufacturers and wholesalers of food by product type and state).

Cahners Publishing Co., 1776 Broadway, New York, N.Y. 10019. *Quick Frozen Foods Directory* (manufacturers, with executives' names).

Gas utility

Moore Publishing Co., Ojibway Building, Duluth, Minn. 55802. *Browns Directory of North American Gas Companies* (executives of United States and Canadian gas utilities).

Glass

National Glass Budget, 912 Empire Building, Pittsburgh, Pa. 15222. *Glass Factory Directory*.

Hotel-motel

Hotel & Motel Red Book, American Hotel Association Directory Corp., 888 7th Avenue, New York, N.Y. 10019.

Import—export

American Register of Importers & Exporters, Inc., 90 West Broadway, New York, N.Y. 10005 *Register* (30,000 importers and exporters classified by product; names of executives).

Imports

The Journal of Commerce, 445 Marshall Street, Phillipsburg, N.J. 08865 *Directory of U.S. Importers* (25,000 companies classified by location and type of product imported; names of owners and key executives).

International

World Trade Academy Press, Inc., 50 East 42nd Street, New York, N.Y. 10017. *Directory of American Firms Operating In Foreign Countries* (4200 United States companies with overseas subsidiaries, classified by product and country; names of United States executives in charge).

International Publications Service, 303 Park Avenue South, New York, N.Y. 10010. *International Businessmen's Who's Who* (executives in international commerce).

Investments

Finance Publishing Corp., 25 East 73rd Street, New York, N.Y. 10021 *Investment Banker Broker Almanac* (400 top bankers/brokers, with key executives).

Labor unions

United States Government Printing Office, Division of Public Documents, Washington, D.C. 20402. *Directory of National & International Labor Unions in the U.S.* (with officers names).

Management consultants

Cornell University Graduate School of Business, Publications Section, Ithaca, N.Y. 14850. *Management Consulting* (2600 consulting firms, with principals and officers' names, arranged by type of consulting and location).

Marketing

Executive Communications, Inc., 54 Park Avenue, New York, N.Y. 10016. *Handbook of Independent Marketing/Advertising Services* (200 consulting firms in marketing).

Metalworking

Dun & Bradstreet, Inc., 99 Church Street, New York, N.Y. 10007 *Metalworking Directory* (45,000 metalworking plants).

Oceanography

Untel, Inc., 1053 National Press Building, Washington, D.C. 20004. *GMT World Register of Oceanographic Products and Services*.

Oil

Burmass Oil Directories, P. O. Box 295, Springtown, Tex. 76082 *Directory* (key executives of Midwest and Gulf area oil companies).

Oil and Gas Guide, Cliborne Towers, New Orleans, La. 70161. *Guide* (oilfield suppliers and service companies by type, with executives).

Midwest Oil Register, Inc., P.O. Drawer 7248, Tulsa, Okla. 74105. *Oil Well Supply Companies* (worldwide listing).

Oildom Publishing Co., 1217 Hudson Boulevard, Bayonne, N.J. 07002. *Pipeline News Annual Directory* (pipeline products and firms, with executives).

The Oil and Gas Journal, Box 1260, Tulsa, Okla. 74101. *Worldwide Personnel Directory of Refining & Gas Processing*.

Overseas

U.S. Dept. of State, Washington, D.C. 20520 *List of U.S. Foreign Service Posts* (explains, eligibility and examination requirements and opportunities by city).

Paper

Paper Industry Management Assn., 2570 Devon Avenue, Des Plaines, Ill. 60018. *Paper Industry Directory* (pulp and paper mill executives).

Plastics

Reinhold Publishing Co., 430 Park Avenue, New York, N.Y. 10022. *Source Book of New Plastics* (leading manufacturers, with executives).

Public relations

PR Publishing Co., Inc., Meriden, N.H. 03770 *PR Blue Book* (PR consultant firms, with owners' names, and 5000 PR directors of major organizations).

Railroads

Simmons-Boardman Publishing Corp., 30 Church Street, New York, N.Y. 10007. *Who's Who in Railroading*.

Research

Gale Research, Book Tower, Detroit, Mich. 48226. *Research Centers Directory (4500 research centers in all fields; names of research directors)*.

Textiles

Davison's Publishing Co., Ridgewood, N.J. 07450. *Davison's Textile Directory*.

PROFESSIONAL RÉSUMÉ
AND CAREER SERVICES

Like doctors, lawyers, and advertising agencies, professional résumé and career services do excellent, mediocre, or poor work. It is therefore important to select your professional résumé service carefully.

In addition to résumé writing, a résumé and career service company may perform the following tasks:

- Reproduction.
- Mailing.
- Supplying mailing lists—custom and standard.
- Broadcast letter writing.
- Interview technique assistance.
- Aptitude testing.
- Psychological testing.
- Third party services.
- Organization of complete job campaigns.
- Corporate "out placement."
- Executive search.
- Career counseling.
- Compensation guidance.

Though some consider professionally prepared résumés to lack the stamp of personality evident in a "homemade" résumé, many successful leaders in business, the professions, and the arts have used them. Writing is a difficult task, requiring knowledge of the rules and practice. Writing about yourself can be even more difficult. You might wish to employ a professional writer for the following reasons:

- You have been unable to organize your employment history.
- You find the task of writing about yourself tedious and exasperating.
- You cannot express ''you'' in a way that you like.
- You speak better than you write.
- You have neither the time nor the patience to write your own résumé.
- You cannot decide what to omit and what to include.
- Your experience is narrow.
- You don't know whether your experience is narrow or comprehensive with respect to the job you want.

Ask the professional résumé service to show you samples of its work. Arrange to meet the individual who will be writing your résumé.

The cost of a résumé varies with the time and expertise required to write it. In a large city such as New York the prices will range from $50 for a single page résumé to $400 for a complex one. Like any business, your résumé service has such overhead expenses as rent, heat, light, taxes, and secretarial help. Preparing a résumé involves its planning, writing and rewriting, proofreading, interviewing, and researching reference material. Fees of $50 an hour are about the minimum needed to run a professional résumé service in a large urban center. The following typical fees for a professionally written résumé are based on information supplied by six résumé writing firms:

By mail
    $25 to $75
    $50 per page (maximum: $150)
    $50 per page (no maximum)
By personal interview
    $50 per page
    $85 for first page, $35 for second page, and $25 for third page
    $36 to $60 per hour
    New entrant to job market: $35 to $50
    Clerical: $50 to $75
    Lower middle management executive: $100
    Upper middle management executive: $150
    Vice-president for small company: $200
    Vice-president for large company: $250
    Chief executive officer or president: $300 to $350.

A professional résumé writer usually provides a résumé that is ready for use as far as its content is concerned, but requires retyping in camera ready form and reproduction. Those résumé services that have their own printing equipment include the cost of typing in their printing cost of the first 100 copies per page.

The typing and printing costs shown below are taken from a survey of eight companies. Quality of printing and paper, accuracy and speed of typing (an experienced résumé typist requires less time than a novice), résumé layout—all affect the cost and all are difficult to assess except based on the firm's reputation.

- 100 copies per page, $3.50 (typing free); 200 copies per page, $5.00.
- 100 copies per page, $4.90 (typing free).
- Typing $5 per page.
- Typing $8 to $10 per page (public stenographer, New York City).
- Typing $8 per hour (public stenographer, suburban area).
- Typing $11 per hour (experienced résumé typist, New York City).
- 100 copies per page, first 100: $10 to $14 depending on quality of paper.
- Additional copies: $3.00 per 100 per page.

INDEX

Accomplishments, identifying your,
129
Accounting, responsibilities checklist,
Appendix B
Accreditations and licenses, 47
Advertising for a position, 168
Advertising space salesmen as source
of leads, 156
Advice visits, 164
Age, 48
Analytical questionnaire, 133
Analyzing your income and position,
13
Analyzing your job personality, 31
Aptitude tests, 188
Art decoration, 49
Articulateness, 170
Auditing, responsibilities check list,
Appendix B

Beginning the interview, 177
Bonuses, 197
Breadth, 37
Broadcasting your resume, 147
Broadcast letter, 147
examples, 149
Business directories, Appendix D

Career planning, 5
ages 18-29, 6
ages 30-39, 12
ages 40-49, 24
ages 50-64, 25
ages 65 and over, 28
Charts and graphs, 50
Choosing an employer, 8, 159

Civil Service grades, 53
Conducting your interview, 176
Corporate measurement of employers,
16
Corporate selection process, 19
Covering letter, 140
examples, 144
typing, 143

Data processing, responsibilities check
list, Appendix B

Earnings and education, 7
Elements of job personality, discus-
sion, 34
Employment agencies, 155
Employment application form, 193
Executive search firms, 155
list of, Appendix C

Finance, responsibilities check list,
Appendix B
Finding a job, 1
Follow-up telephone calls, 162, 187
Forms of address, 142
Four vital steps in the job search, 40
Fringe benefits, 197

Help wanted advertisements, 156
"High-powered rifle" approach, 164
Humor, 166, 178

Ideal manager, 29
Income chart, 17
Industrial relations, responsibilities
check list, Appendix B

Interview, after the, 187
  conducting your, 176
Interview "catch" questions, 173
Interview preparation, 170
Interview questions, examples of, 173
  examples of answers, 178
  you can ask, 186

Job competition, 161
Job personality evaluation test, 32
Job responsibilities, typical, Appendix
  B

Life expectancy, 26

Mailing lists, 157
Marketing, responsibilities check list,
  Appendix B
Measuring your value to an employer,
  16
Miscellanea, 131

Organization charts, 14

Pension planning, 23
Personality, influence of, 171
Personal planning, 5
Personnel, responsibilities check list,
  Appendix B
Ploys for employment, 163
Population changes, 165
Production, responsibilities check list,
  Appendix B
Professional resume and career ser-
  vices, Appendix E
Profit measurement, 18
Psychological testing, relation to
  executive competence, 188
Psychological tests, 192
Purchasing, responsibilities check list,
  Appendix B

Relocation, 164
Resume, elements of, 43
  nature of, 41
  writing, 133
Resume criticisms, 54
Resume examples, by style, accom-
    plishment, 123, 127
  basic, 59, 61
  chronological, 62, 68, 138
    with summary page, 70, 77, 81
    with summary page with variation,
    85
  creative, 109, 111, 112
  functional, 88, 93
    by company, 95, 100, 103
  Harvard, 105
  narrative, 114, 118
  professional, 121
by vocation, administration, aca-
    demic, 103
  health care, 68
  museum director, 118
  communications, 127
  editorial, 110, 111
  entry position, 59
  financial, 64, 112
  general executive, 72, 77, 81, 90,
    93, 96
  law, 121
marketing, 106
operations, 124
personnel, 115
retailer, 100
sales, 85, 138
Resume language, 30, Appendix
    A
Resume length, 57
Retail, responsibilities check list,
    Appendix B
Rewriting and resubmitting resumes,
    152

Salary negotiations, 195
Self-analysis, 133
Standard Industrial Classification
        (S.I.C.) Numbers, 158
Steps in job search, step 1, 41
    step 2, 153
    step 3, 170
    step 4, 176

Ten resumes styles, 55

Types of interviewers, 172
Typical job responsibilities, 209
Typing the covering letter, 143
Typing the resume, 140

Unusual job approaches, 166
Upper management job search, 167
Using your resume, 153

Writing, for publication, 167